Developmental Pei
Psychoanalysis and

MW01484370

Developmental Perspectives in Child Psychoanalysis and Psychotherapy incorporates recent innovations in developmental theory and research into our understanding of the nature of change in child psychotherapy. Diverse psychoanalytic ideas and individual styles are represented, challenging the historical allegiance in analytic child therapy to particular, and so often singular, schools of thought. Each of the distinguished contributors offers a conceptually grounded and clinically rich account of child development, addressing topics such as reflective functioning, the role of play, dreaming, trauma and neglect, the development of recognition and mutuality, autism, adoption, and non-binary conceptions of gender. Extended clinical vignettes offer the reader clear vision into the convergence of theory and practice, demonstrating the potential of psychoanalytic psychotherapy to move child development forward. This book will appeal to all practicing mental health professionals.

Christopher Bonovitz, Psy.D., is a Training and Supervising Analyst at the William Alanson White Institute in New York City and Adjunct Clinical Associate Professor at the New York University Postdoctoral Program in Psychoanalysis and Psychotherapy. He is on the editorial board of *Psychoanalytic Dialogues* and *Contemporary Psychoanalysis* and maintains a psychotherapy and consultation practice with children, adolescents, and adults in New York City.

Andrew Harlem, Ph.D., is Professor of Clinical Psychology at the California Institute for Integral Studies in San Francisco, an instructor at the Psychoanalytic Institute of Northern California (PINC), and faculty member at the Access Institute for Psychological Services. He is on the editorial board of *Psychoanalytic Dialogues* and is a past president of the Northern California Society for Psychoanalytic Psychology. Dr. Harlem maintains a psychotherapy and consultation practice in San Francisco and Oakland, California.

Relational Perspectives Book Series
Lewis Aron & Adrienne Harris
Series Co-Editors

Steven Kuchuck & Eyal Rozmarin
Associate Editors

The *Relational Perspectives Book Series* publishes books that grow out of or contribute to the relational tradition in contemporary psychoanalysis. The term *relational psychoanalysis* was first used by Greenberg and Mitchell[1] to bridge the traditions of interpersonal relations as developed within interpersonal psychoanalysis and object relations, in turn developed within contemporary British theory. But, under the seminal work of the late Stephen A. Mitchell, the term *relational psychoanalysis* grew and began to accrue to itself many other influences and developments. Various tributaries – interpersonal psychoanalysis, object relations theory, self psychology, empirical infancy research, and elements of contemporary Freudian and Kleinian thought – flow into this tradition, which understands relational configurations between self and others, both real and fantasied, as the primary subjects of psychoanalytic investigation.

We refer to the relational tradition, rather than to a relational school, to highlight that we are identifying a trend, a tendency within contemporary psychoanalysis, not a more formally organized or coherent school or system of beliefs. Our use of the term *relational* signifies a dimension of theory and practice that has become salient across the wide spectrum of contemporary psychoanalysis. Now under the editorial supervision of Lewis Aron and Adrienne Harris, with the assistance of Associate Editors Steven Kuchuck and Eyal Rozmarin, the Relational Perspectives Book Series originated in 1990 under the editorial eye of the late Stephen A. Mitchell. Mitchell was the most prolific and influential of the originators of the relational tradition. Committed to dialogue among psychoanalysts, he abhorred the authoritarianism that dictated adherence to a rigid set of beliefs or technical restrictions. He championed open discussion and comparative and integrative approaches and promoted new voices across the generations.

Included in the *Relational Perspectives Book Series* are authors and works that come from within the relational tradition and extend and develop that tradition, as well as works that critique relational approaches or compare and contrast it with alternative points of view. The series includes our most distinguished senior psychoanalysts, along with younger contributors who bring fresh vision. A full list of titles in this series is available at https://www.routledge.com/mentalhealth/series/LEARPBS.

Note

1 Greenberg, J. & Mitchell, S. (1983). *Object relations in psychoanalytic theory.* Cambridge, MA: Harvard University Press.

Developmental Perspectives in Child Psychoanalysis and Psychotherapy

Edited by Christopher Bonovitz
and Andrew Harlem

Routledge
Taylor & Francis Group

LONDON AND NEW YORK

First published 2018
by Routledge
2 Park Square, Milton Park, Abingdon, Oxon OX14 4RN

and by Routledge
711 Third Avenue, New York, NY 10017

Routledge is an imprint of the Taylor & Francis Group, an informa business

© 2018 selection and editorial matter, Christopher Bonovitz and Andrew Harlem; individual chapters, the contributors

British Library Cataloguing in Publication Data
A catalogue record for this book is available from the British Library

Library of Congress Cataloging in Publication Data
Names: Bonovitz, Christopher, editor.
Title: Developmental perspectives in child psychoanalysis and psychotherapy / edited by Christopher Bonovitz and Andrew Harlem.
Description: Milton Park, Abingdon ; New York, NY : Routledge, 2018. |
Series: Relational perspectives book series ; 100 |
Includes bibliographical references and index.
Identifiers: LCCN 2017042155 (print) | LCCN 2017043203 (ebook) |
ISBN 9781351235488 (e-Book) | ISBN 9781351235471 (Mobipocket/Kindle) |
ISBN 9781351235495 (Web PDF) | ISBN 9781351235501 (Master) |
ISBN 9780415742184 (hbk : alk. paper) | ISBN 9780415742191 (pbk : alk. paper) |
ISBN 9781351235501 (ebk)
Subjects: LCSH: Child analysis. | Child psychotherapy.
Classification: LCC RJ504.2 (ebook) | LCC RJ504.2 .D475 2018 (print) |
DDC 618.92/8914–dc23
LC record available at https://lccn.loc.gov/2017042155

ISBN: 978-0-415-74218-4 (hbk)
ISBN: 978-0-415-74219-1 (pbk)
ISBN: 978-1-351-23550-1 (ebk)

Typeset in Times New Roman
by Out of House Publishing

Contents

Contributors

Seth Aronson, Psy.D. is Fellow, Training, and Supervising Analyst, Director of Training, and Faculty and Supervisor in the Child and Adolescent Psychotherapy Training Program, William Alanson White Institute. At Long Island University's doctoral program in clinical psychology, he teaches child and adolescent psychopathology and psychotherapy. For close to 15 years, he has taught at the Institute for Psychoanalytic and Systems Psychotherapy and the International Christian University in Tokyo, Japan. At Yeshivat Chovevei Torah, he facilitates process groups for rabbinical students. His publications cover topics such as mourning in the analyst, working as an Orthodox Jew and a psychoanalyst, and play and supervision. Most recently, he co-edited with Craig Haen, Ph.D., *Handbook of child and adolescent group therapy*. He is in private practice in New York.

Christopher Bonovitz, Psy.D. is Faculty, Supervising, and Training Analyst, William Alanson White Institute; Adjunct Clinical Associate Professor of Psychology and a Clinical Consultant in the New York University (NYU) Postdoctoral Program in Psychotherapy and Psychoanalysis; Faculty and Supervisor, Mitchell Center for Relational Studies and Manhattan Institute for Psychoanalysis; and Associate Editor, *Psychoanalytic Dialogues* and *Journal of Contemporary Psychoanalysis*.

Peter Carnochan, Ph.D. is a graduate of the Psychoanalytic Institute of Northern California, where he is a personal and supervising analyst and a member of the faculty. He serves as voluntary faculty at the University of California at San Francisco (UCSF) and teaches at a number of training programs in the Bay Area. His book, *Looking for* *ground: Countertransference and the problem of value in psychoanalysis*, was published in 2001 by the Analytic Press. He has written numerous papers on analytic theory and technique. His article on infinity, "Containers without lids," was published in 2006 by *Psychoanalytic Dialogues*. He has a private practice in San Francisco for working with children and adults.

Diane Ehrensaft, Ph.D. is a developmental and clinical psychologist, Associate Professor of Pediatrics at University of California San Francisco, and Director of Mental Health of the Child and Adolescent Gender Center, University of California San Francisco (UCSF) Benioff Children's Hospital. She specializes in research, clinical work, and consultation related to gender-nonconforming children and assisted reproductive technology families. She is author of *The gender creative child*; *Gender born, gender made*; *Mommies, daddies, donors, surrogates*; *Building a home within* (co-edited with Toni Heineman); *Spoiling childhood*; *Parenting together*; and *The gender affirmative model: A new approach to supporting gender nonconforming and transgender children* (co-edited with Colt Keo-Meier, in press).

Antonio Ferro, M.D. is a psychiatrist and the current President of the Italian Psychoanalytic Society. He holds full membership in the American Psychoanalytic Association and the International Psychoanalytical Association. He has held supervisions, lectures, and seminars at major psychoanalytic societies in Europe, North America, South America, and Australia. His publications include *Psychoanalysis as therapy and storytelling* (2006), *Mind works* (2009), *Avoiding emotions, and living emotions* (2011), and *Torments of the soul* (2014), all published by Routledge, New Library. In 2007, he received the Mary Sigourney Award.

Andrew Harlem, Ph.D. is Professor of Clinical Psychology at the California Institute for Integral Studies in San Francisco, an instructor at the Psychoanalytic Institute of Northern California (PINC), and faculty member at the Access Institute for Psychological Services. He is on the editorial board of *Psychoanalytic Dialogues* and is a past president of the Northern California Society for Psychoanalytic Psychology.

Barbara Kalmanson, Ph.D. has over 40 years' experience as a clinical psychologist, a special educator, and an infant mental health specialist. She is a founder of the Oak Hill School for children with autism and related disorders, the Interdisciplinary Council on Developmental and Learning Disorders Graduate School, and the KidsAttuned.org website. She was a member of the original faculty of the Infant–Parent Program at the University of California at San Francisco and is a California Infant–Family and Early Childhood Mental Health Specialist Reflective Practice Mentor. Her publications and presentations focus on family-based treatment in infancy and early childhood.

Elena Molinari, M.D. is an Ordinary Analyst of the Italian Psychoanalytic Society and a member of the International Psychoanalytical Association (IPA). She started her professional life working as a pediatrician. Now she works as a private analyst. Continuing her interests, she has carried on working with the unconscious of adult and children. Since 2004, she has been teaching child neuropsychiatry for the postgraduate course in art therapy at the Academy of Fine Arts of Brera in Milan. From 2013 until 2016, she was the editor of *Rivista Italiana di Psicoanalisi*. She has published articles in national and international magazines and books.

Graham Music, Ph.D. is a Consultant Child and Adolescent Psychotherapist at the Tavistock and Portman Clinics and an adult psychotherapist in private practice. His publications include *Nurturing natures: Attachment and children's emotional, sociocultural and brain development* (2016), *Affect and emotion* (2001), and *The good life: Wellbeing and the new science of altruism, selfishness and immorality* (2014). He has a particular interest in exploring the interface between developmental findings and clinical work. Formerly Associate Clinical Director of the Tavistock's child and family department, he has managed a range of services, working with the aftermath of child maltreatment and neglect, and organized many community-based psychotherapy services. He currently works clinically with forensic cases at the Portman Clinic. He teaches, lectures, and supervises on a range of trainings in Britain and abroad.

Bruce Reis, Ph.D. FIPA is a Clinical Assistant Professor in the New York University Postdoctoral Program in Psychotherapy and Psychoanalysis and a Full Member at the Institute for Psychoanalytic Training and Research (IPTAR), where he is also on the teaching faculty. In addition to supervising and practicing full time in Manhattan, Dr. Reis serves on the editorial boards of several psychoanalytic journals, including the *International Journal of Psychoanalysis*, the *Psychoanalytic Quarterly*, and *Psychoanalytic Dialogues*. He has written extensively about the intersection of phenomenological philosophy with psychoanalytic clinical theory, comparative theories of intersubjectivity, masculinities, trauma and witnessing, and infant research and its application to contemporary analytic technique. He is the co-editor (with Robert Grossmark) of the book *Heterosexual masculinities* and he is a member of the Boston Change Process Study Group.

Avgi Saketopoulou, Psy.D. is on the faculty of the New York University (NYU) Postdoctoral Program in Psychotherapy and Psychoanalysis, the William Allanson White Institute, the New York Psychoanalytic Institute, the National Institute for the Psychotherapies (NIP), and the Chicago Center for Psychoanalysis. She serves on the editorial boards of the *Journal of the American Psychoanalytic Association*, *Psychoanalytic Dialogues*, and *Studies in Gender and Sexuality.* She has received the Ruth Stein prize, the Roughton award, the Symonds prize, and the annual prize of the *Journal of the American Psychoanalytic Association.* She has published work on trauma and its representation, on traumatic and normative gender, on psychosexuality and perversion, and on the enigmatics of consent.

Miriam Steele, Ph.D. is a Professor of Psychology at the New School for Social Research. She bridges the world of psychoanalytic thinking and clinical practice with contemporary research in child development. She trained as a child analyst at the Anna Freud Centre London and received her Ph.D. from University College London. Her research began with the study of "intergenerational patterns of attachment," which embodied one of the first prospective, longitudinal studies incorporating the Adult Attachment Interview and Strange Situation protocols. This work was important in initiating the concept of reflective functioning and providing empirical data to demonstrate the importance of parental states of mind in the social and emotional development of their children with a longitudinal focus on their development into adulthood. Currently, Dr. Steele is a co-investigator on a federally funded grant, "Birth to Three: A Pragmatic Clinical Trial for Child Maltreatment Prevention." Her other projects include studies exploring attachment and body representations in adults and mother–child dyads and studies of child development in foster care and adoptive families.

Neal Vorus, Ph.D. is a Training and Supervising Analyst and faculty member at the Institute for Psychoanalytic Training and Research (IPTAR) and Adjunct Assistant Clinical Professor at the New York University (NYU) Postdoctoral Program in Psychotherapy and Psychoanalysis. He has written a number of papers about the integration of contemporary Freudian and modern Kleinian perspectives on therapeutic action and technique. Dr. Vorus is in private practice in Manhattan, where he treats adults, adolescents, and children.

Brent Willock, Ph.D. is Founding President of the Toronto Institute for Contemporary Psychoanalysis; Board Member, Canadian Institute for Child and Adolescent Psychoanalytic Psychotherapy; Faculty, Institute for the Advancement of Self Psychology; Advisory Board Member, International Association for Relational Psychoanalysis and Psychotherapy; Associate Editor, *Psychoanalytic Dialogues*; and author, *Comparative-integrative psychoanalysis*.

Introduction

Toward synthesis

Andrew Harlem, Ph.D.

The field of child psychotherapy has been marked by impassioned debate since its inception. The "controversial discussions" of the early 1940s between Anna Freud and Melanie Klein are well known to students of psychoanalysis. Whether recent discoveries of the Oedipus conflict, transference neurosis, and unconscious sexual wishes could be applied to child treatment and, if so, how established technique ought to be reconfigured to suit the task generated famously heated arguments in the British Psychoanalytic Society. Anna Freud, traditional and scientific, clashed with the more turbulent and unconventional Klein, as the latter boldly challenged some of Sigmund Freud's fundamental assumptions underlying psychoanalytic theory (Likierman, 1995).

Questions such as whether a child patient could develop a transference neurosis or manage an interpretation aimed at his unconscious wishes and anxieties were central to this early debate. Anna Freud stressed the importance of the child's defenses in the service of the ego and adaptation, while Klein advocated deep interpretation of unconscious anxieties. This fundamental disagreement was not merely one of technique, however. Freud and Klein differed on how they understood the child's mind and its development over time. One could argue, in fact, that the psychoanalytic treatment of children has, more than any other area of psychoanalysis, repeatedly over its history drawn our attention to questions involving technique and its conceptual grounding.

Seventy-five years have passed since Freud and Klein made their respective cases to the British Psychoanalytic Society. It is instructive that both perspectives remain instrumental in our understanding of the child – and, more generally, human development. It is also evident to 21st century observers of psychoanalysis, however, that labels like "Kleinian" and "Freudian" have become what Lacan (following Levi-Strauss) termed "master signifiers" – orienting to the subject's identity, but also "empty" or "floating" in relation to their referent. What it meant to call oneself a Kleinian (or Freudian, for that matter) in 1945 is quite different from what it means today. The signified has changed, but the signifier remains the same.

Over the past quarter-century, many changes have occurred in child psychoanalysis. Innovations in infant research, microanalytic obser-vation, and neuroscience have revolutionized our understanding of early life. Baby watchers such as Beatrice Beebe, Alicia Lieberman, Louis Sander, Stephen Seligman, Daniel Stern, and Ed Tronick have articulated theories of child development that emphasize processes of change through the dynamic interplay of mother and baby. The inter-actional choreography of this relationship has yielded greater under-standing of nonverbal communication, as well as the bidirectional and reciprocal influences of mother and baby, analyst and patient. Meanwhile, theory development in psychoanalysis has moved in simi-lar directions. While mid-20th century thinking was bound tightly to the view that fixation along the developmental pathway required regression stimulated by the transference in order for change to occur, contemporary viewpoints tend to chart a broader and less linear path for therapeutic action. The relational turn, nonlinear systems theory, post-modernism and feminism, and reconceptualization of gender development – to name some of the most prominent recent influences on concept development – have expanded psychoanalytic theory and practice in fascinating ways.

It is those expansions that motivated this collection of essays. Each is intended to describe and illustrate (through clinical case material) a synthetic account of child analytic work. What we mean by "syn-thetic" may be useful to you, the reader, in orienting to the individual voices we've included. Signifiers float not only in time, but also across subjects; the "relational" designation, to take a prime example, varies significantly in denotation to different writers and readers. This is not simply a restatement of the fact that individual differences exist in how we think; it is also an acknowledgement that the expanded scope of ideas in today's psychoanalysis requires increased choice and, crucially in our view, the ability to draw together ideas from diverse sources into an individually fashioned (and continually refashioned) account of one's viewpoint on child treatment.

Precisely how one does this is no longer fully evident through the declaration that one is, say, a Kleinian or a self psychologist. Most of us mix and match in unique ways, even when we take ourselves to be working wholly within a single tradition. As such, we suggest, it is often more revealing of any particular therapist's work how she formulates, in word and action, responses to three kinds of questions. In a form unadulterated by jargon (and here purposely lacking in precision in order to accommodate a variety of approaches), these questions are: (1) What does the child want/need (from me)? (2) What structures of mind/self/us are implicated by, and important for my understanding of, that want/need? (3) What has led to this being the case? In other words, we think it useful to conceive of each analytic therapist as operating (although not necessarily consciously or explicitly) within a kind of triadic conceptual universe fashioned from his views of mind, of development, and of technique.[1] This is what we mean by a synthetic account.

It is our view that compelling accounts of psychoanalytic work require, among other things, a coherence of relation between developmental assumptions, models of mind, and the use of particular techniques.[2,3] In the chapters that follow, you will encounter a variety of conceptual emphases and working styles, each intended to describe a particular author's way of linking up some aspect of developmental theory with how one goes about work in the consulting room. With the exception of the first, all of the chapters include detailed clinical material. There is an emphasis on explaining how that material illustrates the author's view of therapeutic action, which we invite you to think of as the primary site of synthesis.

***

The book is divided into four sections.

The first section foregrounds dialogue between research in child/infant development and the consulting room. Contemporary psychoanalytic perspectives on affect regulation, developing the capacity to mourn a significant loss, development of psychological mindedness, interpersonal/relational patterns between child and parent, and working through trauma and neglect are addressed. Ideas about how children develop their capacity to "be with" the other reverberate through these chapters.

In Chapter 1, Bruce Reis explores the concept of "being-with" that originated in Daniel Stern's infant observation work. Reis grounds and extends Stern's ideas through links to phenomenological philosophy. He argues that, at its most elemental level, the idea of being-with refers to our embodiment, the basic constitutional element of our humanity, and with what philosophers refer to as the condition of our "being". Several psychoanalytic uses of being-with are then reviewed, all of which reflect Stern's uncanny sensitivity to the importance and variety of ways-of-being-with others.

Chapter 2 takes us further into the question of how we learn to be with others. By describing infant–parent work with infants showing early signs of autism, Barbara Kalmanson explores the crucial issue of how infants and parents can be helped to make meaning with each other through verbal and nonverbal exchanges. The focus here is on therapeutic interactions that allow a co-construction of experience to unfold from interpersonally arrived-upon patterns of shared experience and mutual regulation. Linking intervention with research findings, Kalmanson focuses on the use of dynamic experience and developmental guidance to help parents understand their infant's unique sensory, motor, and affective profile and its effects on parental experiences of caregiving. Small vignettes from treatment sessions and a case example serve to illustrate how the therapist attends to obstacles to sensorimotor organization and interactive synchrony while simultaneously considering the ghosts in the parents' histories that may constrict parenting. This chapter also grapples with the work of the therapist in holding the family, timing interventions, finding ports of entry, and interpreting the infant's functioning while addressing the parents' internal worlds.

The use of developmental research to ground analytic intervention also orients Chapter 3. Miriam Steele begins by reviewing the increasing roles of attachment, microanalytic, and neuroscience research in clinical practice, with particular attention to Beatrice Beebe's original microanalytic studies and Safran's creative use of Tronick's rupture and repair findings, which inspired a new way of looking at therapeutic alliance. She then turns our attention to Julie, a traumatized nine-year-old who underwent multiple foster care placements early in her life and was eventually adopted at age seven. Steele suggests that the therapeutic context offered a consistent and empathic presence where the terrifying images permeating Julie's internal world could find expression, thereby opening up the possibility of a more flexible internal working model – the hallmark of secure attachment. Steele reflects on ways in which developmental research guided and found extension in her work with Julie, including helping her to utilize the "mid-range" forms of engagement necessary in interactions with traumatized children.

In Chapter 4, Graham Music takes up the issue of emotional neglect, arguing that its long-term impacts may be underestimated. A range of theoretical and research traditions, including developmental psychology, attachment theory, and neuroscience, are used to delineate key features and patterns that arise in the aftermath of neglect. Through his work with ten-year-old Martin, Music illustrates ways in which early neglect reverberates in the consulting room through the evocation of deadening and emotionally flat countertransference. Because neglected children so badly need from us what they also rarely evoke – our passion, interest, enjoyment, and zeal – it is essential, he argues, for us to actively engage them and attend to our own fluctuating vitality.

The second set of chapters focuses on the role of play, variously conceived, in the growth of mind.

In Chapter 5, Peter Carnochan offers a reconfigured account of the parameters of psychoanalytic play therapy. Noting that relational critiques of classical analytic technique have opened the field to a wider understanding of the analyst's subjective participation and to new views of therapeutic action, he argues that child analysis must do more than merely uncover the existing internal world of the child; it must also support the child in developing new affective-relational skills. Carnochan suggests that the analytic field is best understood as a nonfinite, three-dimensional planetary system populated by positive and negative principles. He draws on clinical vignettes from multiple child treatments to illustrate how we strive to draw closer to the gravitational bodies of safety, insight, and aliveness, but steer away from the problematic forces of impingement, despair, and endless repetition.

Antonio Ferro and Elena Molinari also focus our attention on the evolution of psychoanalytic thinking in Chapter 6. Approaching intersubjectivity theory through Bionion concepts, they emphasize elaboration of the game without the need to decode its content. The analyst/therapist, rather, functions as "assistant director" to a daydreaming film in progress, with the recognition that our technique must be adjusted to fit the developmental capacity of a particular child's container. Children who display symptoms that are not very serious need support from the therapist in editing the waking film/dream, starting from the points at which the dream is interrupted; for children who do not know how to play, in contrast, what is needed is the construction together of a place in the mind where dreams are given life. Through a variety of rich clinical examples, Ferro and Molinari describe patient and analyst playing together in the game/film of the session, in some cases restoring images damaged by sudden emotional wildfires. Like the Lumière brothers, who discovered the principle of animated film by observing their mother using a sewing machine, this pair must find the right speed at which to move together to restore the creative feeling of continuity and movement in the mind.

Chapter 7 approaches play from yet another angle, as Christopher Bonovitz locates potential therapeutic action in the emergence of the therapist's childhood and his/her internal struggle to grasp and make sense of the memories, fleeting images, and reminiscences newly contextualized and reconfigured by the dyadic system within the analytic situation. Attention is directed to state changes and shifting patterns within the therapist–child patient dyad in which the therapist comes to know aspects of his own childhood through various transference and countertransference configurations. The focus here is on the nonverbal and procedural level of communication between therapist and child – motor movements, sounds, and visual images – that, in conjunction with verbal content, communicates emotional states and establishes rhythmic dialogue. Bonovitz provides us with a detailed account of his dialogue with Peter, utilizing his own childhood memories to further his patient's self-regulatory capacity and increase his interpersonal flexibility when negotiating social and emotional terrain.

Neal Vorus, in Chapter 8, draws on advances in autism research to articulate a contemporary Freudian perspective that bridges the conceptual divide between interpretive and relational dimensions of child treatment. Therapeutic action is conceived as activating normal developmental processes whereby children acquire the capacity to represent, tolerate, and reflect upon a range of mental states through dialogic engagement with the mind of an adult. From this perspective, the concept of interpretation is redefined as a continuous, meaning-generating dimension of the treatment relationship, rather than a series of discrete verbal statements. Emphasis here is on the analyst's ongoing engagement with the mind of the patient, whether or not formal interpretations are offered; accordingly, defense is reconceived as a process whereby the child independently manages aspects of experience previously felt to be intolerable to the mind of the other. Vorus illustrates his approach through his work with Billy, a three-year-old patient whose father has died.

Mutuality and relatedness provide a conceptual center for the third set of chapters.

Chapters 9 and 10 offer contrasting perspectives on the same clinical case material. In the first of this pair, Christopher Bonovitz provides a detailed account of his work with eight-year-old Jason, who struggles with affect regulation and loss traced to his adoption. Bonovitz focuses on the "inner dialogue" of the therapist's associations, identifications, and tentative formulations as they emerge in relation to Jason's play and utterances. The co-constitutive relationship between the analyst's mind and the analytic field is focal here, as Bonovitz draws on multiple theoretical traditions (including a relational/intersubjective one) to make sense of the transference–countertransference matrix. This kind of participation, Bonovitz suggests, catalyzes the patient's ability to recognize his therapist as a subject, thereby opening what was a "closed system" to new forms of relatedness and understanding.

Brent Willock then offers a contrasting perspective in Chapter 10. Emphasizing the premature disruption of Jason's prenatal development (rather than his adoption), he explores the relevance of Ogden's autistic-contiguous position for working with children (and adults) whose development has been interfered with by very early developmental trauma. Extending that neo-Kleinian construct, Willock underscores the foundational significance of prenatal life, highlighting challenges to the sensory beginnings of the bounded/grounded self/world experience presented by problematic perinatal experience. Psychotherapeutic investigation and remediation of primal deficits and distortions in the core structure of the self and its relational world are explored.

Chapter 11 also offers a contemporary Kleinian viewpoint on therapeutic action. Here, Seth Aronson highlights the therapist's use of reverie to provide containment for the child's projections, while also depicting the therapeutic relationship as inherently interpersonal. From this perspective, meaning is created by the mutual exchange of projections. Most notably, what Aronson terms "positive projective identification" allows the child to begin to integrate previously dissociated aspects of self, as well as between self and other. These ideas are illustrated in the detailed account of Aronson's work with four-year-old Noah.

The two chapters that comprise the book's fourth and final section draw our attention to what has become a particularly fertile area for psychoanalytic thought in recent years. As our models of development have incorporated more room for variety and paradox, the limits of heteronormative conceptions of gender and sexuality have become evident. No longer constrained by categorical binaries and hegemonic understandings of developmental touchstones (e.g. the Oedipal situation), new syntheses have emerged that enable us to more fully imagine gender and sexuality as fluid.

In Chapter 12, Diane Ehrensaft argues that psychoanalysis has simultaneously been at the forefront and behind the times when it comes to the mental health treatment of gender-nonconforming children and adolescents. Summarizing the need to relearn gender as we have been taught it, this chapter outlines a gender affirmative model that can better inform our clinical practices with children of all genders. Applying the theory to the consultation room, the relational techniques of creating a holding environment, listening, mirroring, play and translation, along with exploration of our own countertransference gender angst, are offered as pathways to providing children with the opportunity to work through their gender stress or distress, discover their true gender selves, and fortify gender resilience in the face of a world that is not always so welcoming of gender diversity. The chapter finishes with a description of Ehrensaft's therapeutic work with a gender-exploring child over the course of four years, from the child at age seven to age eleven, to demonstrate the gender affirmative approach to therapeutic action.

In the book's final chapter (13), Avgi Saketopoulou also begins by noting that, historically, gender atypicality and psychopathology have been collapsed into each other, as we've labored under the reflexive supposition that gender variance is necessarily symptomatic of trauma or of the inability to tolerate reality. More recently, however, psychoanalytic thinkers in general and child analysts in particular have worked to question such conflations and to offer us better analytic tools toward understanding what gender wants. In this chapter, Saketopoulou draws on Loewald to show that, in treating such patients, the analyst's work requires (psychic) acts of imagination if the analyst is to hold the tensions of the mismatch between the child's gendered somatic states and the child's bodily materiality. Clinical material from the intensive treatment of a young transgender girl, Jenny, walks the reader through the difficult affects that can be aroused by misalignments between internal experience with the body's contours and illustrates some of their attendant psychic/somatic fragmentations. This treatment illustrates how clinical interventions rooted in contemporary relational psychoanalysis and that keep futurity in mind can help trans children and their families.

Although we've attempted to present these chapters in a meaningful sequence, we expect that they will be read in accordance with individual interests and needs. Some readers may be particularly interested in issues raised by adoption, for instance, and may therefore choose to read Chapters 3 (Steele) and 9 (Bonovitz) in tandem. Those thinking about autism may find Chapters 2 (Kalmanson) and 8 (Vorus) to be a useful pairing. And so on. We hope that this comparative consideration of the interface between developmental theory and clinical intervention serves you well.

Notes

1 Nothing here should be read to suggest that all differences between analytic therapists could be satisfyingly explained through reference to the realm of ideas alone; individual variations in character style, personality, and history are essential contributors. And there is an interaction; our personal

characteristics and histories figure prominently in the ideas to which we are drawn and that subsequently find elaboration in our work.

2 For example, two practitioners invest certain kinds of interpretations with mutative potential, yet for different reasons. For one it might be tied to an understanding of the mind as, say, dissociative, while another locates the efficacy of the same kind of interpretation in the container–contained relation.

3 Some readers may question our emphasis on technique, as there exist excellent arguments against the codification of psychoanalysis into technical prescription. The conceptual space inhabited by "therapeutic action" is, in our usage, a dynamic conjunction whereby what one actually does (i.e. technique) emerges through a kind of implicit, moment-to-moment procedural knowing prefigured by the realm of ideas and yet utterly responsive to the vicissitudes of perception and feeling of a particular clinical moment.

Reference

Likierman, M. (1995). The debate between Anna Freud and Melanie Klein: An historical survey. *Journal of Child Psychotherapy*, 21:313–325.

Infant research, reflective functioning, and mutual regulation

Chapter 1

Being-with

From infancy through philosophy to psychoanalysis

Bruce Reis, Ph.D.

Not long ago, psychoanalysts mostly used the findings of developmentalists to support the validity of existing psychoanalytic theories of pathology. More recently, it seems those theories themselves have been remade under the influence of infant research findings. Developmental theory and observation have transformed contemporary psychoanalytic thinking. Moreover, the adoption of conceptualizations derived from the findings of infant research has led to new visions of the analytic couple and of the analytic task itself. If psychoanalysis had begun by employing a medical model of treatment, it may well have yielded to what might be called a developmental model of treatment in the wake of decades of influence of those whose interest in infants and their caretakers has led to a rethinking of what analysis is – that is to say, what its goals are, how analysis works, and what its methods of therapeutic action are.

The group of infant researchers who have brought this change to psychoanalysis are well known by now, their studies cited by members of every analytic school. The conceptualizations they've introduced have become the new mainstays of analytic thinking. I wish to highlight a particular conceptualization that has only recently migrated into psychoanalytic thinking: that of "being-with". It arises out of the infant research literature and finds spectacular theoretical grounding within the philosophic literature.

The importance of this conception within psychoanalysis resides in a consideration of a facet of the analytic relationship that has heretofore gone largely unremarked upon. At its most elemental level, the idea of being-with has to do with our embodiment, with a basic constitutional element of our humanity, and with issues philosophers refer to as having to do with "being". While most analytic conceptions, supported by different philosophic groundings, have reified a notion of the solitary individual to greater or lesser degrees, the idea of being-with is, in itself, reflective of a condition of relationality, as I will illustrate.

Knowledge and the tissue of experience

I will begin the exploration of the notion of being-with by briefly describing the emergence of this term in the work of Daniel Stern. As a pre-eminent infant researcher, Stern helped to define the relational contexts in which infants come to learn how to do things such as play and engage with another to actualize an intention. Rather than isolate these as separate behaviors, Stern (1998), in the tradition of the attachment theorists, considered the ways in which infants come to learn a "style of relating" that he referred to as "ways of being-with" an other. Stern (2004) always considered this style an implicitly learned disposition, describing that:

> Years of observational research on infants and their mothers, in parallel with the practice of adult psychotherapy, have made us sensitive to the importance of implicit knowledge. Babies do not communicate in the verbal explicit register until after 18 months or so, when they begin to talk. Accordingly, all the rich, analogically nuanced, social and affective interactions that take place in the first 18 months of life occur, by default, in the implicit nonverbal domain. Also, all the considerable knowledge that the baby acquires about what to expect from people, how to deal with them, how to feel about them, and how to *be-with-them* falls into this nonverbal domain.
>
> (p. 113, emphasis added)

For Stern, much of this knowledge is concerned with *how* one does things with others. Yet this is knowledge that, it goes without saying, is neither dynamically unconscious nor conscious; neither is it necessarily verbal. It is instead conceived as non-conscious knowledge on a procedural and affective level. From the very beginning of life, the infant is interacting with significant others. Being-with refers to an organization of the knowledge the infant develops in the process of this interaction. To illustrate, Stern gives examples taken from the work of Ainsworth et al. (1978) of reunions between mothers and children when the infants were only 12 months of age. Focusing on the attachment patterns already in place by this time, Stern (2004) describes that after a short separation from the mother, upon her return:

> The infant implicitly knew what to do with his body, face, feelings, expectations, excitation, inhibitions, redirection of activities, and so on. He "knew whether" to approach her, lifting his arms for an embrace and body contact, or whether to not move and pretend that her return is a non-event, or whether to exaggerate his desire and need for contact to get more from her. He "knows" whether to drop what he was playing with, or to continue to focus on the toys, even half-heartedly. He "knew" if he should anticipate physical–psychological gratification or tolerate a state of stress. He "knew" when to approach her, if he did not immediately, and at what speed, and with steps that were not so large or so fast that she would reject him.
>
> (pp. 114–115)

It is a curious kind of knowing that Stern is referring to here. It is important to understand that this knowing is entirely contextual, in a strongly relational sense. This is not knowledge that one carries around in one's head, as one might a phone number. What one knows is a function of, as well as specific to, the relational contexts one has experienced. It is perhaps better conceived as knowledge that is relational in its nature.[1]

Here, knowing takes on qualities that are different from those one normally attributes to it. It becomes dynamic and fluid rather than fixed and static. Furthermore, there is no reason to assume that such knowing is limited to infancy and childhood. The implicit realm of interaction in adult relationships had largely been unexplored before the late 1990s when researchers such as the members of the Boston Change Process Study Group began to extend the findings of infancy research to the ways in which patient and analyst influence a process occurring between them that is always going on at a non-conscious, embodied level of exchange. At this level, experience is a co-experience where knowledge is not simply of one's self or of another. It is instead knowledge derived within the context of relating. This knowledge is not explicitly learned but is developed within the moment-to-moment therapeutic interaction between analyst and patient; it is an implicit, relational knowing (Lyons-Ruth, 1998; BCPSG, 2010).

Stern et al. (1998) make the distinction between declarative knowledge "which is gained or acquired through verbal interpretations that alter the patient's intrapsychic understanding" and implicit relational knowing, occurring "through interactional, intersubjective processes that alter the relational field within the context of what we will call the shared implicit relationship" (p. 905).

The "knowing" here refers not to any mental contents as such, but to a style or a way of being with others that is learned from birth and continues its development through adult relationships, such as the therapeutic relationship. The infant researcher Louis Sander (2008) placed special emphasis on the importance of the experience of coming to "know" oneself through experiencing being known by another. For Sander, this task was, perhaps paradoxically, at the heart of self-organization for the individual, as increased coherence followed from increased inclusiveness of organization so that more parts (of oneself) are integrated in more complex and adaptive ways into an overall wholeness. The Boston Change Process Study Group (2010) has written:

> Because of the critical role this process of becoming known plays in the individual's sense of integration and well-being, exposing to another the delicate source of self-organizing initiative [remained, in Sander's own words] "a life or death precipice at the heart of self-organization."
>
> (p. 57)

Because of my own commitment to a phenomenological approach, I too think of such "knowledge" as relational in its constitution, similar to the way in which William James (1996) described knowledge when he asked the question: "Why insist that knowing is a static relation out of time when it practically seems so much a function of our active life?" (p. 75). For James, as for Stern et al. (1998), this knowing is a process-oriented conception that relies on experience and embodiment: "Knowledge of sensible realities thus comes to life inside the tissue of experience. It is *made*; and made by relations that unroll themselves in time" (James, 1996, p. 57, original emphasis). Stern (2004) too was intensely interested in the temporal structure of experience as it unfolds, bringing this concentration on experiencing in time into his theorization regarding change in adult psychotherapy. The Boston Change Process Study Group (2010) has gone on to introduce a theory of psychotherapeutic change that emphasizes this type of knowledge made by relations, seeing it as contained within the implicit relating that brings about changes in an individual's ways of being-with others. This paradigm of change suggests a particular function of the analyst to be crucial – his ability to be-with the patient and to live through the often fragile tissue of intense emotional processes occurring between them.

Some philosophic grounding

Before examining how this conception has begun to be used within the clinical realm, it is useful to consider a stream of philosophic thinking that supports the notion of being-with that has just been presented in the work of Stern and other infant researchers.

Arising within the tradition of Continental philosophy and largely born of the dissatisfaction of philosophers with Cartesian trends that define the mind through its isolation and cognitive knowledge and as private and opaque, phenomenological philosophers such as Merleau-Ponty (1945) resituated the mind not as something hidden behind the body or revealed at times within behavior, but rather as itself an intentional, relational subject.

Following Heidegger's situating the human within a human condition of *being*, contemporary philosophers shifted a familiar model of an egocentric individual to a model of a "we-centric" sharing of a condition of being. This ontological approach conceives of the foundation of the human condition in terms of a community rather than in individuality. As an example, consider the work of Continental philosopher Jean-Luc Nancy (1991). Nancy sets out to deconstruct terms such as "individual", "subject", and "intersubjective" in a manner that analysts might term radically relational. Nancy, like the majority of infant researchers, makes sharing the prime condition of human existence. And while Nancy's sharing is philosophically grounded and the sharing described by infant researchers is a psychobiological sharing, their intents are closely related, as will be illustrated.

For Nancy, sharing is not a relation of what he would call "singularities" and is not "intersubjective" in that it does not exist between two individual subjects. What is shared is a condition of being-in-common:

> This means that the relation is not one between human beings, as we might speak of a relation established between two subjects constituted as subjects and as "securing," secondarily, this relation. In this relation, "human beings" are not given – but it is relation alone that can give them "humanity."
>
> (Nancy, 1993, p. 73)

In Nancy's view, sharing is not something that preconstituted individual entities "do" in order to achieve an intersubjective relation. It is rather a non-mediated and non-dialectical relation of encounter in which what is always affirmed is a singular exposure to our mutually shared separation and exteriority, just as much as our connection and proximity. Nancy uses the French verb *"partager"*, meaning both sharing and dividing, to illustrate how our mutual connection lies in our mutual separation and that what most holds us in common is this separating–connecting.

It is rather uncanny how similar Nancy's philosophic conception of this relational space is to descriptions made by infant researchers of the re-embedding of the baby into the social world. Vasu Reddy (2008) writes:

> After all, we (in psychology) often think and talk about understanding other people as if it were a case of one completely separate person – and completely separate mind – trying to understand another. We don't tend to talk about people or minds as already intrinsically connected. But what if we did? What would this mean? What if we think of the starting point for understanding people as being, not isolation and ignorance, but an emotional relation and a psychological awareness?
>
> (pp. 3–4)

Perhaps no Continental philosopher takes Reddy's point so seriously as Nancy.

For Nancy, as for the infant researchers, no experience of "I" comes before the experience of "we". To be an "I" is already to be in an ontological condition of "we"-ness, a condition that Nancy, following Heidegger, would term "being-with". In contrast to many of our analytic theories of intersubjectivity, for Nancy (2000), this condition is not a developmental achievement, but is conceived as a common "exposure" to being:

> Our being-with, as a being-many, is not at all accidental, and it is in no way the secondary and random dispersion of a primordial essence. It forms the proper and necessary status and consistency of originary alterity as such. *The plurality of beings is at the foundation* [fondment] *of Being.*
>
> (p. 12, original emphasis)

This means that the other is outside of the self, but so too is the self outside itself. Indeed, this is how one even comes to have a sense of self. This mutual exposure need not, like Hegelian mutuality, be based upon recognized sameness, given that, in light of Nancy's thinking, sharing is as much a sharing of difference as of sameness.

Within infant studies, Stern and his colleagues (Stern, 1977; 1985; Stern et al., 1984) have developed the idea of affect attunement in a manner that may be said to parallel Nancy's ideas regarding the sharing of difference as well as sameness. Concerned with how each member of the dyad lets the other know about their inner feeling states, Stern wondered how a mother, for instance, might communicate to her infant that she grasped not simply what the infant did behaviorally, but also the feeling the infant experienced that lay behind the action. In this way, Stern shifted emphasis from the overt behavior to the underlying subjective experience. The response would not be an exact matching of the infant's behavior, but rather a response to that behavior that indicates a sharing of the experience by another. Stern (2004) described this responsiveness as a non-conscious, emotional, and bodily based process, "a form of selective and cross-modal imitation, as the path to sharing inner feeling states, in contrast to faithful imitation as the path to sharing overt behavior" (p. 84).

Perhaps we might consider this experience of attunement described by Stern (2004) as being similar to Nancy's thoughts about a being-with that affirms our mutual exposure to separation, distance, and exteriority just as much as our connection and proximity. Reflecting back more than just the infant's own state, the attuned other avows this separation as an originary alterity. She and her infant already find themselves outside of themselves, as it is here that relational experience in the first person plural takes shape.

Being-with in the clinical situation

Winnicott (1960) focused analytic attention on issues of being and breakdowns in the capacity to be. He wrote of the infant's experience of subjective continuity in using the term "going on being" and of a type of being-with another in childhood that stressed the experience of being alone in their presence. He wrote:

> With "the care that it receives from its mother" each infant is able to have a personal existence, and so begins to build up what might be called a continuity of being. On the basis of this continuity of being the inherited potential gradually develops into an individual infant. If maternal care is not good enough then the infant does not really come into existence, since there is no continuity of being; instead the personality becomes built on the basis of reactions to environmental impingement.
>
> (p. 54)

Over several papers (Reis, 2009a; 2009b; 2010; 2012), I have been interested in the clinical applications of the idea derived from infant research and phenomenological philosophy of "being-with". A number of years ago, I utilized the work of several members of the Boston Change Process Study Group in describing a clinical case and in illustrating the importance of an analytic stance of "being-with" the patient. Making use of Sander's (1991) conception of a recognition process and Lyons-Ruth's (2000) extension of that conception into non-conscious forms of coming to know one's self through the way one experiences being known, I suggested that what had been transformative for the analysand in the analytic case I described was the silent accompanying and being-with the patient as painful, traumatic enactments took place in the treatment. Change, I suggested, was not a function of mutative interpretation or a knowing about what had occurred in the patient's past, but rather "an intersubjective experience at the limits of understanding" (Reis, 2009b, p. 1370), similar to what Bach (2006) has described as a mutual living through.

More recently (Reis, 2012), in investigating the differences between analytic silence and analytic quiet, I wrote that "quiet may be the absence of words, but it is not necessarily solitary. Where silence signals withdrawal and withholding, quiet marks a 'withness' between patient and analyst...It is not a withdrawal so much as it is a togetherness without words" (p. 25). Here, again, a deep sharing experience is developed in the being-with another, and it is the relation itself rather than any particular activity that is the source of its power. For this reason, I described analytic quiet as "a more expansive term" that is associated with "lived experience in a relationship between patient and analyst" (p. 24). It is an experience I referred to as embedded in a practice of psychoanalysis rather than a technique, since the former differs in that it is the engagement that takes prominence over the application of a method.

In describing his work with patients in the midst of psychic breakdown, Christopher Bollas (2013) reports the utility of the creation of a different analytic frame, one that is temporally extended and allows patients the room to access early experiences that had been frozen and undigested. Bollas writes that patients seek another with whom this experience can be unfrozen, released, and understood. During this process, he writes, "The mental pain of the individual's suffering is now being released through memory, understanding and evoked emotional experience, and the analyst has just to be there, listening and learning" (p. 82). For Bollas, this is clearly meant to be an experience that is not to be reduced to a patient's increased knowledge. It is rather a fundamental encounter with a person's "being". He goes on:

> These are not moments for rolling insights, the hubbub of dialogue, the articulation of the formations of the self's character through the transference or countertransference. Indeed, it is as if these ordinary features of analysis become mere asides, as the self opens up to the most fundamental dimension of *being*.
>
> (p. 83, original emphasis)

Robert Grossmark (2012) also writes of "accompanying" patients into the depths of their therapeutic regressions without imposing upon them the person of the analyst in order that the patient may find what is truly his or hers to discover. In writing of the importance of "shared states of being", Grossmark, very much in the spirit of Bollas, writes:

> The analyst has to be available to enter and dwell in altered, uncomfortable, and sometimes traumatizing states, which may themselves elude description and elucidation. Acknowledging that my language is insufficient to describe the kinds of bizarre experiences I underwent with [the patient], I can say that feelings of catastrophic fragmentation, aloneness, uselessness, omnipotence, bizarre fantasies, and body dysmorphia were almost commonplace for me over a prolonged period of time. I would suggest that an insistence on intruding my own presence would have obviated the emergence of these phenomena in the analytic relationship and might have amounted to a version of Bion's "obtrusive object analyst" who would introduce interpretations to obviate being the receptacle for the psychotic parts of the patient's personality. I would add that introducing my own experience and pulling for a more mentalized and reflective interaction would have been an attempt to save me, not just from encountering the near-psychotic and fragmented states generated in my own mind.
>
> (p. 640)

In these ways, Grossmark lends himself to an ontological accompaniment of the patient through states of deadness, non-existence, and fragmentation that allows and facilitates the patient's discovery of an increased aliveness, coherence, and being.

Ofra Eshel (2013) has also recently written about the importance of what, like me (Reis, 2012, p. 25), she calls a patient–analyst "withness". She writes of the analyst's deep availability to the patient as a form of "presence", one that focuses on experience-near attunement, receptive capacity, holding, containing, and protection, rather than the proffering of interpretations regarding the analytic relationship and especially of the quality of patient–analyst separateness. She writes:

> I believe that while "presencing" involves each of the above capacities and functions, the experience of "presencing" is a quality that is superordinate to these capacities and functions and must be considered as an aspect of the analytic experience in its own terms. It is primarily an interconnected relatedness rather than an interactive relationship, and it concentrates on the ontological (being) quality of the analytic experience rather than the epistemological and interpretive qualities.
>
> (p. 2)

What I think each of these writers – and myself – are attempting to describe is a quality of being, one that links patient and analyst not on the level of interacting (separate) subjects whose goal is to know themselves and/or the other, but rather on the level of a being-with that subtends such relations. It is an immediate relatedness, a consciousness that is before consciousness, one that does not depend on an "opening up" in order to be in relation, but that is already in relation from the start. Thought of as primary relatedness, this level of consciousness can be conceived as an *a priori* openness to others and to the world that belongs to the very structure of subjectivity itself (Thompson, 2007) prior to any relationship of subject and object.

My own thought about presence goes to the importance Winnicott placed on the idea of maternal presence. Often it is the "maternal" part of the equation that receives the majority of emphasis (i.e. functions of holding or containing or responsiveness), but equally or perhaps more important is the quality of presence evidenced. When, for instance, I think about my work with children, the endless hours of discussion of the intricacies of an online multiplayer game, or other seemingly mundane topics that I have become expert in and consumed with by virtue of participation in a conversation that I know is important to my patient, it is not the symbolic transformation that this play has brought about that allowed my patient to leave a protected psychic area, but rather my presence in the discussion. If, as Winnicott (1952) has written, "the centre of gravity of the being does not start off in the individual. It is in the total set-up" (p. 99), then it seems plausible to me to suppose that one's relation to the "total set-up" may continue as an *a priori* openness to others and the world that belongs to the very structure of subjectivity – that to be a subject will necessarily, therefore, mean to be-with.

Discussion

As analysts, we do not seek to cure persons of the impacts of their experiences. Rather, as psychological companions, we share these experiences in the crucible of the transference–countertransference as it transforms from a relived present to a remembered past. In this reliving, the individual confronts what Sander (2008) called "a life or death precipice at the heart of self-organization" (p. 17) as they expose to another the delicate source of self-organizing initiative that separates them and at the same time is their connection with others. It is from such experiences that patients further come into a personal existence. Those who have raised a child know this mode of connection, as do analysts.

Note

1 As an aside, we could remember here that the word *consciousness* derives from the Greek *suneidesis*, meaning "communal knowledge" or knowledge that can be shared with others. *Suneidesis* was eventually translated into the Latin word *conscientia*, which begins with the preposition <u>con</u> (with) and the substantive *scientia* (knowledge). Taken literally, consciousness can be understood to mean that to be conscious is to have knowledge *with others, knowledge in common, or shared knowledge* (Rochat, 2009). Such a knowledge seems consistent with a conception of the implicit knowledge involved in being-with others.

References

Ainsworth, M.D.S., Blehar, M.C., Waters, E., & Wall, S. (1978). *Patterns of attachment.* Hillsdale, NJ: Relbaum.

Bach, S. (2006). *Getting from here to there.* Hillsdale, NJ: Analytic Press.

Bollas, C. (2013). *Catch them before they fall.* New York, NY: Routledge.

Boston Change Process Study Group (2010). *Change in psychotherapy: A unifying paradigm.* New York, NY: W. W. Norton & Co.

Eshel, O. (2013). Patient–analyst "withness": On analytic "presencing", passion, and compassion in states of breakdown, despair, and deadness. *Psychoanalytic Quarterly*, 82:925–963.

Grossmark, R. (2012). The unobtrusive relational analyst. *Psychoanalytic Dialogues*, 22:629–646.

James, W. (1996). A world of pure experience. In: *Essays in radical empiricism* (pp. 39–91). Lincoln, NE: University of Nebraska Press.

Lyons-Ruth, K. (1998). Implicit relational knowing: Its role in development and psychoanalytic treatment. *Infant Mental Health Journal*, 19:282–289.

Lyons-Ruth, K. (2000). "I sense that you sense that I sense": Sander's recognition process and the specificity of relational moves in the psychotherapeutic setting. *Infant Mental Health Journal*, 21:85–99.

Merleau-Ponty, M. (1945/1962). *The phenomenology of perception*. Trans. C. Smith. London, UK: Routledge Press.

Nancy, J.-L. (2000). *Being singular plural*. Redwood City, CA: Stanford University Press.

Nancy, J.-L. (1993). *The experience of freedom*. Redwood City, CA: Stanford University Press.

Nancy, J.-L. (1991). *The inoperative community*. Minneapolis, MN: University of Minnesota Press.

Reddy, V. (2008). *How infants know minds*. Cambridge, MA: Harvard University Press.

Reis, B. (2009a). We: Commentary on papers by Trevarthen, Ammaniti & Trentini, and Gallese. *Psychoanalytic Dialogues*, 19:565–579.

Reis, B. (2009b). Performative and enactive features of psychoanalytic witnessing: The transference as the scene of address. *International Journal of Psychoanalysis*, 90:1359–1372.

Reis, B. (2010). A human family: Commentary on paper by Elisabeth Fivaz-Depeursinge, Chloe Lavanchy-Scaiola, and Nicolas Favez. *Psychoanalytic Dialogues*, 20:151–157.

Reis, B. (2012). Silence and quiet: A phenomenology of wordlessness. *Division/ Review, The Official Publication of Division of Psychoanalysis (39) of the American Psychological Association*. 6:24–25.

Rochat, P. (2009). *Others in mind*. New York, NY: Cambridge University Press.

Sander, L. (2008). Recognition process: Context and experience of being known. In: G. Amadei & I. Bianchi (Eds.), *Living systems, evolving consciousness, and the emerging person: A selection of papers from the life work of Louis Sander* (pp. 177–192). New York, NY: Analytic Press.

Stern, D.N. (1977). *The first relationship: Infant and mother*. Cambridge, MA: Harvard University Press.

Stern, D.N., Hofer, L, Haft, W., & Dore, J. (1984). Affect attunement: The sharing of feeling states between mother and infant by means of inter-modal fluency. In: T. Field & N. Fox (Eds.), *Social perception in infants* (pp. 249–268). Norwood, NJ: Ablex Publishing.

Stern, D.N. (1985). *The interpersonal world of the infant: A view from psychoanalysis and developmental psychology.* New York, NY: Basic Books.

Stern, D.N. (1998). *The motherhood constellation: A unified view of parent–infant psychotherapy.* London, UK: Karnac Books.

Stern, D.N. (2004). *The present moment in psychotherapy and everyday life.* New York, NY: W. W. Norton & Co.

Thompson, E. (2007). *Mind in life.* Cambridge, MA: Harvard University Press.

Wachtel, P. (2008). *Relational theory and the practice of psychotherapy.* New York, NY: Guilford Press.

Winnicott, D.W. (1952). Anxiety associated with insecurity. In: *The maturational processes and the facilitating environment* (pp. 97–100). Madison, CT: International Universities Press.

Winnicott, D.W. (1960). The theory of parent–infant relationship. In: *The maturational processes and the facilitating environment* (pp. 37–55). Madison, CT: International Universities Press.

Chapter 2

How we know how to be with others

Infant–parent psychotherapy for early indicators of autism spectrum disorders

Barbara Kalmanson, Ph.D.

Some forms of therapeutic action are hidden in full view. When the infant is in the room as the center of treatment, the process of psychotherapy is unique. Attention shifts from the individual to the relationship as the focus of treatment. Once the relationship becomes the focus, therapeutic action comes alive in the nonverbal interaction. The baby cannot talk about dreams or fantasies, past experiences, or even play symbolically – the grist for the mill of traditional child psychotherapies. The infant–parent therapist must find meaning in preverbal systems of communication evident in the choreography of affect cueing, sound making, movement, use of force and space, temporal exchanges, and the demonstration of intention. These elements of dynamic experience that Stern (2010) refers to as forms of vitality are so automatic, one tends to overlook them unless they are absent and violate one's expectations about what it feels like to be with another person. Parents who become perplexed by their infant's lack of warmth and connectedness or failure to seek them out, follow their actions with gaze, move in synchrony, or mold to their body provide a natural opportunity for therapeutic exploration into the essential elements of dynamic experience that form the foundation for building relationships.

The intent of this chapter is to focus on the therapeutic interactions that allow a co-construction of experience to unfold from interpersonally arrived-upon patterns of shared experience and mutual regulation. How the infant and parent are helped to find meaning with each other through their nonverbal exchanges will be illustrated from infant–parent work with infants showing early signs of autism.

Infant–parent psychotherapies with infants and young children who show early signs of not innately knowing how to be with others offer the therapist unique opportunities to apply current developmental research to the therapeutic process. Current research-based psychoanalytic concepts such as forms of vitality (Stern, 2010), intersubjectivity (Trevarthen, 1998; 2009), and implicit relational knowing (Beebe & Lachman, 1994; Tronick, 2007) will be used to link concepts from research and theory to the practice of psychotherapy with infants and parents. The chapter illustrates how this research can be used to devise strategies for establishing connections between parents and infants through the dynamic experiences rooted in affect cueing, pacing, movement, sound, temporal sequences, rhythms, use of space, intensity, and intention. The process of infant–parent psychotherapy will be described, particularly focusing on the use of dynamic experience and developmental guidance to help parents understand their infant's unique sensory, motor, and affective profile and its effect on their caregiving. Small vignettes from treatment sessions and a case example serve to illustrate how the therapist attends to obstacles to sensorimotor organization and interactive synchrony in the timing and intensity of affect cues while simultaneously attending to the ghosts in the parents' histories that are constricting their parenting. Finally, the work of the therapist in holding the family, timing interventions, finding ports of entry, and interpreting the infant's functioning while addressing the parents' internal worlds will be addressed.

Contributions from infant–parent interaction research

Recent work in psychoanalysis and infant development has sparked great interest in the earliest preverbal dynamic interpersonal systems. Clinicians and researchers investigate the origins of interpersonal connection both to learn about how relationships form the fulcrum of infant development and to deepen understanding of the psychotherapeutic process. The work of the Boston Change Process Study Group (BCPSG) (2002, 2010), Stern (1985, 2010), Trevarthen (1998, 2009), Tronick (2007), and Beebe and Lachman (1988, 2002) are examples of inquiries into how we know how to be with others long before we can walk or talk. In the following example, the therapist uses observation of moments of interactional synchrony and moments of mismatch between an infant and parent to understand the infant's constitutional constrictions and the parent's emotional reactions. The therapist is able to translate the internal experience of the infant to the parent, increase the parent's self-awareness of her reaction to her feeling state, and facilitate reconnection between infant and parent, preventing a cycle of affective misalignment from becoming the typical dynamic between them. The therapist can apply research on the origins of interpersonal life to the therapeutic process. Interventions are used to establish intimacy between parent and infant through the dynamic experience.

Freeze reaction in an 11-month-old

An 11-month-old boy is poised on hands and knees about five feet from his mother. He looks up and catches her inviting expression – eyes wide, big smile, open arms, and soft voice calling his name. Accurately reading her affect cues and intention, his facial expression brightens as he begins to crawl toward her. She becomes excited by his approach, which can be observed in the marked increase in her voice volume as she begins to move her body toward him at a quicker tempo than he is moving in her direction. He freezes and drops close to the ground, while his facial expression transforms from excited pleasure to fear. The mother looks confused; her gaze shifts to the periphery of the room and her body stiffens. When the infant shuts down and fails to recover from the feeling of being overwhelmed and mismatched, the mother retreats. She sits up and self-protectively turns her attention to something else in the room, leaving the infant to struggle alone with his internal experience of fright and freeze.

Magnify this experience by the number of natural opportunities for similar misalignment throughout the day, occurring without repair strategies, and one can imagine the vulnerability of this dyad for establishing homeostasis in a dysfunctional dynamic system. In the above example, the parent feels rejected and withdraws. The work of the therapist is to support the parent in the observation of her "good enough" (Winnicott, 1953) invitation to the infant. Most babies would continue to respond positively to the increased intensity in the parent's approach. This baby, however, seems to have a very narrow window of well-regulated arousal, and the slightest unexpected surge in intensity of affect and action violates his anticipation of a rhythmic match of sound and movement. In an effort at self-protection, he shuts out further input.

The parent is helped to see that the obstacle in the way is in the baby's arousal system and registration of sensory input and not his negative feelings toward her. The work of the therapist is to offer the insight and support the parent needs in order to regain the emotional vitality that will enable her to repair the situation by matching the infant's rhythm, use of space, and intensity by slowing down, lowering her body, lowering her voice tone, and tolerating waiting for the baby to recover his movement toward her. Once the baby recovers and sees the invitation has resumed at the right pace, he continues to move toward the parent and ends up in her arms with an embrace that is reassuring to all and gives both parent and infant an experience of repair strategies that serve the growing intimacy of the relationship rather than reinforce a sense of withdrawal. In infant–parent psychotherapy, the therapist is attending to the fundamental central nervous system force of arousal, which initiates action, sharpens perception, brings up cognitions, and makes emotions emerge (Stern, 2010).

Implicit relational knowing

Unlike more traditional forms of psychotherapy where attention to the semantic or symbolic representations in the form of language predominate, in infant–parent work, procedural representations or implicit relational knowing become salient (Beebe & Lachman, 1988, 1994; Lyons-Ruth, 1999; Tronick, 2007). Procedural representation informs us about how to do something, like ride a bicycle, whereas implicit relational knowing refers to knowing how to do things with others that rely on affect and interaction. Infant research and psychoanalytic practice document the presence of this way of knowing long before language emerges. Acting on our understanding of how to be with others operates in full view but often outside our focal attention throughout life. Infants with early signs of autism make the most disorienting social partners. By virtue of their inability to show typical recognition of the mental states of others (Baron-Cohen, Tager-Fusberg, & Cohen, 1993), they bring vitality forms and implicit relational knowing into conscious awareness in their family relationships. By closely examining the early social interactions between these infants and their parents, one can see the effects of attempts and failures in the cycles of mutual regulation that build the sense of knowing and of being known in the relationship. Rather than explore the beginnings of a relationship from the construct of internalized object relations, which connotes a taking in of the other from the outside, the examples in this chapter focus on the co-construction of experience through a process of shared experience and mutual regulation. The infant and parent find each other in their nonverbal exchanges where meanings are derived through rhythm, vision, movement, and sound.

The competent infant

Unlike earlier psychoanalytic conceptions of the infant as merged or undifferentiated from the mother, modern developmental research reveals autonomous, well-differentiated functioning emerging much earlier in development. At between three and five months of age, babies take control over initiating and terminating moments of direct visual engagement in social activities (Stern, 1971; Beebe & Stern, 1977). Although the infant is not walking or talking, or even sitting up, control over gaze is a mature sensory system and a powerful form of social communication. The baby shares almost equal capacity to regulate the same social behavior as the parent. The infant initiates, terminates, sustains, and avoids social contact through the co-regulation of gaze.

The importance of mutual regulation in creating a shared experience between parents and infants is well documented. Brazelton, Koslowski, and Main (1974) describe a narrative cycle between the newborn and parent that includes initiation by infant or parent, visual orientation to voice, acceleration of intensity of expression, a peak of excitement, and deceleration processes. There is choreography between baby and parent with a rhythmicity and mutuality in this moment of shared recognition. Evidence for the importance of the intersynchrony of sound and motion in the development of interpersonal understanding is present in the work of Daniel Stern and Colwyn Trevarthen. Stern, in *Forms of vitality* (2010), describes the dynamic, nonverbal elements of interaction that bring infant and parent together for a matching of inner states that creates a moment of meeting. Temporal elements such as the flow of an interaction, the tempo, and slowing down or speeding up of vocal tone or gesture are the earliest forms of communication. Through affect attunement (Stern, 1985) – a cross-modal parental gesture that matches the vitality affect of the infant – the parent shows the baby that she understands what it felt like to do what the child did. The simultaneous realization of a shared experience joins the infant and parent in a mutually gratifying relationship. The failure of parent and infant to find each other in shared experience creates a different dynamic system. Asynchronous choreography is characterized by physical withdrawal, shutting down of sensory seeking through gaze, flight responses in the motor system, and dis-coordination of rhythmicity in motor and vocal activity.

The following example illustrates the process of mutual regulation unfolding between a ten-month-old girl and her mother following a session during which the parents confessed that they felt Mary was only happy when she was left alone. Tearfully, the mother bemoaned that all mothers want their children to be happy. The therapist suggested that the infant's happiness is meant to include the mother. The work they would embark on together would be focused on making that true.

Pacing and sensory sensitivity in a ten-month-old

Mary is sitting on the rug holding a blanket, with her mother and the therapist seated on the rug nearby. In earlier sessions, we have learned that Mary is more likely to respond to Mom's initiation of mutual gaze when the mother is seated three to four feet from Mary rather than holding her or appearing in close proximity. Mary's over-arousal with too close physical contact or too many sources of sensory input and her subsequent retreat are difficult to understand given the typical infant's pleasure in being held and looked at. The presence of the therapist holds the mother's anxiety that Mary will terminate her gaze and withdraw, happier to be on her own.

As the mother has learned from discussion during other sessions, she must move slowly to invite Mary into closer contact. She either moves or talks, offering sensory information one source at a time in a temporal sequence Mary might absorb. By moving closer to Mary in very small increments of space, Mom is able to sustain their mutual pleasure in gazing at each other. Mom picks up the blanket Mary has dropped and puts it in front of her own face. She initiates a peekaboo game with her daughter, who brightens and chortles with pleasure when Mom reappears.

The therapist knows how long Mom has waited for the sound of her daughter's laughter as a sign of pleasure in the relationship. Anticipating the yearning for closeness will propel Mom into vigorous action and overwhelm Mary, the therapist softly coaches Mom to go slow, repeat the peekaboo, give Mary time to adapt to the game, then come a little closer to her daughter, and a little closer, very slowly. After painstakingly moving toward her daughter, she is finally just in front of her with the blanket hiding her face. The just right pace of the game while holding a facial expression of positive affect and anticipation keeps Mary engaged. It then activates her motor system to take initiative and expand the interaction. Mary reaches toward the blanket and pulls it off her mother's head with a big chuckle and a broad smile, reveling in her sense of agency and capacity to initiate, reciprocate, and co-construct their shared experience.

Mary's mother is overjoyed with her daughter's sustained shared attention and responds with well-calibrated pleasure to Mary's initiation. This exchange is a new experience for mother and child. Mary is neither the passive recipient nor the overwhelmed avoidant responder to her mother's invitations for interaction and emotional connection. Her mother's supported capacity to meet her in just the right rhythm with just the right approach in space and intensity of affect enable Mary to become a co-creator of her experience, mobilizing her motor system and energizing her positive affective response.

Synchronized sound and action

Trevarthen's (1998) conceptualization of the development of intersubjectivity is based on the synchrony of movement and vocalization between the infant and the caregiver. Condon and Sander (1974) first demonstrated the infant's coordinated movement to the sound of the parent's voice. The higher-pitched lilt in the voice of the mother as she says "pretty baby" is matched by the crescendo of the infant's foot reaching high in the air. When the mother picks up the tempo in her voice, the infant's arms bicycle quickly in the air with a motor rhythm that mirrors the voice quality of the mother. Similarly, episodes of spontaneous, sequenced hand movements of a six-week-old create proto-conversations that communicate changing states of vitality (Malloch & Trevarthen, 2008). This research offers a glimpse at how the registration of sensory input is processed across perceptual modalities by the young infant and expressed in attunement with the parent. Sensorimotor activity between the infant and parent come to take on affective meaning as the synchronization of sound and action are experienced as moments of connection and intimacy, or as momentary failures requiring repair, or as disappointments and discomfort requiring self-protective mechanisms of shut down and withdrawal. The rhythms of sensorimotor-based interaction become dual coded with affective experience.

The infant–parent therapeutic process

The process of infant–parent psychotherapy with infants showing early signs of autism expands upon the infant mental health concept of parallel process, in which the therapist's way of being with the parent effects change in the parent's way of being with the infant (Fraiberg, 1980). The job of the therapist is to hold the dyad and support each member's capacity to sustain affective connection. Much of the work in infant mental health is weighted toward resolving the conflicts in the parent's experience that stem from the ghosts in the parent's past that are revisited upon the baby (Fraiberg, 1980; Lieberman & Pawl, 1993). The therapeutic interventions consist of a blend of insight-oriented talk therapy, developmental guidance, and concrete support (Fraiberg, 1980). Developmental guidance requires an expanded working model for infants who are not responding in expectable ways to overtures by parents that would entice most babies into warm, interpersonal exchanges. In these situations, therapists often encounter parents who come to parenting with little conflict or ambivalence, but have begun to feel incompetent, unlovable, frustrated, and rejected by their infant. The infant comes to feel unknowable to the parent, and through a process of self-protective withdrawal from the feelings of helplessness that contact with the infant elicits, the parent unintentionally puts the relationship in peril.

The therapist works as a go-between, understanding the constrictions interfering with the infant's sensory and motor systems, and interpreting to the parents what is being observed and speculating why the infant is struggling with his or her responses. In the moments when parents' natural overtures of affection are not reciprocated, feelings of hurt and confusion are addressed. The therapist thinks developmentally together with the parents to understand from a sensorimotor perspective how the infant is experiencing his or her world and what is getting in the way of coding these sensory and motor experiences as emotionally and socially pleasurable. This form of developmental guidance is combined with the use of an insight-oriented approach to address the parents' immediate distress and historical vulnerabilities. Together, these interventions help parents sustain empathy for the infant's experience, buffer their feelings of inadequacy in engaging their child, and prevent parents from unintentionally withdrawing from the relationship. Here is an example of the use of developmental guidance in the service of emotional support for the relationship.

The conductor of the band

Henry's parents are distraught that they did not recognize his withdrawal from interpersonal contact sooner. At 20 months of age, he is alternately content and irritable; these fluctuations are largely dependent upon whether one of his parents attempts to compete with his current obsession with a particular object. They are aware that Henry loves music and reliably responds to rhythmic sound. During one session, Henry gravitates toward a large container of tinker toys with a metal bottom and lid. Rather than focus on the construction properties of the toy, the therapist follows Henry's natural interests and limited motor repertoire and suggests the sticks inside be turned into drumsticks and the container be used as a drum. Henry, already banging the sticks, responds positively to this idea and repeatedly bangs on the lid. The therapist suggests the parents join him in the activity, finding a moment when he pauses to attune to his rhythm and create a full joint action stop with exaggerated gesture and facial expression. They join him again as he begins banging on the lid.

This shared activity turns Henry into the conductor of the band and opens the door to mutual regulation. The therapist joins the mother to support her in attuning with Henry's rhythm as the leader, as the three of them create an affect-cueing system that regulates the band. Amidst the liveliness in this activity, Mom notices with dismay that Henry looks toward the therapist for a gaze of mutual pleasure and a signal to return to banging whenever they all pause. With no words between them, the therapist catches the sinking expression on the mother's face and her fallen body posture. With nonverbal communication alone, she interprets

the mother's reaction as "he must prefer the therapist to me." Assessing
the reason for Henry's gaze preference, the therapist offers a suggestion
to the mother. "Let's change places on the floor. I think Henry's natural
inclination is to gaze toward the right. If you sit here, he will be able to
see you better." With the mother on Henry's right, he looks to her to
enjoy her matching of his pause in the drumming and beams up at her
lovingly as he begins to drum again. The mother's affect brightens as she
experiences her primary importance to her son.

In the interaction that followed, the therapist was able to assist the
parents in assessing both the sensorimotor processes that may be constricting or derailing Henry's natural inclinations to engage with his
parents and in gaining insight into the vulnerability for misinterpretation of his behavior as having social and emotional intent. In this
situation and others like it, parents are much more likely to internalize
meaning from their own emotional reactions to their child's behavior than they are to look for elusive constitutional explanations about
their otherwise healthy-looking child. When the therapist's interventions help the parents re-experience the child as trapped by his own
body rather than intentionally rejecting their best efforts at parenting,
the parents are able to sustain empathy for the child and begin a journey with the therapist to understand their child's idiosyncrasies and
how to foster engagement.

A case example of infant–parent psychotherapy for early indicators of autism

The following case study of infant–parent therapeutic intervention
with a baby showing early indicators of autism illustrates the therapist's attention to the obstacles to emerging interpersonal synchrony
seen in failures of attunement, temporal matching, and the sharing
of emotional expression in movement. This case considers three areas
of interest in addressing early identification and therapeutic work
with infants with signs of autism. The first is the use of observation
of infant–parent interaction to contribute to our ability to treat early
signs of autism in the first year of life. The second refers to the transactional nature of the infant–caregiver system. The innate constitutional
characteristics of the infant and the parallel innate constitutional

characteristics of each parent constantly provide mutual influence over the dynamic flow, with each parent's internal psychological processes affecting the family dynamics. The third interest is in the overwhelming job of the therapist to hold the hope and health of the family. The therapist functions best when informed across several disciplines. He or she considers the implications of sensory, motor, communication, and affective systems. Although the surface interventions may focus on the practical aspects of the child's functioning, the feelings and conflicts and the ghosts conjured up by the parents' histories are equally the work of the therapeutic process. The focus on rhythmic affective attunement, vitality characteristics, and the music of intersubjectivity as vehicles for therapeutic action enable parents to bring their baby into an engaged and reciprocal relationship.

Family history

I began this journey with a family who then had both new born twins and a 20-month-old boy. The parents were young professionals living in a small suburb of a major Midwestern city. They had many extended family members, but none available nearby as a consistent source of support. The parents employed a part-time babysitter and housekeeper to assist the mother, who had given up her career temporarily to be at home to raise her small children. They were both from big families, which they enjoyed, and they planned to have a large family themselves.

When we first met, the parents were concerned about their son, Blair, because he seemed quite uninterested in them. He was pulling his own hair, flicking the light switches on and off repeatedly, eating only noodles and yogurt, obsessively lining up his small toy animals, crashing his stroller and wheel toys into the walls, staring at the sun, and flapping his hands up and down repetitively. The parents reported that as a newborn and young infant, Blair was cranky and irritable, slept very little, was difficult to soothe, and only calmed when held facing away from his parents' bodies. He seemed to prefer time alone with toys in his crib. Although his parents conscientiously offered enticing smiling, bouncing, and interactive play, they regularly felt rebuffed.

During the initial period of our work together, just a few months prior to his second birthday, the serious nature of these observations about his behavior was sinking in for the parents. By this same time, Mom had given birth to twins, whom they thankfully experienced as easy. They were quiet, especially Chester, who slept all the time. When he was awake, he seemed content to lie in his baby seat and look around. However, it was not long until the regulatory issues presented by this infant became painfully apparent. By nine months of age, the parents had a list of worries about Chester as well. He had an obsessive interest in balls and a preference for lying on his tummy and looking at things sideways. He would arch away from his caregivers when being held close during feedings or when upset and crying. His parents also noted an odd facial expression that seemed to override the social smile and an over-focus on objects that made him slow to turn to the sound of his name, though he did eventually turn and look pleased to see his parents.

With the twins still in their first year, Mom and Dad were overwhelmingly preoccupied with the work they were doing to join their older child and to woo him into the social world. However, Mom was alternately concerned she could never give enough time to the oldest son and guilt-ridden that she was passing her newborns off to the nanny, allowing them to be cared for by her instead of their own mother. She had given up a successful career to raise her own children and longed to be as successful as a mother as she had been in her job. She was torn and suffering. Her personal history revealed that she was the oldest sibling in a large family and had been thrust into a caregiving role long before she'd satisfied her own childhood longings to be cared for. The work with the mother needed to address both the current urgency to understand her sons' developmental issues, her feelings of inadequacy as an effective parent, and her history of being deprived of her own childhood.

Dad had his own suffering. In contrast to his wife, he had not given up his work in technology research when the children were born. He feared if he stepped out now, his career would be derailed and never get back on track. On the other hand, he valued his opportunity to parent his children and was constantly torn between the wish to be with the boys, to be an emotional support to his wife, and to further his career interests. These conflicts contributed to the ordinary tensions a marriage encounters while raising small children, though their conflict was amplified by the special needs of the children. Dad vacillated between responding to his wife's burning requests to attend to the children and to her emotional needs and the intense demands of his career. Dad's history revealed his tendency to retreat to a passive position evolved from competition with his siblings for the meager emotional supplies available from their mother. He both gravitated toward and was repelled by his wife's insistence on order and neatness, which resonated with his childhood experiences of his own mother's obsessions. Although he identified with the warmth and acceptance characterized by his relationship with his father, he also resented his father's relative unavailability due to his work demands and feared the repetition of this dynamic in his relationships with his own sons.

There were worries about heredity as well. Each parent felt certain from all they had now heard and read that one of each of their own parents was "on the autism spectrum." For Mom, it was her father, and for Dad, his mother. Both grandparents relied heavily on their spouse to function in society. Although the maternal grandfather managed a successful business by using his technical expertise, his wife managed him, literally maneuvering him through social situations of the most mundane nature. The paternal grandmother had obsessions, compulsions, and social phobias that made it difficult for her to leave her home to visit her grandchildren. Both grandparents were limited in their capacities for warmth and intimacy, spontaneity, and flexibility, and both stood out for their stiffness and awkwardness in interpersonal relations. Both Mom and Dad were actively concerned about the genetic predispositions they had transmitted to their children.

In their adult lives, each parent was primarily identified with their own warm, more intimate parent. Though concerned about the effects of their identified parent on their own capacities for parenting, their working models for relationships were clearly derived from their experiences with their relationally capable parent. They loved each other, had stable senses of self, worked hard and successfully, loved their children, and experienced strong commitments to their family. Each parent had adequate capacity for warmth, spontaneity, flexibility, and intimacy. They were both exceptionally bright and well educated, but neither was overly intellectualizing.

The arrival of Britt

Let's turn now to the baby in question and explore the therapeutic process over her first five months of life. There were concerns from the beginning that paralleled the parents' early worries about their oldest son. Britt cried the most distressing cry all the time. It was so piercing that the nurses at the pediatrician's office thought it was remarkable and asked the mother if she needed help when she waited for a routine well-baby visit. Experiences like this offer of help and recognition of extreme distress served to mortify the mother, leaving her with feelings of humiliation about her inability to parent her children effectively and causing her to less than graciously withdraw from sincere offers of assistance. Furthermore, helping professionals often attributed the outward signs of her inner experience as aloofness or rejection of their best efforts to assist her. She was wary of attempts to establish a working alliance, feeling that the true underlying meaning of the offer represented proof of her defective parenting.

Soothing and calming were a challenge. Britt did take the breast, but only the breast, refusing a bottle under any circumstances. She had no interest in a pacifier. In the first month, she cried, slept briefly, and nursed. She looked and sounded like a baby in pain. Her facial expressions were somber, deprived of the moments of brightening during quiet, alert states. She was at her best on the breast, satisfied to be in her mother's arms. Nursing calmed her, but it wasn't necessarily nutritive and at times she would become inexplicably frantic. Nevertheless, nursing became the safe haven for this mom, who was extremely sleep deprived and beginning to entertain the possible reality of her future with the boys and this baby.

What does the therapist do at this juncture? We were already up to our eyebrows in the work with the other children. Thankfully, I'd had the months of her pregnancy to deal with my own countertransference feelings about why this couple would invite another child into their lives. The wish for health, the wish for a lively family, the wish for a girl; I worked on myself in my musings, though in my darker moments I struggled to imagine how to keep the family momentum going in the face of intensifying stress and conflicted feelings.

The infant–parent work here involved insight-oriented intervention, examining the conflicts experienced by the parents, and looking at the ghosts from the parents' pasts visited upon their children. Developing a working alliance and an atmosphere of trust allowed us to proceed in partnership to address the very real constitutional issues in the children as the parents faced them daily. The work could be characterized as a blending of infant–parent psychotherapy (Fraiberg, 1980; Lieberman & Pawl, 1993) with a Developmental, Individual Difference, Relationship-based (DIR) approach (Wieder, Greenspan, & Kalmanson, 2008). The parents and I engaged in the triad of therapeutic interventions characteristic of infant–parent psychotherapy: insight-oriented talk therapy, an expansion of non-didactic developmental guidance, and concrete support. Developmental guidance consisted of investigating and understanding each child's individual developmental profile in consideration of obstacles to sensorimotor organization and interactive synchrony in the timing and intensity of affect cues. For these parents, developmental guidance not only focused on what is expectable at the infant's age and stage of development, but also on a sorting-out process of which aspects of development were moving along at an expectable pace, which were delayed, which were atypical or absent, and the feelings elicited in the parents as a result of the child's developmental differences. In the course of sessions with the family, interpretations of the meaning of the baby's behavior in response to the parents' social overtures took into consideration our observations of the infant's constitutional difficulties; for example, registering and integrating sensory input across sensory systems to make a response or integrating movement to facilitate gaze toward a parent.

By the time we were working with Britt, Mom and Dad were already well versed in a developmental therapeutic approach referred to as DIR/Floortime (Greenspan & Wieder, 1998). This family-centered approach to work with infants and young children focuses simultaneously on social-emotional development, individual differences in sensory and motor processing, and the central role of relationships in learning and development. Parents are helped to understand their child's unique developmental profile and are coached in strategies to improve the child's interpersonal connections and development through parent-mediated, emotionally meaningful, playful interactions with their child. Britt's parents understood the importance of considering individual differences while exploring how to reach the expectable emotional-developmental milestones. They already had evidence of the usefulness of this approach from successful efforts with the older boys. The parents shared the belief that the constitutional challenges their children faced could be influenced by shaping particular dynamic qualities in their relationships and interactions with the children.

Britt at two months

We began intensive intervention for Britt by her second month of life. We considered the impact of her unique sensorimotor profile on her capacities to share calm and engaged states of mutual pleasurable attention with her parents. Typically, during the first three months of life, a baby becomes a lively partner in the choreography of mutual engagement. A robust infant is able to integrate and enjoy the simultaneous sensory, motor, and affective input of being held, spoken to, rocked, and looked at, while responding to the salient features of the interpersonal environment and shutting out unnecessary sensory information. How adept the baby is at navigating multiple sources of sensory information influences the quality and clarity of his or her affective signals to the parent.

Parents' perceptions and interpretations of their infant's behavior are rapidly coded into meaningful information about their unfolding relationships with the baby. Parents feel effective and competent in caring for their infants when the baby looks at them intently, when the parent sees the gleam in the baby's eyes, and when the infant's movements are rhythmically synchronized with the parent's vocalizations and actions. But what happens to the unfolding relationship when the parent perceives the infant's gaze as glazed over? Or when the parent interprets the infant's gaze as focused on the sleeve of their shirt, but not on the parent's face? Or when the infant's movements are delayed and asynchronous, leaving the parent searching for a response or feeling abandoned? These were the early observations of Britt's parents. At two months of age, they were already apprehensive about their abilities to woo her into affective contact. Britt had not begun to develop the dance to move in synchrony with her parents' voices. She did not orient her gaze to look for the source of the sound of her parent's voice. Her facial expression was somber, lacking the expectable brightening around the eyes and action in the lips. Her arm and leg movements were stiff and delayed. She extended her arm when she turned her head and was unable to sustain eye contact because her neck did not elongate or allow her to lower her chin.

Reflux was diagnosed by the second month of life. We hoped that medication would help regulate the baby and her crying would subside. It was, at best, of modest help. These physical constrictions were not as obvious to her parents as were their impressions that intimate contact did not feel good to this baby. From the outset, we collaborated with a pediatric physical therapist. She assisted us in understanding how to support sensorimotor development in the service of affective contact. Following her advice, we noticed that even when Britt's body was fully supported on the floor and there was no demand to integrate voice with touch and vision, she still tended to look away from her parents and only rarely and fleetingly toward their faces. Neither Mom nor Dad with baby looked or felt like a synchronous, dynamic system.

The combination of the sense of apprehension and the reality of such fleeting contact worked together to generate feeling states that undermined the potential for connection between this baby and her parents. Although Mom and Dad knew how to brighten their voices, hold facial expression, and slow their pace while heightening affect, strong feelings of concern did show on Britt's parents' faces. The inner feelings of sadness and worry betrayed their attempts to look cheerful, such that smiling lips often accompanied sadness in their eyes. The sadness made sense to them and to me. In the context of our sessions, we were able to think together about the multiple layers of hope and despair they were experiencing and to relieve some of the weight of these feelings. But from Britt's perspective, I wondered how an infant who was having trouble encoding complex facial displays could make meaning from the mixed affect apparent on her parents' faces.

Mom and Dad worked as a team, switching the baby from one to the other whenever they had an idea the other parent might be more successful. They noted every fleeting moment of connection with comments like, "What a nice smile you gave me." Their effort to capture and amplify these moments stood in stark contrast to the more typical developmental experience of cascading pleasure taken in shared looking, vocalizing, and movement. While the typical dyad becomes a system of co-regulation of affect and excitation, Britt and her parents looked more like a system of tentative and anxious miscues with celebrated moments of fleeting mutuality.

Britt at three months

By the third month, the parents and I were working toward extending hard-won moments of mutual gaze and attention. In our sessions, we looked for the most comfortable physical positions to facilitate Britt's capacity to orient visually to voice. At the same time, I was conscious of faltering resilience in the parents and a vulnerability to take this baby's somber face and lack of responsiveness personally. Comments such as, "Are you interested in something else?" or, "Sometimes you like me more than this," began to seep into the fabric of our sessions. With empathy for their experience and support in holding on to our conviction that Britt was struggling with issues of sensory and motor integration that occluded her attempts to engage with her parents, we forged ahead in our efforts to discover just how to ignite and hold this baby's attention and affect.

Just when a human partner should hold the most appeal for an infant, we found ourselves competing with her visual interest in objects like her receiving blanket. This led us to focus more wholeheartedly on interpersonal play without toys. The therapist's spoken observations of what drew Britt's attention worked to help Mom and Dad to become the focus, and gradually Britt's attention was brought back to them. When Britt turned away, her parents followed her gaze and joined her interest, literally lowering their bodies to appear in her visual field. With the therapist's coaching, they focused on becoming available to be seen rather than creating a bob-and-weave avoidance pattern. The parents learned to comment on whatever Britt seemed to be looking at and drew her back to them by pouring heightened feeling tone into their voices and pleasure in seeing her look toward their faces.

The therapeutic work was focused on bearing witness to fleeting moments of emotional attunement, recognizing and naming moments of sensorimotor disorganization, and holding the parents through stark moments of unfulfilled emotional anticipation. Thankfully, these parents were capable of taking pleasure in brief moments of meeting. With therapeutic support, they were able to use those moments to re-energize themselves emotionally and sustain their efforts to hold their daughter's engagement.

Calming and soothing Britt was challenging. She could not take comfort in chest-to-chest body contact or cuddling into a parent's shoulder. Efforts to sooth Britt's frantic cries required holding her looking outward, away from her parent's face while bouncing her up and down. She began to cry again as soon as the movement stopped. She was unable to calm with gaze because she did not look for her parents' faces. A strong layer of vestibular stimulation calmed but did not regulate her because she continued to need the repeated external input. The bouncing failed to organize her. She could only use it to calm her in the moment. Both parents were painfully aware of the long periods of time they spent calming their baby. The impact of these efforts was compounded by the grief they experienced with an infant who seemed not to want to cuddle up close to them when she was in distress.

Britt at five months

With therapeutic support, the parents continued their heroic efforts and sustained empathy for this very difficult and disorganized baby. By five months, we began to experience more than a fleeting gaze and an emerging capacity in Britt to seek and sustain contact with her parents when her body was supported and her sensory surroundings were optimal. The quiet of my office was an ideal haven for interactions that helped the parents invest in hopefulness and begin to experience joy with this baby. We found that Britt felt well supported when propped against her parent's bent legs and tucked into the "V" of their seated body. This distance also provided an optimal visual field for seeking out her parents' faces and controlling the rhythm of gazing and looking away.

Britt was developing an intermittent and easily constricted sense of agency in her relationships and interactions. There was still a tentative choreography to their interactions, with Mom at times wishing for more intimacy and violating Britt's fragile sense of self-agency. For example, the sheer joy of seeing her baby look lovingly into her eyes and brighten with a smile created a yearning in Mom. She reached her head in closer to Britt's face with a wide smile, heightened intensity in her voice, and physical contact, drawing Britt toward her body, kissing her cheek. In this moment, Britt's inability to tolerate the affective intensity and physical closeness caused her to twist away, raise an arm as a barrier, and settle into an expression of distress. However, both parent and infant became more resilient and able to recover pleasurable contact, making good use of touch, vocalization, and baby games like raspberries on the tummy.

Britt's development of a more stable physical base of support allowed her more fluid movement and comfortable weight shifting as she was motivated by affect cues to lean toward and away from her parents. She began to reach for her parents' faces with pleasure in her own facial expression. Both parents became increasingly able to tolerate the moments that felt too fleeting or were experienced as avoidance. They could hold in mind the moments of connection that were building between themselves and their baby. The parents experienced expanded periods of synchronized movement with Britt. Mom could move and vocalize and show joyful affect in her face as Britt responded positively with movement and vocalizations.

What follows is an example of a moment of achievement toward interactive synchrony:

> Mom's eyes widen and her voice lilts while she talks to Britt. In response to the rhythm of Mom's voice, and matching her cadence and crescendo, Britt's foot extends upward and toward Mom's hand as she vocalizes in return. She leaves her foot in her mother's hand long enough for Mom to reach in and kiss her toes. Britt squeals with glee, kicks outward, and now shows evidence of her own yearning for intimacy. She leans her trunk toward Mom with her arms reaching for her mother's face. Britt holds her mother's cheeks between her hands and moves her own face closer to her mother's. Such moments of intimacy, the standard fare of relatedness in most households with babies, were cultivated and cherished by this family. Tears of joy surfaced in her mother's eyes and stories about this micro-event were celebrated for days following.

Britt at two years

We will never know what Britt would have been like without intervention. By age two, she had become a lively, verbal, warmly related toddler. She used gaze to regulate interaction, including joint attention. She delightedly engaged in sensorimotor activity and began to represent ideas with toys in play. She enjoyed family playtime with her parents and siblings. Britt remained sensitive to some sensory stimulation, recoiling from feeling messy or sticky. She was slow to process affectionate touch and looked away and stiffened for a moment when she received a hug. But if her parent continued to hold her with stable proprioceptive pressure and without escalating the expectation for a response, she softened and molded into their arms.

At the park or participating in "Mommy and Me" classes, Britt maintained her position as an onlooker until she became comfortable enough with her surroundings to engage with a group. The vulnerabilities observed at this point in her development appeared idiosyncratic, but well within the normal range expected of a healthy toddler characterized as shy or by a slow to warm temperament type. Most importantly, both parents felt confident and competent in responding to their daughter. Their understanding of her unique developmental attributes formed a protective shield around their vulnerabilities to feeling rejected or helpless.

Discussion: Next steps in our understanding

Case examples like those presented in this chapter may be useful in developing hypotheses about which behavioral indicators are worth investigation as early signs of autism. Although most children with autism do not receive a positive diagnosis until they are well into the second or third years of life, early indications may be more visible than is commonly thought if we look at the dynamic feedback system between the infant and parent rather than focusing on the behavior of the child (St. Clair, Danon-Boileau, & Trevarthen, 2007). Much of the current research in the autism field is focused on discrete behavioral markers in the infant, such as failure to turn to his or her name at 12 months (Nadig et al., 2007). Reformulating the question from what the baby is or is not doing to looking at the dynamic interactional synchrony of gaze, pace, sound, rhythm, and movement between parent and infant may give us a better vehicle for discerning these early signs. Refocusing research on the interpersonal process reveals techniques for improving identification during the first year of life and offers positive direction for expanding strategies for effective intervention.

Powerful clues are available in the observations of the infant's interactive relationship with the parent. Early indicators are evident in the synchrony of vocalization and movement between the dyad, the timing and intensity matching of affectively rich cues between parent and baby, and the communication and reception of intention. Further, we have to take note of the reactions of the infant in relation to the accruing feelings and emerging meanings in the infant–parent interaction and in the potential behavioral sequelae to the parents' mounting worries and fears.

In these case examples, experience in the body and in sensory registration was transmitted into affective meanings for both parents and baby. For example, constrictions in the development of a stable physical base impede the development of fluid movement. The infant then struggles to coordinate the turning, looking, reaching, and positive affective facial displays parents perceive as early signs of relatedness and interest in them. These physical challenges are compounded by sensory sensitivities and difficulties integrating sensory input across modalities, the conduit for affect attunement. The pleasure most infants take in the simultaneous orchestration of looking and being looked at while being held close and spoken to are absent. The typical experience of feeling warmth, intimacy, and reciprocity is transformed into feeling overwhelmed, fearful, disorganized, and sad. This leads to physical and emotional withdrawal by the infant and the parent. Both baby and parent are responding to feelings that are constructed from thousands of micro-moments of daily life together, during which a look or a body movement are the signals we call upon to make meaning of our experiences and internalize feeling states that grow into our mental images of ourselves in relation to others and our internalized knowledge of how to be with another person.

As therapists, we have neither the risk model nor the diagnostic criteria to do more than share in the parents' concerns about the ultimate diagnostic meaning of their infant's early responses. However, when parents are worried about how difficult it is to capture their baby's attention to their faces and voices, when the baby calms better if left alone or arches away from his or her parent's body, or when the baby turns away from the parent's face at close proximity, we have enough information to offer therapeutic support and developmental expertise. When parents find themselves withdrawing from the relationship with their child, the therapist is able to validate the parents' concerns as real and worthy of attention.

My position alongside these babies and parents allows me to lend my vitality affect to the experiences of the parent and the infant (Stern,

1985, 2010). My reassuring posture or vocal tone, a slow-paced comment, or a long-held facial expression gives parents a nonverbal interpretation that alters the rhythmic asynchrony or intensity of affects and allows the parent to recalibrate their internal experience of being with their baby. This allows the infant to rest, to modulate the arousal, and to find the self-regulation needed to receive or initiate contact with the parent. I reassure parents that the difficulties they experience creating intimate contact with their babies are due to the infants' unique constitutional qualities. Identifying a child's specific constrictions and addressing them through the therapeutic relationship makes room for the parents to sustain empathy for the child, overcome their own discouragement and sense of loss, and maintain their heroic efforts on behalf of the child.

References

Baron-Cohen, S. Tager-Fusberg, H., Cohen, D. (Eds.) (1993). *Understanding other minds: Perspectives from autism*. Oxford, UK: Oxford University Press.

Beebe, B. & Lachman, F. (1988). The contribution of mother–infant mutual influence to the origins of self and object representations. *Psychoanalytic Psychology*, 5:305–337.

Beebe, B. & Lachman, F. (1994). Representation and internalization in infancy: Three principles of salience. *Psychoanalytic Psychology*, 11:127–165.

Beebe, B. & Lachman, F. (2002). *Infant research and adult treatment: Co-constructing interactions*. Hillsdale, NJ: Analytic Press.

Beebe, B. & Stern, D. (1977). Engagement–disengagement and early object experiences. In: M. Freedman & S. Grand (Eds.), *Communicative structures and psychic structures*. (pp. 35–55) New York, NY: Plenum Press.

Boston Change Process Study Group (2002). Explicating the implicit: The local level and the microprocess of change in the analytic situation. *International Journal of Psychoanalysis*, 83:1051–1062.

Boston Change Process Study Group (2010). *Change in psychotherapy: A unifying paradigm*. New York, NY: W.W. Norton & Company.

Brazelton, T.B., Koslowski, B., & Main, M. (1974). The origins of reciprocity: The early mother–infant interaction. In: M. Lewis & L.A. Rosenblum (Eds.), *The effect of the infant on its caregiver* (pp. 49–76). New York, NY: Wiley.

Condon, W.S. & Sander, L.S. (1974). Neonate movement is synchronized with adult speech: Interactional participation and language acquisition. *Science*, 183:99–101.

Fraiberg, S. (1980). *Clinical studies in infant mental health: The first year of life.* New York, NY: Basic Books.

Greenspan, S.I. & Wieder, S. (1998). *The child with special needs.* Reading, MA: Addison-Wesley.

Lieberman, A. & Pawl, J. (1993). Infant–parent psychotherapy. In: C.H. Zeanah (Ed.), *The handbook of infant mental health.* (pp. 472–484) New York, NY: Guilford Press.

Lyons-Ruth, K. (1999). The two-person unconscious: Intersubjective dialogue, enactive relational representation, and the emergence of new forms of relational organization. *Psychoanalytic Inquiry,* 19:576–617.

Malloch, S. & Trevarthen, C. (2008). *Communicative musicality: Exploring the basis of human companionship.* Oxford, UK: Oxford University Press.

Nadig, A.S., Ozonoff, S., Young, G.S., Rozga, A., Sigman, M., & Rogers, S.J. (2007). A prospective study of response to name in infants at risk for autism. *Archives of Pediatric and Adolescent Medicine,* 161:378–383.

St. Clair, C., Danon-Boileau, L., & Trevarthen, C. (2007). Signs of autism in infancy: Sensitivity for rhythms of expression in communication. In: S. Acquarone (Ed.), *Signs of autism in infants: Recognition and early intervention* (pp. 21–45). London, UK: Karnac.

Stern, D. (1971). A microanalysis of mother–infant interaction: Behaviors regulating social contact between a mother and her three-and-a-half year old twins. *Journal of American Academy of Child Psychiatry,* 10:501–517.

Stern, D. (1985). *The interpersonal world of the infant.* New York, NY: Basic Books.

Stern, D. (2010). *Forms of vitality.* New York, NY: Oxford University Press.

Trevarthen, C. (1998). The concept and foundations of infant intersubjectivity. In: S. Braten (Ed.), *Intersubjective communication and emotion in early ontogeny* (pp. 15–46). Cambridge, MA: Cambridge University Press.

Trevarthen, C. (2009). The functions of emotion in infancy. In: D. Fosha, D.J. Siegel, & M. Solomon (Eds.), *The healing power of emotion* (pp. 55–85). New York, NY: W.W. Norton & Company.

Tronick, E. (2007). *The neurobehavioral and social-emotional development of infants and children.* New York, NY: W.W. Norton & Company.

Wieder, S., Greenspan, S., & Kalmanson, B. (2007). Autism assessment and intervention: The developmental individual difference, relationship-based DIR/ Floortime model. *Zero to Three Journal,* 28:31–37.

Winnicott, D. (1953). Transitional objects and transitional phenomena. *International Journal of Psychoanalysis,* 34:89–97.

Chapter 3

Trauma and attachment

Clinical techniques to enhance reflective functioning

Miriam Steele, Ph.D.

When John Bowlby established the Child and Family Department at The Tavistock Clinic, and with it a training in child psychotherapy, it was with the following motto in mind: "No therapy without research, and no research without therapy" (Dicks, 1970, p. 142). This chapter is an attempt to show the ongoing relevance of Bowlby's words. The interplay between clinical and developmental exploration, especially attachment theory and research, and psychodynamically oriented child clinical treatment is the unifying theme across this chapter.

The chapter follows a well-trodden path of clinical writings that have been informed by developmental research and clinical work. This is a vital dialogue that depends upon new and useful ways of approaching both clinical problems and research endeavors. In terms of adult treatment, developmental research has eloquently furthered our understanding. Beatrice Beebe's use of her original microanalytic studies informs her clinical work and that of a myriad of adult analysts and therapists (Beebe & Lachmann, 2002; Beebe, 2004; Seligman, 2012). Safran's (Safran & Muran, 1996; Safran, 2002) creative use of Tronick's rupture and repair findings (Tronick & Weinberg, 1997; Tronick, 2007) inspired a new way of looking at therapeutic alliance and the development of a modality of adult treatment focused on this concept. Clinicians working with children utilize attachment theory and research (Hopkins, 1996; Slade, 1999, 2004), developmental and neuroscience research (Alvarez, 1992, 2012; Music, 2014), and microanalytic mother–infant research (Bonovitz, 2003). The focus of this chapter is to present a psychodynamically oriented treatment case of a nine-year-old girl who suffered trauma as young child, with multiple moves in foster care until she was adopted at age seven. Paying close attention to specific aspects of a psychotherapeutic intervention can highlight how developmental research complements clinical understanding and alerts us to some possible sources for promoting therapeutic action.

The field of attachment theory and research, with its roots in psychoanalytic thinking coupled with decades of empirical research, has led to several key concepts that can inform our clinical enterprise. These include Mary Ainsworth's groundbreaking work delineating the construct of maternal sensitivity and the development of the Strange Situation paradigm. Ainsworth's innovative contribution to attachment theory was her initiation of an empirically based assessment of parent–infant attachment, operationalized with the coding of infant proximity seeking, contact maintenance, avoidance, and resistance in relation to caregiver separation and reunion (Ainsworth, Blehar, Waters, & Wall, 1978). While we don't often have the luxury of having formal Strange Situation assessments of our patients, many clinicians intuitively make a point of observing the child and parent's responses to separations and reunions.

Mary Main, a student of Mary Ainsworth's, shifted our conceptual frameworks both in developmental research as well as in the clinical domain as she identified and described disorganized–disoriented responses (the natural grief response to loss in adults) among one-year-old infants upon reunion with the mother in the Strange Situation (Main & Solomon, 1990). And around the same time, Main, Kaplan, and Cassidy (1985) introduced the Adult Attachment Interview, which signaled a paradigmatic shift in the field of developmental attachment research beyond an exclusive focus on the behavior of preverbal infants with their caregivers (at home or in the Strange Situation procedure).

Widely appreciated is the way responses to Adult Attachment Interviews, transcribed verbatim from audio recordings, reveal four or five typical broad patterns of response that resonate with psychoanalytic writings on the regulation of anxiety and guilt via defensive strategies: (1) the typical healthy response of autonomy, flexibility with regard to the regulation of anxiety and guilt, and credible consistency in the narrative; (2) insecure–dismissing responses that typically deny anxiety and guilt, maintaining all was well and is well despite evidence of childhood attachment difficulties that may be inferred from inconsistencies (excessive defensiveness) in the narrative; and

(3) insecure–preoccupied responses that present attachment difficulties, but in a way governed by anger, passivity, or unremitting fearfulness, despite an urgent wish to connect meaningfully with others that typically includes, or ends with, persisting disappointment. Adult Attachment Interviews are also given a rating for evidence of unresolved mourning with respect to loss and/or trauma, which occurs in approximately 10% of the typical population, but up to 80% in clinical samples. The Adult Attachment Interview inspired the concept of "reflective functioning", which has particular resonance amongst psychodynamic clinicians with its unique value in examining therapeutic goals and the techniques employed to establish this competency (Fonagy & Bateman, 2006; Steele et al., 2010; Rossouw & Fonagy, 2012).

The concept of reflective functioning

Reflective functioning (RF) is defined as the capacity to envision and think about mental states in oneself and others in the service of building realistic models of why people behave, think, and feel as they do. RF is a unique construct in part because of its detailed dimensional scoring procedure, outlined in a 60-page manual, applied to Adult Attachment Interviews (Fonagy, Target, Steele, & Steele, 1998) with relevance to other narrative material (e.g. psychotherapy transcripts).

The capacity for RF is crucial to the development of the self, as both psychoanalytic and developmental theorists have connected the nature of the experiences within the parent–infant relationship and the ability to regulate affect, which are formed into mental representations (Greenacre, 1952; Spitz, 1959). Links between quality of attachment and quality of play have also been made by many, but in this context of the development of RF, it is worth noting Fonagy's (1999) assertion that the "parent of the secure child engages in behaviors such as pretend play, which almost obliges the child to contemplate the existence of mental states" (p. 460). These connections are central to psychotherapeutic work and prompt the question: how do we promote the capacity for RF in both child and adult patients? This remains the *sine qua non* to understanding therapeutic action; that is, the "why and how" of therapy. Identifying what clinicians actually *do* in the consulting room and tracking the impact of their interventions in terms of changes in our patients' internal and external worlds are crucial if we are to provide evidence for the effectiveness of our model and for training the next generation of psychodynamically oriented child clinicians.

Accounts of the psychoanalytic treatment of adopted children elucidate unique aspects of the interplay between these children's external reality, namely that they were given up by biological parents, and their internal representations that reflect this reality (Hodges, 1991; Olesker, 2003; Kenrick, 2006). These provide exceptional opportunities to study clinical material where there is a commonality amongst the cases, thereby allowing for interesting contrasts. Studying the processes inherent in the psychodynamic treatment of such cases also allows for the possibility to synthesize the knowledge base gleaned from empirically derived developmental research and to explore some of the pertinent issues, such as children's response to distress, tolerating negative affect, and qualities of their attachment representations (Steele et al., 2003; Hodges, Steele, Hillman, Henderson, & Kaniuk, 2005; Steele, Hodges, Kaniuk, & Steele, 2010).

Along these lines of bringing about a dialogue between an attachment research perspective and psychodynamic treatment, I present a case of a ten-year-old girl who had suffered a series of traumatic events until her removal at age five from her biological parents and later adoption. Within the rich context of child analytic work at the Anna Freud Center, including a tradition of analyzing children who had been adopted (Hodges et al., 1984), the case provides an opportunity to engage in a dialogue between attachment theory research and clinically derived understanding.

Clinical case: Julie

Background

Julie was ten years old when she began twice-weekly psychotherapy that took place over a three-year period. She and her two years older brother were adopted from an Eastern European country by Mr. and Mrs. B., a childless couple in their late forties. Mr. B was a medical researcher; Mrs. B. was a nurse who had family in the children's country of origin. Both Julie and her brother experienced early trauma. When she was three, Julie and her brother were taken into care after her biological father was arrested and charged with the murder of her one-year-old sister. The children were placed in a foster home with a view to adopting them; however, after the foster mother became ill, they were moved to a therapeutic facility. A psychological report from an insightful psychologist working for the institution wrote about Julie, then five years of age:

> Julie entered the room, sat down, frozen. She does not try to establish eye contact, and plays with the first thing that comes to hand, some play dough that she forms into what looks like a gun. Her play is solitary and infantile. She does not talk and answers only when she has been directly asked a question. In her drawing, she is not able to do more than the most basic scribbles – there is no relationship to the various images and her conceptualization is retarded. Julie demonstrates what appears to be post-traumatic stress disorder as she remains introverted, fearful of strangers, especially men, and most worrying, is repressed of any affective content. She also shows a strong wish to please, to be a good girl, and not attract attention.
>
> It is clear that she has not yet mourned the losses she has experienced – first of her sister, then her father and finally of her mother when she was placed in care. She seems to be a child whose world has collapsed. She sits daydreaming, like an automaton, jumping up to answer or carry out a task requested of her, with no expression of affect. At each meeting, she behaves as if it were the first.

The report concludes:

> I have no doubt that the two children are aware that their sister was battered to death by their father and that this killing was preceded by a long period of violence. It is unclear to what extent they were also abused.

With the help of relatives, Mr. and Mrs. B. were put in touch with the children's home and negotiated the adoptions when Julie was ten years old. Both children were referred for treatment, where the major concern was her brother's sexually promiscuous behavior with Julie. It was Julie's response of marked passivity, both in relation to her brother's sexual overtures but also more generally in her aloofness and lack of relatedness, that motivated her parents to seek treatment for her. There were concerns about her level of cognitive functioning, as she seemed to be functioning at school by doing the minimum: achieving passing grades but showing little interest in her work. In terms of peer relationships, she had few friends inside or outside of school. Most of her time was spent at home watching television or aimlessly flipping through stashes of magazines. Mr. and Mrs. B. presented as invested and loving parents who wanted to facilitate their daughter's development in any way they could. They supported treatment and brought her consistently. They engaged in parent work with a clinician at the Anna Freud Center, which focused on enhancing a reflective stance in them regarding their daughter, despite many occasions where they would convey feeling like it was hard to really reach and understand Julie.

First session with Julie

My impression of Julie upon our first meeting was of an attractive child with shoulder-length, dark hair and huge, dark eyes. She seemed rather expressionless, as if smiling went against her better judgment, so she didn't smile, or at least not often. She seemed to take care of her appearance. While I introduced myself in English, I explained that I had some facility in her mother tongue, and as her eyes lit up with this information, I had an inkling that this might help initiate a therapeutic alliance. It turned out that for Julie to have the upper hand in something, with my many grammatical mistakes and her corrections, was very important. Still, I soon learned that most of my verbal communications were experienced as intrusive and unwelcome. I invited Julie to have a look at the contents of our standard-issue child therapy box of board games, play dough, doll figures, and drawing materials. She sat across from me, staring down, showing no interest in engaging with me or with the box. I tried to inquire about her journey to see me that day, and then mused, as if to myself, as I looked into the box about whether we could find something of interest in the materials.

During the awkward first sessions, I recalled the seminal work of Colwyn Trevarthen, one of the original "baby watchers", whose work centered on describing mother–infant intersubjectivity as embedded in the human infant's propensity for relating to the "other". Trevarthen commented that "good parenting is defined by reticence on the part of the parent" (1977, p. 343). His observations of mothers who are able to follow their infants' leads – that is, not to display overly intrusive or withdrawn behavior, a hallmark of a secure attachment relationship – is of enormous clinical relevance. Using reticence as a strategy in a psychotherapeutic context involves the ability to tolerate uncertainty about what is going to happen. Reticence also has an impact on affect regulation. This resonates with the art of observation and of slowing down so that thinking and feeling can take place in the service of effective clinical work (Schlesinger, 2013).

I looked for strategies to connect to Julie, to have her feel like I was trying to understand and to make my presence felt. Fortunately, I did discover a way to connect, or at least in the beginning, a way to be with her that didn't seem characterized by palpable fear. I learned not to start our session with many words, but to allow our time together to unfold, with her leading the way. This meant my placing the box of our materials in front of her and letting her sort through the items. A pattern soon emerged and it seemed we each understood how our sessions were to unfold. The less talking I did, the better. The ritual of my setting out the paper and colored pencils was initiated and became our medium for communication throughout treatment. Drawing was our form of play. My aims for the treatment were to connect and to form an alliance with Julie so that we could discover thoughts and feelings to do with her early traumatic experiences and, more importantly, move them to a level of representation that was accessible to change and where exploration and relating could be deemed as safer.

Many child clinicians (Alvarez, 1992, 2012; Bonovitz, 2003) have described creative techniques for reaching children and providing a therapeutic context where words seem to be experienced more as weapons than as effective tools of the trade. The child clinician often relies on ingenuity for ways of "being-with" that entice and eventually end up defining communication and presence. In my work with Julie, it was the realm of drawing where we could forge a link.

The first phase of treatment: Access through drawing

Julie was amazingly consistent in what she did in our sessions, always choosing to communicate through the medium of drawing, as a much younger child might choose to do. But there were discernible shifts when the consolidation of a therapeutic alliance formed and the drawing and art-making morphed into meaning making. It was only after many months with very minimal verbal communication and much drawing that words, including talking about Julie's traumatic experiences, became possible.

The first phase lasted nearly a year. It did not take long for me to be silenced when I tried to connect with words. Even a benign, "How are things?" would engender a look of terror, which was contagious. So, as Julie picked up paper and pencil, I did the same. The drawings Julie created were carefully executed but low on imagination. With a ruler she would draw a square, then subdivide it and continue with the ruler to place an X in each square. These were done in pencil, and if she strayed, the "delinquent" line would be erased and she would try again. Session after session, square after square. I commented on the squares, but received no response. Were they part of a game? I copied Julie's squares, even as she remained seemingly uninterested in what I was doing. It was clear that her reliance on ruler and pencil and eraser seemed to convey, in an almost desperate way, her need to keep me within the lines and to not dare let much out in the open space between us. Once or twice I verbalized this sentiment, how we each can keep safe by working so hard to stay in the lines. I had no acknowledgment from Julie that she heard me.

We continued, slowly and quietly, for many weeks, which made for rather barren sessions and seemed far from a therapeutic context that I thought might actually help Julie. But, practicing reticence, going slowly, and seeing each session as an opportunity to connect did seem, especially in retrospect, to aid in establishing a therapeutic relationship. By having in mind how one might ignite Julie's capacity for curiosity as the road to RF, even in the most rudimentary form, I found it helpful to relax and try and "just be with" Julie. If I could get her to "look" at me – that is, to consider that I was there as a person who was interested in her, who had thoughts, feelings, and intentions separate from her own – I believed I could gain some access to her internal world. My time during our sessions was spent watching and imagining ways of reaching out that would be tolerated. Sparking her curiosity seemed key. Working in the same modality as the one she chose was an obvious choice. Each session, as we walked to the consulting room, there was a growing ease between us, a brief smile as we greeted each other, sat down, and picked up pencil and paper. I would comment out loud, as if to myself, on what I thought she was doing. Musings such as, "Drawing these boxes gives us time to think, and I am thinking about you and what *you* might be thinking."

After weeks of these boxes, devoid of anything that resembled much that I could find meaning in, I ventured to drawing outside of the box by adding a triangle on top of the box – turning it into a house. When I described my drawing of houses, Julie did pick up her head to look, but I received no overt acknowledgment that I or my drawing registered with her. I often wondered if all of this solitary activity was a safe way of being in the presence of "another" that demanded little of Julie. She seemed so determined to structure her time with me in a way that would bring her to a place of being in control, of feeling safe. She initiated all the activities in the consulting room and I was placed in the role of audience. In our respective roles, Julie did show a readiness to engage, albeit on her terms, and she did convey a wish to be liked by me, as she would look up and show me her drawings. But the painstakingly slow pace of the work often made me feel like there wasn't much I was offering in terms of therapeutic input.

Just when I was feeling ready to acknowledge that I was of little help, Julie picked up the ruler and drew a triangle on her box. In the next session, I drew a window in the house and mused about who might live in such a house. Julie responded by drawing windows, which appeared open. This ushered in weeks of Julie and me drawing houses. It seemed I had finally gained entrance into some aspect of her inner world.

I ventured to moving us along to more object-related territory by drawing figures – a person first, and then a family. Julie responded by drawing people, mainly women. These were quite extraordinary figures of women, dressed in glamorous, almost bawdy outfits, cleavage showing, adorned with jewelry, fishnet stockings, and heels. These women, I mused, seemed almost like photographs from some other time that maybe Julie was remembering or thinking about. Sometimes these comments would be acknowledged with a look, but often not. I took to drawing-in-kind. My lack of artistic skills would often evoke a sympathetic smile from Julie. But I did try and convey that I was a "thinking presence" in the room. I was careful in not talking too much, but was intent on my continued effort to promote a reflective stance. When Julie drew purses for her "ladies", I mused that what women keep in their purses can often tell us something about them. I then embarked on trying to convey that I was interested in Julie, so I drew my best rendition of Julie and then drew a purse.

In each session, I mused about creating a replica of something I knew about her; for example, her outfit, the pencil, paper, the plate of cookies, the cup of juice she liked to bring to our sessions. Each of these I cut out and carefully placed in the purse I titled "Julie". While Julie showed minimal curiosity in this activity, I would ponder out loud about what it was I was getting to know about her just by being with her and noticing different things about her – that she likes to draw, eat cookies, and wear a favorite sweater. At one point, Julie looked up at me suspiciously and smiled. Amazingly, as I was fidgeting with the purse/envelope, she picked up some of my drawings and began cutting out the various images and placed them next to the envelope. I said, "Perhaps the envelope is a safe place to keep the bits of you I have come to know."

In this way, I was initiated into my job of providing an endless supply of just-the-right-size pieces of Scotch tape to ensure her ongoing cutting and sticking together. With so much quiet between us, my feeling so very closely watched by her, and her no doubt feeling watched by me, this seemed like a joint activity that brought relief to both of us as it offered something 'in-between". My willingness to be available and to be useful in the way that Julie decided she needed seemed to usher in a safer place where I could sometimes comment. I verbalized how my role was to help think about Julie and how all the different places that she had lived and all the changes might feel like a jumble and need to be separated out and then put back together. I am not sure how helpful my verbal commentary was, but all the physical sticking together of the various bits seemed very important to her.

A shift in the treatment with Julie: Her past comes more fully into view

One can never be totally sure as to the actual agents for change or aspects of a therapeutic intervention that bring about therapeutic action in treatment. What we are looking for is a link between the often-subtle interchanges that happen with our patients where we engage our understanding of their experience and they respond by signaling that they "heard" us and that they feel understood. In less esoteric terms, we see them move toward more adaptive responses in their relating to us and to others or show a growing ability to tolerate negative affect. Or we can notice that they move from their rigid, highly defended, and constricted stance to one of experiencing a wider array of affects. This can be evident both in the consulting room and also in demonstrable shifts outside of treatment. In this particular case with Julie, it was shortly after this period of our connecting over the drawings that a significant event in Julie's narrative building was marked.

In a telephone call, Julie's parents told me that she had for the first time told them that she had witnessed the murder of her sibling. The trigger for her disclosure was in the context of learning about some Bible stories at school, including the story of the Binding of Isaac. Julie had been upset when she was picked up at school, and that evening said to her parents, "It is not always true that parents don't kill their children." Julie cried that night, which was quite unusual for her. While the narrative describing the trauma was at times unclear, putting the event and what ensued into words seemed to have heralded a shift in Julie. In the weeks that followed, her parents noticed this shift; they reported that she seemed "to be relaxed, more focused, and more willing to be a part of school and family."

In treatment, I saw a shift as well. I let Julie know that I knew about her disclosure and she retold the account to me. We talked about her courage in talking about this terrible event, which was a secret she had kept to herself for so long. She was more willing to exchange eye contact and show the occasional smile, as well as frowning when I said or did something she didn't like. Importantly, Julie seemed interested in building a narrative around some of the events that haunted her. This phase of treatment ushered in new forms of drawing. Weeks were spent on a story in pictures about a school bus trip that ended with an accident where all the children and teachers were injured. There were children on crutches and others with eye patches or missing limbs. This allowed many opportunities to describe different ways of being hurt, some visible on the outside, some only known from the inside. This new capacity for conveying a wish to share her sense of hurt and damage showed a willingness to trust and also heralded a willingness to tolerate mental pain.

Two years into treatment: The challenge presented by puberty

My sessions with Julie continued with the familiar drawing activity and with some verbal exchanges between us – usually about school, or sometimes a complaint about her brother or being in trouble for not helping at home. Verbal communication was a challenge for Julie. Julie reached menarche around her 11th birthday, which coincided with what sounded like an intensification of difficulties. Julie's adoptive mother complained about her passivity, that she seemed to be in her own world, describing her as "prone to dissociation." When asked for an example, she told of how Julie had recently begun to menstruate and would refuse to engage in any self-care. Instead, "I would find her in the morning, in a pool of blood. She seems unable or unwilling to take care, and so I end up helping to get her clean." Mrs. B. also recounted how Julie and two cousins had gone to see a film a few blocks from their house and Julie had gone to the bathroom and disappeared, having decided without telling anyone she was going home. When confronted, Julie seemed confused by the concern. Indeed, these examples did seem to indicate that Julie had a propensity for entering into dissociated states. We know from attachment research studies that trauma in parents predicts disorganized attachment in their infants and that there is an association between infant disorganization and adolescent symptoms of dissociation (Carlson, 1998).

From my experience of working with Julie, it was not hard to imagine that dissociation was in her repertoire of strategies to regulate internally generated and overwhelming affect. But I was also feeling that therapeutic change, while elusive, could still be registered, especially if one stayed modest on the unit of change by focusing on a widening of scope of expressing feeling states and engaging meaningfully with another. As Karp (1997) suggested:

> In a patient who has limited verbal communication for one reason or another, drawing can be a good way to establish an alliance between patient and therapist. It seems that once the symbol is on

the page, it is already externalized to some degree and can then become part of the play. Because drawings are highly personal, the process seems to heighten the patient's sense of being understood.

(p. 267)

The next few weeks of drawings continued along the lines of Julie expressing pain and damage as the theme of injured children permeated. In terms of the backdrop to the drawings, there was a palpable shift in Julie toward a tolerance for talking with me, what felt like a determined effort to "work" on her drawings, and, I think, to have me understand some of what lay beneath the surface. As she drew in a slow and meticulous way her scenes of chaos and injury, I drew ambulances, doctors, and nurses and verbalized the fear that comes from being hurt when there isn't help available. While not verbally responding, Julie would look up, directly making eye contact, and then return to her drawing, expanding its reach to a seemingly new level of disclosure. During one session, Julie picked up from where we had left off, adding yet another injured figure – this time a boy with an eye patch with a speech bubble, "I can't see with just one eye," and then a girl with her arm in a sling, saying, "That hurt [spelled 'heart'] very much." I thought about how clearly Julie was communicating to me that there are obvious injuries we can observe, but that the injuries she carries as images and thoughts continue to be present for her. Her drawing and my "counter-drawing" seemed the best way to have her express herself and share this aspect of her internal world with me.

As she was coloring these figures in, she became frustrated with the pack of colored markers and yelled at them for not easily fitting back into the pack. She said in a rather chilling voice, "Get back in there or I will kill you." I commented on her wanting to show me what it looks like when she gets angry, maybe not just with the markers, but with people too. Julie wanted to retract her unusual affective display by retorting, "I was only joking." I said sometimes jokes are good clues to how we are feeling inside and that her joke about killing, or maybe about being killed, was not so far from her mind. Julie responded by drawing a picture of a lady lying face down, telling me that she is the children's teacher. I asked about this figure and she said the lady fainted or maybe is dead. I said that sometimes when terrible and frightening things happen it is enough just to have watched for us to feel very hurt and injured, especially if someone close to us has been hurt. Here I was thinking of the research findings that children who witness domestic violence are impacted and suffer from the negative consequence much like those who are victims of physical abuse (Osofsky, 1995). Julie looked up, discernibly sad, her eyes welling with tears. She then drew a caption underneath this figure that read, "Miss are you ok?" I said that it seemed she might even be worried about what it will mean if she shows me some of her "hurts"; will I faint or even die from all that she has to tell me? Julie turned back to her drawing, determined to color in this figure's shoes.

In the following session, Julie added more "injured" children, gave the teacher figure long, black hair, and cut her out so that she was isolated. Julie told me she didn't just faint, she is dead. I commented that people who faint can look like they are dead and that I knew that she had seen some terrible things happen in her family from a long time ago. Julie then drew a cemetery, as if to show me what happens when people die. I sat quietly as she drew graves and added a church with a bell and a figure with two captions, "Why can't I go there? That is private." I asked her about this and she said what happened in her family is private. She then drew a small figure, adding a caption, "God is with her." I said it seems like she has a lot of thoughts and feelings about what happens when people die and she said clearly, "Yes." Julie then drew a fairy-like figure over the graves with a caption that read, "Don't worry children – I can make people wake up." Julie then talked about how hard it is to understand what happened to her sister and what happened to her biological father. "Is he still in jail?" she asked. I clarified with her as much as I could and discussed with her adoptive mother the need to be available to Julie to hear her should she raise the issue of her biological family and to clarify what she could concerning the fate of her biological father.

Over the next few weeks and months, Julie continued to draw many figures. Eventually, she drew her current family. Treatment continued for a further six months. Mrs. B. reported that Julie's tendency to "space out" had lessened, and as she made the transition to a new school, they had hopes that her learning challenges could be addressed in a more supportive environment. While the multilayered traumas she suffered left their mark over the course of treatment, there was movement toward a more enlivened and related self.

While a formal assessment of Julie's parents in terms of their attachment representations was not done, the question is *how* their daily caregiving of Julie, which would have been experienced as more sensitive and consistent than what she had been exposed to previously, played a crucial role in helping her change from their description of her as an "automaton" to a more adaptive child/adolescent. The case of Julie exemplifies how the powerful intervention of adoption can help set a child back on a healthier trajectory and highlights our interest in the possible mechanisms of change, namely the link between attachment relationships and the regulation of affect, including the metabolizing of negative affect and providing opportunities to experience a semblance of joy within the relationships.

Understanding therapeutic action

The therapeutic context offered a consistent and empathic presence where some of the terrifying images that inhabited Julie's internal world could be expressed and thereby opened up the possibility of a more flexible internal working model, the hallmark of secure attachment. When we look to the therapeutic context and what might have led to changes, it seems clear progress was made within the scope of a relationship that veered much more to waiting and following rather than intruding. Empirical studies of the mother–infant relationship that focus on closely observing the small units of behavior in mothers and infants as they interact with one another find that profitable analysis is possible through a microanalytic lens (Tronick & Weinberg, 1997; Beebe & Lachmann, 2002). These studies helped guide this clinical work in terms of noticing how important it is to titrate the flow of engagement as much as possible and to allow one's partner to have their turn. We could surmise from Julie's traumatic past that she would have had disorganized attachment relationships with her biological parents. The rounds of cumulative trauma would have left her with an internal working model that was compromised, inflexible, and prone to dissociation beyond infancy. Julie needed to be engaged slowly, and one only need read the eloquent descriptions of the careful work of Anne Alvarez (1992, 2012) with traumatized children to be inspired regarding how moving slowly, waiting to catch the attention of the child, and being alert to "tiny beginnings of feeling at ease or comfortable" (2012, p. 72) can yield therapeutic action.

As Beebe et al. (2000) have demonstrated in their empirical studies of mother–infant relationships, the contingency in the modalities of interaction, namely gaze, touch, and vocal rhythms, is the building block to the development of attachment and mutual regulation. They describe these as follows:

> Systems can shift into new forms only if the system is sufficiently variable and flexible that perturbations can shake up old forms. The openness of the system leads to "preparedness" to pick up on perturbations. Change happens only when there is sufficient variability to explore options, and there is the opportunity to find new patterns. A small change can build on itself, exponentially, in a nonlinear way.
>
> (p. 115)

Moreover, Beebe et al. (2000) demonstrated across a range of studies that it is not too much or too little tracking of the "other" that is optimal in mother–infant interactions, but rather those characterized in the mid-range. When working with children, especially those who have suffered trauma, being mindful of working in the mid-range in engagement would seem most likely to be experienced as therapeutic. This translates into matching communications at the intensity or level of the patient. In the case of Julie, that meant slow and nonverbal, especially at the beginning.

Conclusion

With the positive caregiving from Julie's parents that she hopefully internalized, alongside a therapeutic intervention that allowed the expression of negative affect and an experience of meaning making through verbal and nonverbal means, it seemed that Julie's development could unfold more smoothly to include more positive attachment representations. We also have reason to believe that the negative representations were not totally extinguished. As one of the child analysts, Anne Hurry (1998) from the Anna Freud Center, commented, "New models of self with others built up in treatment do not obliterate old models. They are built up alongside the old: the potential activation of the old remains, particularly under conditions of stress" (p. 51). This realistic sentiment very much resonates with the myriad challenges inherent in both the parenting and treating of children who have suffered from early experiences of trauma that are well known in the field of adoption studies[1] (Hodges et al., 1984; Hodges, 1991; Olesker, 2003; Hodges et al., 2005; Kenrick, 2006; Steele et al., 2009; Steele et al., 2010).

Engaging in the dialogue between clinical work and research is always a laudable if also ambitious goal. It becomes impossible to tease apart where one's formulations either in the clinical realm or as researcher begin and end, as they can overlap and feel intrinsic. There is much to be gained from this dialogue, but it is also a challenge with the vastly different frames of references in each discipline. In the case presented of Julie, there were moments of our work that relied heavily on an appreciation of an attachment theory and research perspective and on developmental psychological research. The knowledge about the impact of emotional availability as a conduit through which change can happen, especially for patients who missed out on optimal parenting at some point in their histories, is an obvious tool in the clinician's way of working. To experience "being-with" Julie, and then to link it with an understanding of the conceptual framework and actual coding of Strange Situation observations, enhanced my clinical work and my understanding of attachment-related behavior. Specifically, sensing Julie's fear, I conjured images of Mary Main's (Main & Solomon, 1990) description of the disorganized–disoriented pattern of attachment. And then, sitting side-by-side with Julie, I tried to provide an experience of what the infants described by Beebe had with mothers operating in the mid-range of affective engagement – not too much and not too little (Beebe, 2005). Tracking Julie's affect and following her lead rather than intruding paid off and a therapeutic alliance was set in motion.

Through slowing down, watching, waiting, and working within the realm of nonverbal activity – namely, play and drawing – I felt like I reached Julie and came to understand something of her experience. My work with Julie and with patients like her has also informed my research work, with an interest in charting the development of attachment relationships in adopted and maltreated children, as well as in better understanding the "why" and "how" of therapeutic action across a range of clinical settings.

Note

1 In our empirical study of previously maltreated children who were aged between four and eight years, we found a significant association between adoptive parents' Adult Attachment Interview classifications collected prior to placement and their children's story stem narratives collected soon after placement one year and two years later. Across all the families, regardless of their parents' attachment status (secure, dismissing, preoccupied, or unresolved), there were changes in the children's story stem themes across the first two years of the adoptive placement, whereby all the children in the previously maltreated group showed increases in their "secure" themes (Hodges et al., 2005). However, the children who had been placed with parents who were classified as insecurely attached in terms of the Adult Attachment Interview responses – those with dismissing, preoccupied, and/or unresolved status with regard to past trauma or loss – continued to show elevated levels of avoidance and disorganized themes as a strategy to resolve the dilemmas in the stories. This difference remained even at the two-year follow-up.

References

Ainsworth, M.D., Blehar, M.C., Waters, E., & Wall, S. (1978). *Patterns of attachment: Assessed in the strange situation and at home*. Hillsdale, NJ: Lawrence Erlbaum.

Alvarez, A. (1992). *Live company: Psychoanalytic psychotherapy with autistic, borderline, deprived, and abused children*. Brighton, UK: Psychology Press.

Alvarez, A. (2012). *The thinking heart: Three levels of psychoanalytic therapy with disturbed children*. London, UK: Routledge.

Bakermans-Kranenburg, M. & Van IJzendoorn, M. (2009). The first 10,000 Adult Attachment Interviews: Distributions of adult attachment representations in clinical and non-clinical groups. *Attachment & Human Development*, 11:223–263.

Beebe, B. (2004). Symposium on intersubjectivity in infant research and its implications for adult treatment. IV. Faces-in-relation: A case study. *Psychoanalytic Dialogues*, 14:1–51.

Beebe, B. & Lachmann, F. (2002). *Infant research and adult treatment: Co-constructing interactions*. Hillsdale, NJ: The Analytic Press.

Beebe, B. (2005). Mother–infant research informs mother–infant treatment. *Psychoanalytic Study of the Child*, 60:7–46.

Beebe, B., Jaffe, J., Lachmann, F., Feldstein, F., Crown, C., & Jasnow, M. (2000). Systems models in development and psychoanalysis: The case of vocal rhythm coordination and attachment. *Infant Mental Health Journal*, 21:99–122.

Bonovitz, C. (2003). Treating children who do not play or talk: Finding a pathway to intersubjective relatedness. *Psychoanalytic Psychology*, 20:315–328.

Bowlby, J. (1969/1982). *Attachment and loss: Vol. 1. Attachment.* London, UK: Hogarth Press and the Institute of Psychoanalysis.

Carlson, E.A. (1998). A prospective longitudinal study of attachment disorganization/disorientation. *Child Development*, 69:1107–1128.

Dicks, H.V. (1970). *Fifty years of the Tavistock Clinic.* London, UK: Routledge & K. Paul.

Fonagy, P. (1999). Points of contact and divergence between psychoanalytic and attachment theories: Is psychoanalytic theory truly different? *Psychoanalytic Inquiry*, 19:448–480.

Fonagy, P., Leigh, T., Steele, M., Steele, H., Kennedy, R, Matoon, G., Target, M., & Gerber, A. (1996). The relation of attachment status, psychiatric classification, and response to psychotherapy. *Journal of Consulting and Clinical Psychology*, 64:22–31.

Fonagy, P., Target, M., Steele, H., Steele, M., Kennedy, R, Matoon, G., Target, M., & Gerber, A. (1996). *Reflective functioning manual. Version 5 for application to Adult Attachment Interviews.* London, UK: University College London.

Fonagy, P., & Bateman, A. (2006). Mechanism of change in mentalisation based treatment of borderline personality disorder. *Journal of clinical Psychology*, 62:411–430.

Freud, A. (1965). *Normality and pathology in childhood.* New York, NY: International Universities Press.

Greenacre, P. (2006). Pregenital patterning. *International Journal of Psychoanalysis*, 33:410–415.

Hodges, J., Berger, M., Melzak, S., Oldeschulte, R., Rabb, S., & Salo, F. (1984). Two crucial questions: Adopted children in psychoanalytic treatment. *Journal of Child Psychotherapy*, 10:47–56.

Hodges, J. (1991). On castaways and some effects of early experience. *Bulletin of the Anna Freud Centre*, 14:79–94.

Hodges, J., Steele, M., Hillman, S., Henderson, K., & Kaniuk, J. (2005). Change and continuity in mental representations of attachment after adoption. In: D.M. Brodzinsky & J. Palacios (Eds.), *Psychological issues in adoption – Research and practice* (pp. 93–116). Santa Barbara, CA: Praeger Publishers.

Hopkins, J. (1996). The dangers and deprivations of too-good mothering. *Journal of Child Psychotherapy*, 22:407–422.

Hurry, A. (Ed.) (1998). *Psychoanalysis and developmental theory*. London: Karnac Books.

Jacobson, E. (1964). *The self and the object world*. London, UK: The Hogarth Press.

Karp, M.R. (1997). Symbolic participation: The role of projective drawings in a case of child abuse. *Psychoanalytic Study of the Child*, 52:260–300.

Kenrick, J. (2006). Psychoanalytic framework for therapeutic work with looked-after and adopted children. In: J. Kenrick, L. Tollemache, & C. Lindsey (Eds.), *Creating new families: Therapeutic approaches to fostering, adoption and kinship care* (pp. 24–32). London, UK: Karnac.

Lieberman, A.F., Van Horn, P., & Ghosh Ippen, C. (2005). Toward evidence-based treatment: Child–parent psychotherapy with preschoolers exposed to marital violence. *Journal of the American Academy of Child and Adolescent Psychiatry*, 44:1241–1248.

Lieberman, A.F., Van Horn, P., & Ghosh Ippen, C. (2006). Child–parent psychotherapy: 6-month follow-up of a randomized control trial. *Journal of the American Academy of Child and Adolescent Psychiatry*, 45:913–918.

Mahler, M.S., Pine, F., & Bergman, A. (1973). *The psychological birth of the human infant*. New York, NY: Basic Books.

Main, M., Kaplan, N., & Cassidy, J. (1985). Security in infancy, childhood and adulthood: A move to the level of representation. In: I. Bretherton & E. Waters (Eds.), *Growing points in attachment, Monograph of the Society for Research in Child Development*, 50: 66–104.

Main, M., & Solomon J. (1990). Procedures for identifying infants as disorganised/disoriented during the Ainsworth Strange Situation. In: M.T. Greenberg, D. Cicchetti, & E.M. Cummings (Eds.), *Attachment in the preschool years* (pp. 121–160). Chicago, IL: University of Chicago Press.

Music, G. (2014). Top down and bottom up: Trauma, executive functioning, emotional regulation, the brain and child psychotherapy. *Journal of Child Psychotherapy*, 40:3–19.

Olesker, W. (2003). An analysis of a developmentally delayed young girl: Coordinating analytic and developmental processes. *Psychoanalytic Study of the Child*, 58:89–111.

Osofsky, J.D. (1995). Children who witness domestic violence: The invisible victims. *Social Policy Report*, 9:1–16.

Rossouw, T. & Fonagy, P. (2012). Mentalization-based treatment for self-harm in adolescents: A randomized controlled trial. *Journal of the American Academy of Child & Adolescent Psychiatry*, 51:1304–1313.

Safran, J.D. & Muran, J.C. (1996). The resolution of ruptures in the therapeutic alliance. *Journal of Consulting and Clinical Psychology*, 64:447–458.

Safran, J.D. (2002). Brief relational psychoanalytic treatment. *Psychoanalytic Dialogues*, 12:171–196.

Sandler, A.M. (1975). Comments on the significance of Piaget's work for psychoanalysis. *International Review of Psycho-Analysis*, 2:365–377.

Sandler, J. & Rosenblatt, B. (1962). The concept of the representational world. *Psychoanalytic Study of the Child*, 17:128–188.

Sandler, J., (1976). Countertransference and role-responsiveness. *International Review of Psycho-Analysis*, 3:43–47.

Sandler, J. (1987). *From safety to superego*. New York, NY/London, UK: Guilford Press.

Schlesinger, H.J. (2013). *The texture of treatment: On the matter of psychoanalytic technique*. London, UK: Routledge.

Seligman, S. (2003). The developmental perspective in relational psychoanalysis. *Contemporary Psychoanalysis*, 39:477–508.

Seligman, S. (2012). The baby out of the bathwater: Microseconds, psychic structure, and psychotherapy. *Psychoanalytic Dialogues: The International Journal of Relationship Perspectives*, 22:499–509.

Slade, A. (2004). Two therapies: Attachment organization and the clinical process. In: L. Atkinson & S. Goldberg (Eds.), *Attachment, psychopathology and intervention* (pp. 181–206). Hillsdale, NJ: Erlbaum Press.

Slade, A. (1999). Representation, symbolization and affect regulations in concomitant treatment of mother and child: Attachment theory and child psychotherapy. *Psychoanalytic Inquiry*, 19:797–830.

Spitz, R. (1945). Hospitalism: An inquiry into the genesis of psychiatric conditions in early childhood. *Psychoanalytic Study of the Child*, 1:53–73.

Spitz, R. (1950). Anxiety in infancy: A study of its manifestations in the first year of life. *International Journal of Psychoanalysis*, 31:138–143.

Spitz, R. (1959). *A genetic field theory of ego formation: Its implications for pathology*. New York, NY: International Universities Press.

Steele, M., Hodges, J., Kaniuk, J., Hillman, S., & Henderson, K. (2010). Attachment representations in newly adopted maltreated children and their adoptive parents: Implications for placement and support. *Journal of Child Psychotherapy*, 29:187–205.

Steele, M., Hodges, J., Kaniuk, J., Steele, H., Hillman, S., & Asquith, K. (2008). Forecasting outcomes in previously maltreated children: The use of the AAI in a longitudinal adoption study. In: H. Steele & M. Steele (Eds.), *Clinical application of the Adult Attachment Interview* (pp. 427–451). New York, NY: Guilford Press.

Steele, M., Hodges, J., Kaniuk, J., & Steele, H. (2010). Mental representations and change: Developing attachment relationships in an adoption context. *Psychoanalytic Inquiry*, 30:25–40.

Steele, M. Hodges, J., Kaniuk, J., Steele, H., Asquith, K., & Hillman, S. (2009). Attachment representations and adoption outcome: On the use of narrative assessments to track the adaptation of previously maltreated children in their new families. In: B. Neil & G. Wrobel (Eds.), *International Advances in Adoption Research for Practice* (pp. 193–216). New York, NY: Wiley.

Steele, M., Murphy, A., & Steele, H. (2010). Identifying therapeutic action in an attachment based intervention. *Journal of Clinical Social Work*, 38:61–72.

Trevarthen, C.B. (1979). Communication and cooperation in early infancy: A description of primary intersubjectivity. In: M. Bullowa (Ed.) *Before Speech* (p. 343). Cambridge, UK: Cambridge University Press.

Tronick, E., & Weinberg, K. (1997). Depressed mothers and infants: Failure to form dyadic states of consciousness. In: L. Murray & P.J. Cooper (Eds.) *Postpartum depression and child development* (pp. 54–81). New York, NY: The Guildford Press.

Tronick, E. (2007). *The neurobehavioral and social-emotional development of infants and children.* New York, NY: W. W. Norton & Co.

Wilson, A., & Weinstein, L. (1992). An investigation into some implications of a Vygotskian perspective on the origins of the mind: Psychoanalysis and Vygotskian psychology, Part I. *Journal of the American Psychoanalytic Association*, 40:357–387.

Chapter 4

Neglect and its neglect

Developmental science, psychoanalytic thinking, and countertransference vitality

Graham Music, Ph.D.

Introduction

This chapter describes the difficulties of working with emotionally neglected children. I delineate a patient group who can challenge conventional psychoanalytic technique and also challenge us personally. They evoke a particular range of countertransference feelings that are hard to admit to, but are the most vital clues to how we must approach the work. These include boredom, deadness, and cut-off, dulled-down states in which thoughts can become wooden and bodily feelings flat. I will suggest that it is easy with such patients to be unwittingly drawn into enactments (Aron, 2001) and a form of role-responsiveness (Sandler, 1993) whereby there are two dulled people in the room and little real therapy being done.

I suggest that in such work we need to substantially adapt our technique. Work with such children requires an understanding of how normal developmental trajectories might have been stymied by the lack of good, "expectable" experiences and how such stalled trajectories can be restarted. As Alvarez (1992) says, these children are not withdrawn but rather can be thought of as "undrawn" and require a particular kind of "Live Company" to come alive and grow a mind.

Thus, a developmentally informed psychoanalytic approach (Hurry, 1998) is needed, allied with astute observational skills. Fraiberg's early work (1974), particularly with blind babies, provides an excellent example of the need to be alert to and amplify tiny and easy-to-miss, but hopeful, signs. Such work also requires helping patients experience and bear the positive as well as the negative emotional states that are the usual fare in psychoanalytic work (Music, 2009).

Other deviations from the usual emphases in psychoanalytic psycho-therapy include being prepared to speak with authenticity and spontaneity, as many in both the British Independent (Symington, 1983; Klauber, 1987; Coltart, 1992) and relational (Bromberg, 1998; Aron, 2001; Altman et al., 2002) traditions have asserted. This avoids the dangers of overusing interpretations with such children defensively, making one believe that one is doing something called therapy when one is in fact going through the motions.

Work with this group is also helped by facilitating interoception, the awareness of body sensations, as too many neglected children are cut off from the kind of body awareness that allows them to read and respond to their own signals. Furthermore, I will suggest that as such children become more alive, we might witness unpalatable forms of aliveness, such as aggression and shocking cruelty, on the road to their becoming more ordinarily socialized and interpersonally adept.

I will use psychoanalytic ideas as well as research from neuroscience, attachment, and developmental psychology to try to make sense of emotionally neglected children. Here, I do not describe the kind of neglect that quite rightly often preoccupies social workers, such as children coming to school dirty and hungry or living in squalor and poverty. Physical neglect is a very serious and too common issue, but I concentrate on the psychological sequelae of emotional neglect, which are often more serious.

I allow the term "neglect" to cover a broad spectrum, from relatively mild neglect to more extreme examples, such as children brought up in deprived institutional care.

A final caveat is that I am all too aware that one must not confuse symptomatology with etiology. Not all neglected children end up the same, and of course temperament, genetic inheritance, and a host of other factors will influence outcomes. Nonetheless, I do think that there are enough commonalities to justify trying to make clinical sense of this group of children and the very particular challenges that they pose.

Countertransference monitoring

A big therapeutic challenge is to remain alive and curious with children who so easily slip out of our minds. Such children can be experienced as deadened, inhibited, passive, and overly self-contained. They often have little ability to reflect on emotions (their own and others'), their narrative capacity is limited, and they experience little pleasure. Indeed, they rarely inspire hope, affection, or enjoyment in those around them.

In sessions with neglected children, I often find myself thinking about mundane things like chores. In fact, my cognitive countertransference is rarely alive with fantasies and reveries useful to the work. Rather, it is my somatic countertransference that gives me the important clues – my listlessness and lack of presence, my boredom and dullness. Winnicott (1994) exhorted us to be alive to and bear our "hate in the countertransference." With these patients we might add the need to be alert to "boredom in the countertransference."

The patients I describe have not suffered terrible abuse or obvious trauma, such as being beaten or sexually abused, or witnessing violence. These children are marked out not by what happened *to* them, but rather by what *did not* happen to them – in other words, neglect. They have lacked the good experiences that foster healthy emotional development.

An example from a typical clinical day illustrates something of the response often evoked in such work. One morning, my second patient is a very neglected and cut-off boy I call Josh. We do not have very much information about Josh's early life, but we know he was adopted from a South American orphanage at the age of nearly three. Reports suggest that his early environment provided at best for his basic physical needs, but not his emotional development. We do not know at what age he entered the orphanage or anything about his biological parents.

When the receptionist informs me of Josh's arrival, I feel a deadening thud inside as I slowly reach for the phone. I walk down the corridor lethargically, nearly dragging my feet. My breathing is shallow and, indeed, so is my mind. I feel a kind of dread and am certainly not looking forward to the session. I barely remember what happened last time, but know it was all too similar to the session before. My main intention is to try to keep myself psychologically alive. In the waiting room, Josh is sitting where he sits every time, reading from the same set of comics. He looks up in the same way he always does, his predictability inducing dullness, and languidly gets up and follows me to the therapy room. There is a robotic feel to all this. My reactions to Josh are, I think, typical of what often happens in the presence of children who have been emotionally neglected.

This is in stark contrast to my previous patient, who I call Tommy. He is not the kind of child this chapter describes and was overtly abused and traumatized rather than neglected. The contrast in countertransference responses between abused children like Tommy and neglected ones like Josh is very telling. There is rarely a dull moment in therapy with Tommy. On the previous week, I left the session with bruised shins, a battered therapy room, and my psyche similarly battered. Six-year-old Tommy cannot be still for even a few seconds. He is a real handful not only for me, but also for his teachers, his social worker, and especially his adoptive parents. Yet with Tommy, very differently from neglected children like Josh, I feel alive and interested. When the receptionist tells me of his arrival, my heart begins to beat fast, partly from anxious sympathetic nervous system arousal, but also from a modicum of eager anticipation. Something about Tommy evokes warm feelings in those who know him, a warmth one rarely experiences in response to dulled-down, "undrawn" children like Josh.

Psychoanalytic thinking

In thinking about neglect, we can build on helpful psychoanalytic ideas about "cut-off" and unpsychologically minded patients. In adult psychoanalysis, Bollas (1987) uses the concept "normotic" to describe patients he sees as psychologically "unborn." He found that they were often raised in families where their "real selves" were not mirrored, with parents not alive to their children's inner reality. Bollas describes normotic patients as having little capacity for identification or empathy and as "strangely objectless." They rarely introject much, nor project into others, hence being so often ignored. Our words spoken with meaning, life, and energy can quickly become denuded of significance. These are not patients who are attacking links in Bion's (1959) sense, but rather links have simply not developed, something that recent neuroscience seems to be corroborating (Siegel, 2012).

McDougall (1992) describes similar patients whom she calls "normopaths," often "alexythmic" patients who lack an affective or interior life or "personal psychic theater" (p. 156). Her writing about such patients is full of metaphors such as "armor-plated shells." She argues that it can take years before such "rejected representations and the stifled affects which surround this 'sterilized' space become visible and available to verbal thought and psychic elaboration" (p. 443).

In clinical writings about such patients, there is often an almost despairing thread about how the therapist is affected. Ogden (1999) writes that one's sense of aliveness or deadness is the central measure of the status of the therapy. He argues that the analyst has to work hard to be honest about the countertransference in order to generate ways of relating meaningfully. He writes with candor about, for example, fantasies of feigning illness "to escape the stagnant deadness of the sessions." I certainly find that such patients give rise to similar "heart-sink" moments. Flat inner worlds, lack of fantasy and imaginary play, and little empathy can make for unrewarding sessions.

In child psychotherapy, much writing about autistic spectrum patients is directly relevant. Several psychoanalytic writers have focused on the need for a more "active" technique, the use of an enlivening "reclamation" (Alvarez, 1992), as well as the importance of not colluding with lifeless and empty behavior (Alvarez & Reid, 1999; Rhode & Klauber, 2004).

Neglected children have, by definition, received little attention from their parents and caregivers. They then suffer from what the child psychotherapist Gianna Henry (2004) calls "double-deprivation," as they tragically do not use or even recognize the existence of helpfulness in the adults in their lives. In fact, we often also see what Louise Emanuel (2002) calls "triple deprivation," as these children can also get ignored or neglected by adults and other professionals. These are the children sitting in the back of class causing no trouble, but almost vegetating, while all the attention goes to the bright, sharp ones or the acting-out, misbehaving ones.

A view from developmental science

From the works of Lou Sander (1972, 2007), Daniel Stern (1985), and onward, infancy research has in recent decades outlined the conditions for optimal emotional development. Even if there remain debates about exactly what children need, and even if there are huge cultural differences about exactly what constitutes good parenting (Keller, 2007;

Music, 2016), we know much more about the effects of particular early experiences. We know which kinds of parenting lead to secure attachment and that various forms of emotional trauma give rise to specific psychobiological effects. We know that infant minds grow in response to attuned and emotionally sensitive caregiving and that mind-minded (Meins et al., 2002) input from parents and emotional responsiveness give rise to a host of hopeful developments. This includes secure attachment and the capacity for self-regulation (Fonagy et al., 2004; Schore, 2005; Bakermans-Kranenburg et al., 2008). We know that babies need to have their difficult feelings understood and that they feel held and contained when they know they are in the presence of adults who are trying to understand them.

This is of course partly why the work of psychoanalytically informed infancy researchers such as Beebe and Lachmann (2002), Tronick (2007), and Stern (1985) has been so important. Experimental situations have proven what we have long known from the traditions of infant observation (Bick, 1968; Miller, 1989): that being held in mind is a growth-enhancing experience. Children, of course, thrive not through having perfect care, but through experiencing a relationship in which the other person is sensitive to them and tries to repair mismatches and get miscommunications back on track.

Such repairs give rise to a sense of agency in infants and children (Broucek, 1991; Alvarez, 1992). They learn that if something goes wrong, it is not the end of the world. They come to believe that repair is possible, that they can play a part in facilitating this, and are players in relationships. This links with the emphasis relational psychoanalysts place on becoming aware of enactments and stepping outside of them. With neglected children who have lacked attuned early experiences, the therapist's feelings of dullness or boredom and consequent lack of active responsiveness to the patient can be viewed as a form of enactment.

Throughout the first year of life, in cases where care is good enough, imitative capacities transform into more sophisticated mutual understanding. By just four months of age, infants come to know they are the object of another's attention, showing coyness, for example (Reddy, 2000), and, if lucky, by eight months, they can attain sufficient understanding of other minds to be able to "tease and muck about"

(Reddy, 2008). By about nine months, "joint attention" and "social referencing" are seen. This is what Trevarthen (Trevarthen & Aitken, 2001) originally called secondary intersubjectivity, in which both parties understand and appreciate what is in the other's mind. Already the building blocks of empathy (Decety et al., 2012), altruism (Tomasello, 2009), and mutuality are in place. This is all built on early reciprocity and what Anne Alvarez, after Colwyn Trevarthen, called "Live Company" (1992), something so many neglected children lack.

Such experiences, incrementally built up over the seconds, minutes, hours, and then days, weeks, months, and years of a young life, are what give rise to an internal world full of richness and trust and interest in the external world. Infants are born other-centered (Bråten, 2006) as opposed to ego-centered. Or, as Emde (2009) might put it, an ego depends on first forming a "we-go." We might be born with a preconception of what Trevarthen (2001) calls a companion in meaning making, but if reality does not deliver such companionship, then infants adapt to their reality, however bleak.

This is when we see presentations common in the worst cases of neglect: staring into space, rocking, dead eyes, and little responsiveness. These are the kinds of symptoms that led Rutter (2007) to realize that a large number of the Romanian orphans he researched showed symptoms indistinguishable from autism. Several cases of neglected children I have seen were misdiagnosed with Asperger's syndrome. At the age of 14, one adopted former Romanian orphan rocked when distressed, struggled with relationships, and took great interest in categorizing and lists. Another would memorize car manuals and shopping catalogues and said that this was what he most liked doing. Research such as by Spitz (1945), Tizard and Hodges (1978), and Rutter (2007) has outlined the terrible longitudinal effects of neglect. While luckier children are held, touched, talked to, played with, loved, and held in mind, neglected children can be left in a desultory world, stagnating and "undrawn" (Alvarez, 2012).

We now know that neglect can have a profound effect on children's developing brains and hormonal systems. Bruce Perry (1995) was one of the first to draw attention to how neglected children's chronically understimulated brains do not grow ordinarily. Scans show that they react less to pictures of faces, particularly faces showing emotion

(Parker & Nelson, 2005). They show less metabolic activity in many brain areas (Marshall et al., 2004) and less connectivity between different brain regions, including regions central to both social and emotional as well as cognitive development (Eluvathingal et al., 2006). Deficits have shown up consistently in the prefrontal cortex (Maheu et al., 2010), central for empathy, concentration, and self-regulation. Institutional deprivation is also associated with atypical development of other brain regions such as the amygdala, which is so central to fear and anxiety (Tottenham et al., 2010), and also with decreases in cortical white matter (Sheridan et al., 2012).

The hormonal systems of severely neglected children also become programmed differently. Lane Strathearn (2011, 2009), probably more than anyone, has examined the effects of neglect. He linked it with lower activation of the oxytocin system and also brain regions associated with rewards, particularly the dopamine system. An earlier study of neglected Romanian orphans found that the adopted children released less oxytocin and vasopressin when cuddled by their adoptive mothers than a control group of birth children (Fries et al., 2005), presumably due to poor early nurturing experiences. Their stress systems also show abnormalities.

However, there is room for hope. The Bucharest Early Intervention Project found that children adopted into foster placements do much better on many measures than those who remain in orphanages, showing higher levels of executive functioning and enhanced development of its neural correlates in prefrontal brain areas (McDermott et al., 2012).

Of course, in real life, we rarely see a pure form of neglect. Most neglected children have had some good input alongside the neglect and often also suffered more overt abuse. There are also degrees of neglect, ranging from very depriving orphanages to some forms of avoidant attachment, as well as the very deadening forms of maternal depression, particularly when mothers are unable to interact much (Field et al., 2006). Lynne Murray's research on depressed mothers described effects we might expect, with children being more passive, with less sense of agency, more withdrawn, less interested in the world, and less inclined to reach out to people (Murray & Cooper, 1999).

The deadened or uninterested object

Before a typical session with ten-year-old Martin, 18 months into his weekly therapy, I already felt flat when the receptionist called. Martin politely came shuffling along, having given a compliant smile that seemed to lead my mind to go blank. Once in the room, he sat and looked at me expectantly – and paradoxically with a total lack of expectation. By this point, I was already feeling despondent, plummeting back to the feeling of other weeks that the burden of anything "alive" happening was down to me. I felt a less than proper therapist if I stayed silent, but when I tried to make interpretations, these disappeared into a chilling silence. I had learnt that to have any impact, what I said and did must come from a genuine "feeling-fullness" inside myself and words needed to be spoken with emotional honesty. I could console myself with the knowledge that I had "comrades in feeling" in most of the adults who had contact with Martin, most notably his parents and teachers.

Martin was the oldest of three children, the younger ones seeming to develop relatively normally. He was born a few weeks prematurely with some complications, but apparently no organic damage, and he remained in the hospital for several weeks, alone much of the time. At birth, his maternal grandmother was terminally ill and she died soon afterwards. His mother was physically absent, but also depressed and preoccupied with needing to look after her bereaved father and adjusting to her new marriage. Martin lacked a mind attuned to his emotional states and was left alone more than was good for him.

He was described as a "good" and "quiet" baby, but presumably was "too good" for his own good. He was frequently left with family and neighbors. Physically, he reached all the usual milestones, but he demanded and received less input than one would hope. As he grew up, he showed little interest in other children, did not play in an imaginary or "make-believe" way, and was described as being a loner. His parents experienced little pleasure from him, and he spent hours in his room in aimless activities. Children like Martin have not been given a sense of themselves as continuing over time in anyone else's mind and have not introjected an object that is attentive to them. Indeed, they have a deadened and uninterested internal object. In attachment and developmental psychology terms, such children lack a narrative sense of themselves or a developed autobiographical self and they can live in an eerily timeless realm.

My hunch is that such cases rarely get referred to services and those that make it are often closed more quickly than others. We can justify this to ourselves by arguing that they seem "just fine", that they seem not to want help and certainly do not ask for it. Furthermore, we can experience such children as rejecting. It is difficult to admit to, but we can sometimes be relieved at the idea of not working with them, thus perpetuating their neglect.

Martin did not understand ordinary social cues and, for example, looked "uncool", wearing clothes that his parents might choose. He had been bullied at school, but had no words to describe his feelings about this. He would say, "I am one of those fidgety sorts of people," as his legs twitched and his hands tapped, his body working at a speed that belied the apparent slowness of his mind. I understood his fidgeting as his way of holding himself together, a form of second-skin defense (Bick, 1968) or self-soothing, compensating for the lack of a containing internal object or recognition of good external ones.

I spent quite a lot of time in the early stages of Martin's treatment trying to show interest in such body states of which he was unaware. This might include copying his gestures as kindly as I could and talking about what I thought he might be feeling or, in time, asking him to describe such states. He would get a bit more agitated toward the ends of sessions, but interpreting his anger at breaks or endings went nowhere and at this stage had no conscious meaning for him. Attending to smaller gestures such as checking what the increased twitching was like and whether his heart was beating faster did, though, help him develop some interest in himself. It could also be fun and enlivening, which was important in itself.

In my attention to body states, I drew on lessons from attachment theory. We know, for example, that children categorized as avoidant tend to seem very self-sufficient and barely respond when their caregivers come and go (Ainsworth, 1978). Yet on their mothers' departure in Strange Situation tests, they show similar physiological responsiveness as secure children, such as faster heart rates. However, they act as if they are not experiencing such bodily symptoms. Presumably, they cannot afford to notice such signals to themselves and a split develops in their personality so that they cut off from such signs of distress. It makes no sense to feel and express distress to unresponsive parents. With them, it pays to develop a deactivated attachment style, which in effect means neglecting one's own and other people's signs of upset or distress (Holmes, 2001).

Not surprisingly, Martin had no friends, although he did mention another boy who was as obsessed with trains and timetables as he was. Cozolino (2006) suggests that, in such patients, right hemisphere emotional functions might be not very connected to left brain, more rational, and logical ones. These children can sometimes be logical, but have little emotional depth. When I tried to speak in my usual way – imagining his feelings, for example – my comments were generally brushed aside or ignored. I often felt myself becoming enveloped in a cotton wool-like deadness. At times, I spoke just to feel that I was alive. I think that often such patients do not so much ignore what we say as not really notice it, irrespective of how empathic or accurate it is, as they lack an idea of a mind interested in them. Their internal object is similarly uninterested (Alvarez, 2012). Neglected children and many classified as avoidant have a "dampened down" *hypo*active system, the opposite of the *hyper*active and acting-out children with heightened "sympathetic" nervous systems. As opposed to children who have suffered trauma or intrusion, they do not have to bother much with others, of whom they have few expectations.

Sustaining thinking, empathy, and internal freedom

I often draw on the writings of British Independent Psychoanalysts Coltart (1992) and Symington (1983) about "inner acts of freedom" and how our internal mental work is the most crucial aspect of maintaining aliveness. This means being on guard to avoid the trap of doing work that can feel like psychotherapy, but really is a form of pseudo-therapy. As Morgan (2005), a mindfulness psychotherapist, wrote, "… the task is first and foremost not to be killed off. We are killed off when we are not present in the moment" (p. 141).

The deadness we often feel is not, I think, a result of having such feelings projected into us, but is rather a form of role responsiveness, a non-conscious mirroring of a patient's experiences and gestures, maybe "emotional contagion" (Hatfield et al., 1993), maybe mirror neuron responsiveness (Rizzolatti et al., 2006). Often, our seemingly well-intentioned therapeutic interventions are a defensive retreat from the grim reality of a patient's internal world. This is a paradox, as we need to be sufficiently empathic to bear their psychic states in our countertransference without being drawn too far into their deadness. Often, empathy is the last thing one feels and so it is a huge challenge to use countertransference to help these patients.

Martin was typical. He was reluctantly dragged to therapy by parents unnerved by their feelings about him, such as frustration and hopelessness – feelings I soon understood. At school, too, he was viewed as odd, a loner, and sometimes as "lazy" and "stubborn". In sessions, he would sit and stare compliantly. Often, each session was neatly divided up. He might start by saying, "I will talk about my dreams for three minutes, things at home for four minutes, play a game of hangman for five minutes, talk about worries for four minutes."

I realized what a different world he inhabited from the one that I took for granted. One week, he came in acting the same as other weeks, making his list of "things that happened this week", which included the death of his grandfather. I was shocked and disturbed and tried to show what I believed was empathy. However, he looked at me blankly and told me some factual details about the funeral. Martin was far away from experiencing the feelings I wrongly assumed he might have.

What made a difference was when I concentrated on what it really felt like to be in a room with him, bearing my feelings, whether of boredom, irritation, wanting to shake him up, or drifting away. Once, when in a kind of half-alive torpor, I managed to concentrate hard on what he seemed to be experiencing, imagining what it might feel like to be him. I soon surprised myself by feeling some sympathy. I am fairly sure in response to just this change in my feeling tone he looked up and smiled, a small moment to cherish, one from which some genuine relating followed. His smile seemed real, not compliant. At such moments, I know my voice had more urgency, but also genuineness. I was "calling him back," "reclaiming" (Alvarez, 1992) him, and he could respond. I wonder what a magnetic resonance imaging scan might have revealed in his or my prefrontal cortex at such moments or what measurements a skin conductivity test would have shown, but I feel fairly sure that something would have registered in a way that was unusual in our therapy.

Slowly, Martin slightly loosened up as I found a way to empathize and feel my way into his world. As a result, I realized I found myself liking him. Then I could be more actively challenging of him in a way that he would not experience as judgmental. Sometimes my frustration crept in and then my less than sympathetic tone precluded real contact. When my attempts to reach him had urgency but not frustration, when I challenged him warmly, then real contact was possible. When, for example, I leaned forward slightly and said, "Oh, wow, this bouncing leg keeps Martin from feeling nervy, but it keeps him from noticing that Mr. Music is really interested in him," he looked up and his tone changed. Such shifts came from immersing myself in an aspect of his being that I found almost unbearable.

As he bounced his leg, I bounced mine in response. He looked up at me and awkwardly smiled, but clearly some rudimentary "reciprocity" (Brazelton & Cramer, 1991) was emerging. As he stopped jigging his leg and I did too, he looked up again, jigged and waited for me to respond. This was akin to the ordinary rhythmic to-and-fro that most babies engage in but that Martin had lacked. He was developing some capacity for conversations in which slightly more difficult feelings could be processed. In contrast, it made no sense to him when I talked, as I did too much, of breaks between sessions or holidays. However, when in a game I enacted being suddenly stopped in my tracks and expressed frustration, he seemed to enjoy me showing I could bear these feelings, even if he could not as yet bear them himself. He looked awkward, then laughed, and in the next session he did a slightly wooden version of the same thing, showing a capacity for both introjections and for "deferred imitation" (Meltzoff, 1988). He had also become slightly humorous, which, as Canham (1999) states, means that a patient "has a benign observing function on another part" (p. 168).

I have also found that when such deadened patients start to "thaw out", I often witness both aggression and sadism. This can be hard to stay with, yet I think expressing such unsavory aspects of their personalities can ironically be part of their very lifeblood. Eigen (1995) illustrates a therapeutic approach that is genuinely allowing of all aspects of a patient's psyche, suggesting that some patients need to act psychopathically while "on the road" to achieving a more moral and "depressive" outlook. If we too quickly interpret the destructiveness or aggression in a way that smacks of being judgmental, then a developmental opportunity is lost. Freud's theory suggests that we need to accept "id" impulses, which can then be used in the service of the life instinct. Sometimes, our disquiet at cruel aspects of the personality can lead to pseudo-interpretations that stymie the development of something more "feelingful" and "alive".

As Martin became livelier, I sometimes saw disturbing and sickly scenes enacted, such as horrible deaths and torture. If I revealed any hint of disapproval, his play ground to a halt. At times, I needed to speak to, or even for, the sadistic, aggressive voice, empathically saying things like, "Yes, he really wants to beat him up as hard as he can. That's what he wants." As unsavory as this might seem, there was at least some "desire" here that needed encouraging. In this and other cases, tolerating such abhorrent feelings can be a stepping stone in development, not an unleashing of psychopathic monsters. A big part of such work is encouraging "aliveness", and as psychoanalysis has always shown, life is not always nice or pleasant.

Pleasure and enjoyment

Over time, Martin became somewhat playful. He would sit behind a chair, wave his leg around, and wait for me to respond. He began to show initiative, a sense of agency, and, maybe more importantly, the beginnings of fun. I often felt guilty, hearing a psychoanalytic superego telling me that if it was enjoyable, it was not psychoanalytic. However, I now think that a range of emotions are neglected in the psychoanalytic literature (Music, 2009). These include enjoyment, pleasure, excitement, liveliness, and joy. Neglected children generally experience too few of these feelings. They also lack much sense of agency (Broucek, 1991) or belief that they can be active partners in social interactions, something that in itself is pleasurable. Infancy research describes how babies love making things happen, whether making a noise by pulling a cord or making the mother come with a cry or laugh. When all goes well, babies are active participants in lively, enjoyable interpersonal encounters. Neglected children rarely have this capacity for pleasure and enjoyment.

Alvarez (1992) in particular has cautioned against mistaking manic defenses for developmental opportunities. She suggests that with certain deprived children, if we interpret what we see as defenses too quickly, then we simply deflate patients. Some children who jump on a chair and shout, "I am king of the castle!" might be being omnipotently defensive, but for others this could be a first experience of feeling strong and confident. They might revert to a more hopeless state if we interpret something like, "You want to be strong but really inside you feel little and hopeless."

Children, when young, tend to think they can climb higher mountains, balance more balls, score more goals, and perform better than they really can (Bjorklund, 2007). Not experiencing such feelings can even be a sign of depression in children. Confidence, in fact, increases resilience, both of which are often lacking in severely neglected children who have had no one believing in their capacities or that they are special. Such "protective optimism" is not just a defensive process used to deny a painful reality, but is also necessary for children to experiment with hope and to persist at tasks that otherwise feel too difficult.

Martin began to not give up so easily, developing belief that he could make things happen. Often when he struggled to do something, like build a tower, he would quickly give up. I actively encouraged him – "Yes, you can do it. No need to give up. Wow, you are doing well." Such support actively spurred him on. His face would beam when he succeeded in making something happen rather than just giving up and retreating. At the start of his therapy, he was rather like the children of depressed mothers that Murray (1992) or Field et al. (2006) studied, who tend to be passive and lacking self-belief, but by the end he was showing more initiative and, indeed, enjoyment. Obviously, there can be dangers in overestimating one's ability, but children like Martin run the opposite risk of becoming hopeless, with little belief that they can make an impact on the world.

As well as lacking confidence, many neglected children have not been much enjoyed and do not easily experience pleasure. Psychoanalysis and attachment theory have tended to privilege our defensive systems and the managing of difficult experiences. Yet the "appetitive" or "seeking" systems (Panksepp, 2005) of such neglected children also need stimulating, and it is playful, mutually enjoyable interactions that do this. We need to help patients process positive as well as negative affects, "tip-toe up to pleasure" as well as pain, given that pleasurable experience can be dysregulating for such children.

When Martin smiled slightly, I could occasionally meet that feeling and respond, maybe with an, "Oh, yes, that is exciting," or, "Wow, you really want to do that very much." This allowed him to believe that he could have a feeling that we might call "excitement" or "pleasure". In turn, this led him to become more obviously resilient, determined, and even pleasure-seeking. At times, toward the end of his therapy, he made gestures that clearly showed active desire. On one occasion, we were playing cricket. As he forcefully hit the foam ball with a ruler being used as a makeshift cricket bat, I exaggerated the gesture, almost screeching with excitement at his successful shot. I could almost feel his skin tingle with excitement in response. The next shot had a new-found looseness about it and a gesture that could almost be taken for aplomb.

The trick was being alive to signs of life that were faint and hard to detect (Fraiberg, 1974), as well as gauging and enabling a tolerable level of excitement. I hate to think about the signs that have bypassed me over the years. When we amplify or "mark" such signs of life (Fonagy, 2002), they can become the building blocks of lively mutuality. By the end, there were certainly moments when I enjoyed being with Martin, and he with me.

Neglected children often do not experience the enjoyable reciprocity that leads to a sense of playfulness, agency, and a sophisticated communicative dance. They struggle to be "Live Company" (Alvarez, 1992). Learning to be outgoing and positive and to have a sense of agency activate completely different brain regions (Davidson, 2004) from those used in processing negative emotions. While both are important, psychoanalysis has possibly under-theorized positive experiences. For patients like Martin, blank screens can breed more blankness, which is certainly not what they need.

Like many neglected children, as Martin thawed out, he became livelier, more enjoyable to be with, and even at times naughty. Indeed, parents and teachers are not universally pleased that a child who was quiet but caused no trouble can turn into one who demands attention and can get upset when their wishes are not responded to. However, on the positive side, they often become more interesting, more interested in other people, and start to show some empathy. Their stories about themselves become richer and more finely nuanced, with more emotional depth, sometimes even laced with humor. Martin, by the end, often made me smile, sometimes even laugh, and that for me is clear evidence of movement in the right direction.

Conclusions

I have suggested that a number of common factors make neglected children a clinical group worthy of our attention. They can leave caregivers and professionals feeling deskilled, dehumanized, even bored or apathetic. They often lack much awareness of minds and mental states, of stories and imagination, and they struggle with emotional expression, have little sense of agency, and, maybe most importantly, lack much capacity for ordinary enjoyment.

Neglect does not affect all children the same way. Some children can, it seems, make do with less, as recent epigenetic research has shown (Belsky, 2005; Bakermans-Kranenburg et al., 2008). Maybe not all children, given similar circumstances, would have withdrawn in the way that Martin did. Yet whatever our genetic inheritance, all humans need a degree of good early interactive care. We have learnt from orphanage studies about the "deadly" effect of a lack of early interpersonal input. The impact of too little interaction can be more pernicious than overt abuse and trauma.

Field (2006) compared the infants of withdrawn, depressed mothers with infants whose mothers' forms of depression were more intrusive. Those with withdrawn, depressed mothers were less exploratory at one year of age, and by three were not showing empathy, were passive and withdrawn, and were doing worse cognitively. Intrusion is at least stimulating, whereas neglect is deadening. We are born with "preconceptions," as Bion (1962) stated. Or, in other language, we start life experience "expectant," and if such an "evolutionarily-expectable environment" (Cicchetti & Valentino, 2006) is absent, then certain capacities simply do not develop.

I have attempted to delineate a group of children who pose a particular puzzle for psychoanalytic work. I have alluded to a few areas of technique that I find challenging. These include tolerating boredom in the countertransference. Such work also entails finding a way to encourage agency and positive affect and the paradoxical task of stepping back from a lifeless encounter in order to be empathically in touch with the patient. Spontaneity and authenticity are essential aspects of this, as are attention to body states and somatic counter-transference. One also has to bear immature and sadistic states of mind when these children begin to "thaw out". These only touch the surface of developing an effective therapeutic technique with such neglected children. We walk a delicate tightrope between being there to amplify aliveness, but not being intrusive. Similarly, we need to find a way to foster a sense of agency and enjoyment, while being neither too manic nor seductive. Our countertransference is always central to such work, particularly when it involves bearing uncomfortable experiences and the threat of being enveloped by a numbing atmosphere. A big challenge is ensuring that our interpretations and interventions are infused with emotional aliveness, relying less than usual on more cognitively based levels of work (Alvarez, 2012).

The neglected children I have known, like Martin, have not all undergone complete personality transformations through therapy, although the younger they are when they are offered help, the more dramatic are the changes seen. They often slowly "warm up", becoming livelier and slightly more real. Parallel work with parents is crucial in learning to identify and amplify any slight developmental signs, which in turn can lead to more rewarding experiences. Sometimes parents, teachers, and therapists might not be pleased that our work leads to children moving from being dull and cut off to becoming more lively, aggressive, and challenging, but at least some life is forming. Neglected children do not generally inspire passion and therapeutic zeal and have not only been neglected emotionally in their early lives, but are often further neglected later by other adults and professionals. If we do not provide them with the help they need, then their prognosis is particularly bad. Neglected children so badly need from us what they also rarely evoke – our passion, interest, enjoyment, and zeal.

References

Ainsworth, M.D.S. (1978). *Patterns of attachment: A psychological study of the strange situation*. Mahwah, NJ: Lawrence Erlbaum Associates.

Altman, N., Briggs, R., Frankel, J., Gensler, D., & Pantone, P. (2002). *Relational child psychotherapy*. New York, NY: Other Press.

Alvarez, A. (1992). *Live company*. London, UK: Routledge.

Alvarez, A. (2012). *The thinking heart: Three levels of psychoanalytic therapy with disturbed children*. 1st edition. Oxford, UK: Routledge.

Alvarez, A. & Reid, S. (1999). *Autism and personality: Findings from the Tavistock Autism Workshop*. 1st edition. London, UK: Routledge.

Aron, L. (2001). *A meeting of minds: Mutuality in psychoanalysis*. New York, NY: Analytic Press.

Bakermans-Kranenburg, M.J., Van IJzendoorn, M.H., Mesman, J., Alink, A.R., & Juffer, F. (2008). Effects of an attachment-based intervention on daily cortisol moderated by dopamine receptor D4: A randomized control trial on 1- to 3-year-olds screened for externalizing behaviour. *Development and Psychopathology*, 20:805–820.

Bakermans-Kranenburg, M.J. Van IJzendoorn, M.H., Pijlman, F.T., Mesman, J., & Juffer, F. (2008). Differential susceptibility to intervention: Dopamine D4 receptor polymorphism (DRD4 VNTR) moderates effects on toddlers' externalizing behavior in a randomized control trial. *Developmental Psychology*, 44:293–300.

Beebe, B. & Lachmann, F.M. (2002). *Infant research and adult treatment: Co-constructing interactions*. New York, NY: Analytic Press.

Belsky, J. (2005). Differential susceptibility to rearing influence. In: B. Ellis & D. Bjorklund (Eds.), *Origins of the social mind: Evolutionary psychology and child development* (pp. 139–163). New York, NY: Guilford Press.

Bick, E. (1968). The experience of the skin in early object relations. *International Journal of Psycho-Analysis*, 49:484–486.

Bion, W.R. (1959). Attacks on linking. *International Journal of Psycho-Analysis*, 40:308.

Bion, W.R. (1962). *Learning from experience*. London, UK: Heinemann.

Bjorklund, D.F. (2007). *Why youth is not wasted on the young: Immaturity in human development*. Oxford, UK: Blackwell.

Bollas, C. (1987). *The shadow of the object: Psychoanalysis of the unthought known*. London, UK: Free Association Books.

Bråten, S. (Ed.) (2006). *Intersubjective communication and emotion in early ontogeny*. Cambridge, MA: Cambridge University Press.

Brazelton, T.B. & Cramer, B.G. (1991). *The earliest relationship: Parents, infants, and the drama of early attachment*. London, UK: Karnac Books.

Bromberg, P.M. (1998). *Standing in the spaces: Essays on clinical process, trauma, and dissociation*. New York, NY: Analytic Press.

Broucek, F.J. (1991). *Shame and the self*. New York, NY: Guilford Press.

Canham, H. (1999). The development of the concept of time in fostered and adopted children. *Psychoanalytic Inquiry*, 19:160–171.

Cicchetti, D. & Valentino, K. (2006). An ecological–transactional perspective on child maltreatment: Failure of the average expectable environment and its influence on child development. In: D. Cicchetti & D. Cohen (Eds.), *Developmental psychopathology: Risk, disorder, and adaptation* (pp. 129–201). New York, NY: Wiley.

Coltart, N. (1992). *Slouching towards Bethlehem*. London, UK: Free Association Books.

Cozolino, L. (2006). *The neuroscience of human relationships: Attachment and the developing social brain*. New York, NY: W. W. Norton & Co.

Davidson, R.J. (2004). Well-being and affective style: Neural substrates and biobehavioural correlates. *Philosophical Transactions: Biological Sciences*. 359:1395–1411.

Decety, J., Morman, G.J., Berntson, G.G., & Cacioppo, J.T. (2012). A neurobehavioral evolutionary perspective on the mechanisms underlying empathy. *Progress in Neurobiology*, 98:38–48.

Eigen, M. (1995). *Electrified tightrope*. New York, NY: Aronson.

Eluvathingal, T.J. et al. (2006). Abnormal brain connectivity in children after early severe socioemotional deprivation: A diffusion tensor imaging study. *Pediatrics*, 117:2093–2100.

Emanuel, L. (2002). Deprivation× 3. *Journal of Child Psychotherapy*, 28: 163–179.

Emde, R.N. (2009). From ego to "we-go": Neurobiology and questions for psychoanalysis: Commentary on papers by Trevarthen, Gallese, and Ammaniti & Trentini. *Psychoanalytic Dialogues*. 19:556–564.

Field, T., Diego, M., & Hernandez-Reif, M. (2006). Prenatal depression effects on the fetus and newborn: A review. *Infant Behavior and Development*, 29:445–455.

Fonagy, P. (2002). *Affect regulation, mentalization, and the development of the self*. New York, NY: Other Press.

Fonagy, P., Gergely, G., Jurist, E.L., & Target, M. (2004). *Affect regulation, mentalization, and the development of the self*. New edition. London, UK: Karnac Books.

Fraiberg, S. (1974). Blind infants and their mothers: An examination of the sign system. In M. Lewis & L.A. Rosenblum (Eds.), *The effect of the infant on its caregiver* (pp. 215–232). New York, NY: Wiley-Interscience.

Fries, A.B.W., Ziegler, T.E., Kurian, J.R., Jacoris, S., & Pollak, S.D. (2005). Early experience in humans is associated with changes in neuropeptides critical for regulating social behavior. *Proceedings of the National Academy of Sciences*, 102:17237–17240.

Hatfield, E. et al. (1993). Emotional contagion. *Current Directions in Psychological Science*, 2:96–99.

Henry, G. (2004). Doubly deprived. In: P. Barrows (Ed.), *Key papers from the Journal of Child Psychotherapy* (p. 105). London, UK: Routledge.

Holmes, J. (2001). *The search for the secure base: Attachment theory and psychotherapy.* London, UK: Routledge.

Hurry, A. (1998). *Psychoanalysis and developmental therapy.* London, UK: Karnac Books.

Keller, H. (2007). *Cultures of infancy.* Mahwah, NJ: Lawrence Erlbaum.

Klauber, J. (1987). *Illusion and spontaneity in psychoanalysis.* London, UK: Free Association Books.

Maheu, F.S. et al. (2010). A preliminary study of medial temporal lobe function in youths with a history of caregiver deprivation and emotional neglect. *Cognitive, Affective & Behavioral Neuroscience,* 10:34–49.

Marshall, P.J., Fox, N.A., & Bucharest Early Intervention Project Core Group (2004). A comparison of the electroencephalogram between institutionalized and community children in Romania. *Journal of Cognitive Neuroscience,* 16:1327–1338.

McDermott, J.M., Westerlund, A., Zeanah, C.H., Nelson, C.A., & Fox, N.A. (2012). Early adversity and neural correlates of executive function: Implications for academic adjustment. *Developmental Cognitive Neuroscience,* 2:S59–S66.

McDougall, J. (1992). *Plea for a measure of abnormality.* 1st edition. London, UK: Routledge.

Meins, E. et al. (2002). Maternal mind-mindedness and attachment security as predictors of theory of mind understanding. *Child Development,* 73:1715–1726.

Meltzoff, A.N. (1988). Infant imitation and memory: Nine-month-olds in immediate and deferred tests. *Child Development,* 59:217–225.

Miller, L. (1989). *Closely observed infants.* London, UK: Duckworth.

Morgan, S.P. (2005). Depression: Turning toward life. In: K. Christopher et al. (Eds.), *Mindfulness and psychotherapy.* New York, NY: Guilford Press.

Murray, L. (1992). The impact of postnatal depression on infant development. *Journal of Child Psychology and Psychiatry,* 33:543–561.

Murray, L. & Cooper, P. (1999). *Postpartum depression and child development.* New York, NY: Guilford Press.

Music, G. (2016). *Nurturing natures: Attachment and children's emotional, social and brain development.* London, UK: Psychology Press.

Music, G. (2009). What has psychoanalysis got to do with happiness? Reclaiming the positive in psychoanalytic psychotherapy. *British Journal of Psychotherapy,* 25:435–455.

Ogden, T.H. (1999). *Reverie and interpretation: Sensing something human.* London, UK: Karnac Books.

Panksepp, J. (2005). Affective consciousness: Core emotional feelings in animals and humans. *Consciousness and Cognition*, 14:30–80.

Parker, S.W. & Nelson, C.A. (2005). The impact of early institutional rearing on the ability to discriminate facial expressions of emotion: An event-related potential study. *Child Development*, 76:54–72.

Perry, B.D., Pollard, R.N., Blakley, T.L., Baker, W.L., & Vigilante, D. (1995). Childhood trauma, the neurobiology of adaptation, and "use-dependent" development of the brain: How states "become traits". *Infant Mental Health Journal*, 16:271–291.

Reddy, V. (2000). Coyness in early infancy. *Developmental Science*, 3:186–192.

Reddy, V. (2008). *How infants know minds*. Cambridge, MA: Harvard University Press.

Rhode, M. & Klauber, T. (2004). *The many faces of Asperger's syndrome*. London, UK: Karnac Books.

Rizzolatti, G. et al. (2006). Mirrors in the mind: Mirror neurons, a special class of cells in the brain, may mediate our ability to mimic, learn and understand the actions and intentions of others. *Scientific American*, 295:54–61.

Rutter, M. et al. (2007). Effects of profound early institutional deprivation: An overview of findings from a UK longitudinal study of Romanian adoptees. *European Journal of Developmental Psychology*, 4:332–350.

Sander, L., Julia, H.L., Stechler, G., & Burns, P., (1972). Continuous 24-hour interactional monitoring in infants reared in two caretaking environments. *Psychosomatic Medicine*, 34:270–282.

Sander, L. (2007). *Living systems, evolving consciousness, and the emerging person: A selection of papers from the life work of Louis Sander.* London, UK: Routledge.

Sandler, J. (1993). On communication from patient to analyst: Not everything is projective identification. *International Journal of Psycho-Analysis*, 74:1097–1107.

Schore, A.N. (2005). Back to basics: Attachment, affect regulation, and the developing right brain: Linking developmental neuroscience to pediatrics. *Pediatrics in Review*, 26:204–217.

Sheridan, M.A., Fox, N.A., Zeanah, C.H., McLaughlin, K.A., & Nelson, 3rd, C.A. (2012). Variation in neural development as a result of exposure to institutionalization early in childhood. *Proceedings of the National Academy of Sciences*, 109:12927–12932.

Siegel, D.J. (2012). *The developing mind: Toward a neurobiology of interpersonal experience*. New York, NY: Guilford Press.

Spitz, R.A. (1945). Hospitalism: An inquiry into the genesis of psychiatric conditions in early childhood. *Psychoanalytic Study of the Child*, 1:53–74.

Stern, D.N. (1985). *The interpersonal world of the infant*. New York, NY: Basic Books.

Strathearn, L., Fonagy, P., Amico, J., & Montague, P.R. (2009). Adult attachment predicts maternal brain and oxytocin response to infant cues. *Neuropsychopharmacology*, 34:2655–2666.

Strathearn, L. (2011). Maternal neglect: Oxytocin, dopamine and the neurobiology of attachment. *Journal of Neuroendocrinology*, 23:1054–1065.

Symington, N. (1983). The analyst's act of freedom as agent of therapeutic change. *International Review of Psycho-Analysis*, 10:283–291.

Tizard, B. & Hodges, J. (1978). The effect of early institutional rearing on the development of eight year old children. *Journal of Child Psychology and Psychiatry*, 19:99–118.

Tomasello, M. (2009). *Why we cooperate*. Cambridge, MA: MIT Press.

Tottenham, N. et al. (2010). Prolonged institutional rearing is associated with atypically large amygdala volume and difficulties in emotion regulation. *Developmental Science*, 13:46–61.

Trevarthen, C. (2001). Intrinsic motives for companionship in understanding: Their origin, development, and significance for infant mental health. *Infant Mental Health Journal*, 22:95–131.

Trevarthen, C. & Aitken, K.J. (2001). Infant intersubjectivity: Research, theory, and clinical applications. *The Journal of Child Psychology and Psychiatry and Allied Disciplines*, 42:3–48.

Trevarthen, C. & Hubley, P. (1978). Secondary intersubjectivity: Confidence, confiding and acts of meaning in the first year. *Language*, 183–229.

Tronick, E. (2007). *The neurobehavioral and social emotional development of infants and children*. New York, NY: W.W. Norton & Co.

Winnicott, D.W. (1994). Hate in the counter-transference. *Journal of Psychotherapy Practice and Research*, 3:348.

Play, dreaming, and the growth of mind

Chapter 5

The universe of play

Technique in contemporary child therapy

Peter Carnochan, Ph.D.

A chapter on the technique of play therapy might seem a contradiction in terms. Play lays claim to the spontaneous, suggests a respite from the demands of the serious. Requiring this most free domain of living to submit to laws of technique could be a premise from Dr. Seuss: the animals of the jungle demanding, "Boil that dust ball." But a theory of technique does not need to be read merely as prescription and limit. The thoroughgoing evolution in psychoanalytic theory has reshaped analytic practice (Carnochan, 2001). The evolution has been driven both by discoveries within the analytic consulting room and also by advances in our understanding of infant and child development. This broader view of what leads to disturbance and what is required for a vibrant sanity has lessened the rigidity of the prescriptions and pro-scriptions of contemporary technique.

Here, I offer something of how I understand the terrain of play in contemporary psychoanalytic child therapy. In this view, technique must both help illuminate children as they have come to us and invite them into more expansive and flexible ways of living. Psychoanalysis, I argue, is concerned with helping children develop radiant affective-relational skills. To understand this asks us to orient ourselves newly in the way we view the frame of the consulting room and bring our subjectivity to the time with a child patient.

Therapists often come to psychoanalytic play therapy with a romantic notion of how the work will unfold. In this imagining, the child comes to therapy with a story about concerns and worries that seek expression. When children find the security of the analytic play-room coupled with the empathic attention of the analyst, they natu-rally begin to express themselves in narrative play. The therapist's role, then, is to translate the play into a story about the child's origins and internal life. Within this imagining of a therapy, the analyst's technique is anchored by the twin principles of receptivity and concern and it is the analyst's offering of understanding that drives therapeutic action.

In practice, though, play therapy is often more jagged. Many children who come for therapy show inhibitions and deficits in their ability to use play as a way to express their emotional situation. Children on the autistic spectrum, those who have suffered from neglect and trauma, or those have other more addictive or dissociative defenses challenge the viability of the classical model. These children may show limitations in their symbolic capacity, may be at a loss for how to play, may engage in repetitive and addictive play, or may push against the limits of the analytic frame. With these cases, the therapist must find more active and engaging ways to meet the child and bring about tangible change. Technique cannot be anchored merely by the principles of receptivity and concern. To help some children, the therapist may need to locate the vitality of feeling, help build a foundation for subjective experience, set limits, confront addictive forms of avoidance that masquerade as play, and even introduce new ways of playing together.

This expanded account of therapeutic action, I argue, follows naturally from changes in contemporary theories of psychoanalysis and child development. Child therapy, if it is to be of real help, must do more than uncover the child's existing emotional landscape; it must also help children develop new and more expansive affective-relational skills. I will argue that the technical principles of child therapy, rather than being understood as a fixed pier where we try to stay properly moored, are better imagined as a three-dimensional gravitational universe. Within the therapeutic space, there is a non-finite set of technical values that function as gravitational bodies that the therapist seeks to move closer to: empathy, aliveness, the capacity to think, mentalization, and others. These planetary bodies are suspended in a space intermixed with those negative principles that the therapist endeavors to avoid: intrusion, prolonged boredom, stasis, and other problematic enactments. In this view of technique, there is no fixed or secure ground. This view asks us to tolerate uncertainty and requires a willingness to regularly reimagine what we are up to in our play and what may be required to help a particular child.

***

When I was a teenager, my father, a professor of English, brought home a copy of Winnicott's *The Piggle* (1977). He was drawing on the case history for an article on childhood in the 18th century. I picked up the book and was immediately drawn in by Winnicott's telling of the Piggle's struggles with the birth of her younger sister. In ways that seemed mysterious and uncanny, he saw a narrative about the maternal breast and rivalry in the middle of the Piggle's play. At the end of the case, the Piggle wants to bring in her little sister to meet Winnicott, but is conflicted about sharing the doctor who had been her own. Winnicott, as I remember it, said that even if the sister came in, she would meet a separate version of himself, that the Piggle's doctor would remain hers alone. I was quite taken by Winnicott's ways of understanding and speaking to this little girl; as a boy who had struggled with the birth of my own younger sister, the story had deep resonance.

As I began working therapeutically with children, I imagined that my work might look something like Winnicott's. At a therapeutic school where I worked, there was a boy named Greg who had an overworked mother and an absent father. I brought in a set of toys that I imagined would allow this boy to tell me about himself through play. There were figures from a rescue team: paramedics, fire engines, helicopters. Greg liked these toys, but he didn't use them to tell a story. The gadgets of the toys kept his attention more than their possible use as a narrative vehicle. Like the early analysts who struggled to conduct an analysis after reading one of Freud's case histories, I thought Greg wasn't playing by the rules of therapy. We kept working, and Greg began to build a kite. He found a slinky and proposed attaching it to the kite so that it would bounce off trees. I thought, "You can't put a spring on a kite. It will never be kept up by the wind." I didn't yet know how to see the reasonable wish in the dream. If you have to find a way to love a father who regularly misses his commitments to visit, a spring to help you rebound from the collision with disappointment would be a good thing. I didn't understand the ejecting springs he used to keep out interpretations that were too much. In my earnestness and zeal, I think I helped Greg, but I was still learning how to play with a child, how to help a boy play in ways that opened the field of living.

Winnicott (1971) writes that when patients don't know how to play, we must first help them learn. It's statements like this, so full of possibility and enigma, that keep Winnicott at the forefront of psychoanalytic imagining. We are conditioned by preconception and romantic story to think that children are born knowing how to play; in films like *Big* or *Elf*, it is the child who often must help an adult relearn how to play. But the ability to play emerges only after a foundation of care and self has developed. To play, there needs to be a window between urgent need and calamitous danger. Only in this intermediate realm, where the continuity of going-on-being has established itself, can the imagining and pleasure of play take shape. In *The bi-personal field* (1999), Ferro argues that the fundamental task of analysis is not to uncover an already existing narrative, but, by offering an experience of containment, to help the child develop the capacity to convert raw elements of experience – beta elements in Bion's language – into dream thoughts that lay the foundation for the capacity to think – for alpha function. It is an account of the therapeutic action of psychoanalysis, I argue, that stresses how relational experience and provision in the therapy help the child develop foundational affective-relational skills.

***

Psychoanalysis has gone through a deep revolution in theory and practice. From the beginning, the gap between the patient analysts *imagined* they would find and the patient they *actually* encountered has required rethinking the meaning of psychoanalysis. This evolutionary pressure is something I have detailed at length in *Looking for ground: Countertransference and the problem of value in psychoanalysis* (Carnochan, 2001). There, I sought to provide a foundation for a postmodern psychoanalysis through an investigation of the history, epistemology, and metapsychology – what I call the moral architecture – of psychoanalysis. Freud, after his initial forays into hypnotism, was committed to the principle that analysis cured through insight rather than suggestion. He saw the task of analysis as removing the obstacles to objective perception, the unconscious attachments and repressions that kept the neurotic living in a transferential fantasy. He felt that if analysis could expose the cathected and problematic phantasy, then the synthetic capacity of thought would naturally arrive at a clear view of the real. For Freud, this marked the apotheosis of health, to abide in a courageous acceptance of the imperfect excellence of the real. It is a framework for analytic work that I call Transcendent Virtue.

Over the last hundred years, however, we have come to understand that the structure of the self is an achievement that depends on a host of provisions from the developmental environment. The work of Klein, Winnicott, and Bion has shifted our attention to earlier periods of infantile development and exposed the complex relational events that undergird the development of a capacity to think and organize experience. The capacity to experience feelings as internal and essential, the ability to soothe oneself, the faculty to engage in dream thought that is meaningful and creative – all these require key experiences of provision with our earliest caretakers. We need adequate mirroring, reliable attachment figures, and sustained experiences of containment. To understand this is to see that sanity cannot rely merely on undoing confusion or conflict. We cannot rely on an unclouded access to reality (the aim of Transcendent Virtue) or on an unperturbed relationship to a core self (the romantic hope of Natural Virtue). It depends on the construction of core developmental skills, what I call "affective-relational skills",[1] to navigate the subjective and interpersonal environments. When we try to help children who suffer from greater disturbance, who have endured neglect or trauma, we must have ways of working that offer them understanding and experience that redress the core deficits that make them unable to take in ordinary help.

Perhaps the clearest challenge to traditional accounts of analytic technique has come from the American Relational School of analysis. Its sustained critique of objectivist epistemologies and its willingness to accept the primacy of relationship over drive have led it to reimagine the analytic project and the limits of technique. I describe this emergent view as resting on a theory of Constructed Virtue. The advances in our understanding of developmental psychology, the profound shifts in our cultural values, and the progressive dialogue between psychoanalytic theorists have shown that the skills that allow us to negotiate a life are complex and developed over a lifetime. While the body provides the biological parameters of what it means to be human, we are still in the process of inventing ways to live that allow more stability, vitality, and creativity.

Constructed Virtue sees the project of imagining what it can mean to be human as an evolving and esthetic enterprise. To be well requires that a deep array of affective-relational skills be learned. The development of alpha function, the ability to tolerate rather than evade frustration, the capacity to integrate intensely affectively imbued perceptions of the other, amongst others, are foundational skills that have been brought to light by the work of pioneering psychoanalysts. Each of these skills can only be learned in the context of key relational provisions; these are also necessary preconditions for higher-order skills to be developed. Without the capacity to tolerate frustration, there is no chance that a child can see beyond the horizon of envy to accept a younger sibling as a playmate and ally, rather than merely as a hated rival.

Within the conversation of psychoanalysts, to talk of skill evokes suspicion. Psychoanalysis is founded on Freud's recognition that hysteria was a reaction to the constrictive world of the bourgeois. In this light, "skill" could seem another way of teaching the capacity to adapt and submit. In the modern era, new forms of therapy have emerged – cognitive behavioral therapy and stress reduction, amongst others – that suggest that the length and depth of an analysis is not needed. The slow work of uncovering and relational attunement, proponents argue, is inefficient and can be bypassed by learning ways to think, by learning skills that offer immediate help. Analysts know, however, that to veneer didactic learning over unconscious difficulties, over unresolved trauma or neglect, is palliative rather than transformative. To my mind, what defines the analytic project is the commitment to radiant rather than veneered change. Radiant change proceeds from the center of our agency and feels like it is in accord with our desire and subjectivity, rather than an outside-in attempt to make our given subjectivity more adaptable. When I talk about Constructed Virtue and its concern with affective-relational skills, I mean to point toward the radiant skills of subjectivity, rather than the more instrumental skills that might be taught through a manual or explicit instruction.

***

This account of the moral architecture of psychoanalysis is condensed. I offer it to clarify my approach to analysis and the technique of play therapy. When children come to therapy, we must discover how they have already organized a deep array of skills, both adaptive and problematic. We must determine how their difficulties have developed and be prepared to help them find alternate pathways for handling their feelings and relationships.

Thomas was a boy who made clear the need for additional parameters in our theory of technique. When he first came into my playroom, he showed a bold confidence as he quickly explored the room and began to engage in play. Yet this confidence contained defiance and a reactive willingness to fight. When the first session came to its end and I signaled that our time was up, Thomas said "No," and anchored himself under my analytic couch. To his mind, the rules were determined by might and he was determined to be the mightiest. He was quick to tell me I was stupid, to try out powerful expletives whose meaning he did not understand. When I tried to talk about the feelings that gave rise to his violent response, he shut me down with further vitriol.

Thomas had learned a set of skills to deal with a world where he expected others to humiliate him or dominate him with perceptions and concepts beyond his grasp. The first step in helping him required bringing the structure and sense of his affective-relational skills to light. Only when the great peril he had experienced could be known could these skills be suspended and the possibility of learning alternatives emerge. The first steps, though, could not happen through a verbal modality. His conviction that I would use my thinking to triumph over him prevented him from listening, from thinking about my interpretations as something that might be of help rather than trouble. As it became clear how volatile Thomas could be, I began to steer away from competitive play; I brought in a Lego model with which he could show his substantial concentration and mechanical skill. I would watch him build, genuinely impressed, trying to find ways to be of help that did not evoke his fear that I was doubting his ability or trying to make him feel diminished.

The evolution in psychoanalytic theory, when linked to insights from developmental psychology, shows that we need a more multifaceted theory of technique. If this view of Constructed Virtue is coherent, then it becomes clear that analytic practice cannot be governed by the inherited principles of abstinence and neutrality. Modern analytic play therapy must keep in mind the deep array of skills that are required in sanity and see the multiple and sometimes conflicting goals within a given therapy. Thomas needed an experience of safety and provision, but he also needed to see that therapy was not governed by rules of violence and subjugation. To let the session continue until he felt ready for it to be over – a way of proceeding that might be suggested if we felt the task was to create a holding environment, a feed that would mirror what we would want to provide a newborn – would reinforce the idea that the spoils of war go to the most violent, the most insistent.

***

As my thinking on psychoanalysis as a therapy of Constructed Virtue has evolved, a different calculus of analytic technique has taken shape. Rather than seeing analytic technique as anchored by Transcendent Virtue principles of objectivity and neutrality or the Natural Virtue principles of safety and provision, I now see the domain as a three-dimensional gravitational field shaped by a non-finite set of analytic principles. I have imagined these as a set of planetary bodies suspended in the universe of analytic space. At the core of the work are those planetary bodies that are hospitable to the life of an analytic therapy. These are positive principles that guide our work, the qualities of presence and action to which we aspire. On this list, I would include foundational principles like "containment", "holding", "safety", "understanding", and other modes of setting an analytic frame. At a less central position are other positive principles of technique that are sometimes vital. Here, we might include things like "liveliness", "holding limits", and "confrontation". The universe of technique is also governed by the need to avoid the problematic forms of engagement whose atmosphere cannot sustain the life of a caring therapy. These negative principles are gravitational fields that are to be avoided to protect the therapy from destructive enactment. Here, we find things like "impingement", "overstimulation", "intellectualization", and "shaming".

If the positive planets of technique were all grouped at one end of the space and the negative planets at the other, navigation would be relatively straightforward. But the gravitational principles are intermixed within a three-dimensional space. Sometimes, trying to make orbit around one positive principle puts us close to the gravitational pull of its negative cousin. Safety is a necessary principle of a transformative child therapy.

But what allows some children to feel safe may also keep them mired in addictive and avoidant modes of play. The negative planet "avoidance" is a close cousin to the positive planet "safety". To avoid stasis, other principles need to be brought forward. Perhaps something must be confronted, a limit must be set on addictive play; both of these, though, take us much closer to the negative planet of "danger". Given the complexity of the valorous skills of Constructed Virtue and the deeply held nature of problematic skills functioning as defense, it should be clear that the therapeutic action of child analysis is not singular. There are many things to be understood, softened, and relearned. The list of principles guiding analytic technique is not finite. We must be willing to find new ways to reach and help children. In the process of expanding our vocabulary of therapeutic play, we must look carefully at how our approach is positioned relative to the whole array of positive and negative principles. We must be willing to accept the inevitable moments of enactment and error that a bold therapy will encounter and realize that this requires a deep willingness to take responsibility and to redirect the course of our work to avoid collision and impasse.

To show how this model of the three-dimensional gravitational field operates in practice, I will tell a story about a young boy named Mike. The younger of two brothers, Mike had gone through a lot. His parents had undergone a painful and acrimonious divorce. His mother had remarried and begun to spend half her time with her new husband in a distant city. His father had to move twice because of financial pressures. Then, in the middle of first grade, an evaluation confirmed that his troubles at school were caused in part by significant dyslexia. Mike was not wrong when he angrily stated that unfair things kept happening to him. He had to move, and move again; he had to go through tutoring and attend a summer program for dyslexic children. He didn't have many ways to fight back, so he began to find ways to refuse. In the morning, he would drag his heels and delay getting ready. At school, he would excuse himself to go to the bathroom and stay there for extended periods of time. He would only agree to work on reading with the direct help of a teacher. All these complex strategies to protect himself from the humiliation of dyslexia, from the problem of being dominated by adult demand, were partially effective in that regard, but were not helping him learn to read, and they risked getting him expelled from his caring private school.

Mike was happy to come to session and play games on my iPad, build things from Lego, or draw cartoons. He felt good about his capacity in these domains; they were a respite from the more painful demands of school. But over quite some time, this did not change Mike's effort to read. We spoke about how he was good at these other skills and how that helped him feel proud. We talked about how alone he felt in having to carry the burden of dyslexia. His brother didn't have it; I didn't have it. I spoke with him about finding ways of fighting the dyslexia other than the strategy of avoidance. I noticed his determination and courage in other domains and I thought he could bring those qualities to bear as he struggled to decode reading and writing. But none of this awakened a true conviction that he wanted to put in the hard and vulnerable effort to read.

After I met with his teachers and counselors at school, it became clear that they were reaching their limits with his extra demands and that if he couldn't find a new way he would be asked to leave the school. This was a truth that Mike had been evading just as he evaded the worksheets and reading assignments. But he was deeply attached to this school. It was one of the few things that had stayed constant in his life; it was where his loved and admired older brother went; it was where his friends were. Losing this school would be one more unfair loss. At this point, I felt that Mike needed to confront the genuine danger he faced. In the following session, I spoke to him in plain language about the school's position. I told him that if he wanted to stay at the school, he needed to commit to working independently, even if this sometimes left him feeling unsure or worried that his wrong answers might be humiliations.

Mike hated my telling him this. It was a moment of flying close to the problematic bodies of danger and humiliation. But I felt this was necessary to locate the more obscure comet of galvanizing motivation, of the capacity to accept the privations of a painful reality that could only be ameliorated, in the long run, by effort and confrontation. When I brought this reality to bear, and I brought it to bear in a strong way, part of my goal was to awaken a realistic and potentially useful fear. Sometimes, change is motivated by safety and understanding. If I knew how, I would have all change move through this door. But sometimes change comes because of danger, grief, and realistic fear. There are times when it takes these more highly charged affects to push through the tightly held and known forms of preserving safety. Mike was upset and spent much of the session inconsolable in his mother's arms. For that time, I became the focused embodiment of much that plagued him. Yet, despite the contravening of immediate safety, I believe this was a useful intervention. It depended on the long foundation of safety developed over years of work. In the following weeks, Mike began to do independent work at school and take further steps to shoulder the burdens of learning to read with dyslexia. In taking this action, I believe I allied with other parts of Mike, future versions of himself that I think will be glad I confronted his evasions and helped put him on the path toward literacy. In this way – and I said this to him – I was trying to protect him from future humiliations and disappointments.

***

The analytic encounter with a child is a peculiar meeting between people at the intersection of multiple dimensions. The therapeutic relationship is both real and unreal. It concerns the past and its echoes, the present, and vistas of the future. For therapy to work, there must be a frame that helps maintain clarity between these dimensions and allows the work to touch on dangerous thoughts and feelings without puncturing the container in too perilous ways. In more traditional accounts of analytic technique, the frame concerns formal arrangements that organize the setting of the therapy. The regular appointment time, the capacity to start and stop a session on time, the financial arrangements, the agreements around confidentiality, the use of the couch – these things create a setting that allows the transference to be analyzed, not merely enacted. For Freud, the analytic frame was designed to show the unreality of the transference. The analytic encounter was a place of medical help rather than personal intimacy. It was a place where the unconscious could be made conscious without the risk of fantasy bleeding into the realm of action and actuality. In this way, the analytic frame functioned like a frame around a painting, marking the division between the wall and the art.

But just as in contemporary art – where progression in the field has challenged the easy distinction between art and non-art, where the frame has been deliberately disrupted – contemporary psychoanalysis cannot accept a singular conception of the frame. The frame cannot and should not function to keep out the subjectivity of the analyst. Our furnishings, the toys we offer, the way we play – all reveal aspects of the therapist's self. Rather than offering a single version of the frame, then, we do better to understand its meaning and the ways it can help represent and articulate the different dimensions of reality. As I understand contemporary psychoanalysis, there is not one prescription for how the frame should be shaped. Instead, there are multiple ways it can be constructed, and our task is to understand how these choices reverberate in the work.

For play to be possible, there needs to be a preliminary division between the real and the imaginary. Without some clarity about these two realms, what can be imagined – what can be admitted into play – is necessarily quite narrow. When Daniel came to therapy, he was working to handle the aftermath of a contentious divorce in which his mother had become delusional about his father's actions and character. Learning to distinguish between what we imagine and what is actual is hard enough under ordinary circumstances. When your mother regularly asserts that the imagined trumps the real, however, it becomes an even more confusing boundary. In our sessions, Daniel was wary about play. At moments, he would drop out of sight behind my desk. With other children, this might have been the beginning of a game of hide-and-go-seek, but for Daniel it seemed more to mark his need to protect himself from becoming the object of someone else's imagination. He would rest behind the desk while I spoke out loud what I thought might be happening to the boy who disappeared. After a time, Daniel began to make forays out from the desk. He wanted to sneak up on me, creeping from behind the desk to behind the chair. At times, he wanted me to pretend that I didn't see him.

Within the logic of invisibility, as he came forward, the objects he was holding would move as though by magic; it would seem there was a ghost in the room. In the play, then, I would say something like: "Oh my gosh, what's happening? It must be a ghost!" showing surprise and fear. When I began to give voice to this part of the play, however, Daniel would become frightened. He would tell me to stop talking like that and make sure that I didn't really think there was a ghost in the room. His own confusion about the boundary between the real and the imaginary and his reasonable concern that adults might also be blurry about the distinction kept the realm of the imaginary constricted for Daniel. He was one of those boys Winnicott might say needed preliminary help in learning how to play.

Without some clarity about the distinction between the non-rigid boundary between the real and the imaginary, the world becomes an extremely dangerous place, where what is imagined constantly is felt as something becoming real. This is Klein's key insight about the paranoid–schizoid position. The child imagines making all kinds of angry attacks, and then, feeling that these have been actual, becomes paranoid as he or she waits for the inevitable retaliation. When this happens, the imaginary can become a place of too much danger and constriction sets in. But curtailing of the imaginary is problematic for development. While the imaginary differs from the real, it is where an ability to understand intense feeling begins. This is what Bion meant when he said that alpha function depends on dream thought for representation to take shape. Access to the imaginary is necessary for creative thought, to begin thinking about the daunting elements of the real. The imaginary is also the launching pad for all new realities. To change, we must first imagine a new way of being, a different way of approaching the world. The frame establishes the boundary between the real and the imaginary. Part of its function in play therapy is to help children articulate more fully their understanding of the real and the imaginary and how to move between them. When this boundary becomes clearer, the imaginary becomes a space where the past can be represented, where the present can be faced, and where new possibilities for the future can be conceived.

In play therapy, the rules of the playroom necessarily convey something of how the analyst understands these different dimensions of reality. In my office, a place where I see both children and adults, some spaces are fully available for play and others are where the demands of reality hold. The first split is between speaking and acting. I am clear that kids can say anything in my office, but there are limits to what they are allowed to do. They can tell me they hate me and want to kill me, they can try out forbidden words – all of it must be made welcome in the analytic space. Words belong to the representational realm, to the imaginary; they are not the same as doing. While anything can be said, it cannot be shouted. When kids begin to yell, I tell them it is too much, that it is not fair to my therapeutic neighbors, to the siblings of the setting. In the physical realm, however, the boundary between play and the real is subtler and requires more complex rules. At the first level of understanding, we might say that almost everything in the office can be played with, but the property of the office can't be destroyed. Children may use the toys freely. They can remove the cushions from the couch and build a fort. But they can't wreck my property. I don't let children take scissors to the upholstery or pens to the paint. This limit is clearly for my benefit. I don't want my office destroyed. But it is a useful limit because it naturally holds the boundary between the real and the imaginary.

***

Ellen had spent the first year of her life in a relatively good orphanage, perhaps good enough to let her risk the rage of not being able to hang on to a good caretaker. She would often ask me, "What's your favorite color?" If I answered, "Blue," she would then say, "Well, what if you couldn't say that color, what would your favorite be then?" I came to understand this as a way of bringing into dream what it might be like to be an infant in the care of a loving nurse – a favorite color – and then have to endure the shift change – the next nurse. After an initial phase where her loving transference held sway, where she drew pictures of flowers and wrote, "I love playing with your toys," her rage emerged. When children need to make attacks on me, on my space, they often make use of string. Ellen found that string was something she could use up, cut to pieces, or take all of it, leaving me with none. She would tie the toy chest to the desk, the desk to the couch, all of it to me. She would divide the room into sections and allow me only the smallest quarter of space where she would occasionally toss me an almond for sustenance. In this play, she made me know deeply what she had endured, let me understand and speak of all forms of torment.

   At times, Ellen would push through this realm of play, of the imaginary, where there was freedom to assert and reverse past trauma, and push up against the limits of the real. She would want to tie me up too tight; she would want to attach the string to something too fragile, liable to break. Here, I would say, "No," and hold that line against her very strenuous attempts to push past the limit. We can say that the play was a way that Ellen communicated something of what she had endured.

Through intense and vibrant projective identification, she gave me the experience of being helpless in the face of a tantalizing world. Yet it was also true that, in this play, Ellen had deeply identified with the aggressor. If the world was divided into tyrants and subjects, she was clear which side she would be on. Over the course of years, I lived through this extremely creative and painful play in many iterations.

At some point, the danger is that the play becomes a way of rehearsing the pattern. At first, I began to try to fight my way out of the pattern from within the play. I would talk about my predicament and the cruel helplessness to which I was subjected. All of this helped articulate experiences that I believed Ellen had endured during the earliest moments of her life, experience from the reflex and sensorimotor tiers of development. But child therapy has to do more than merely articulate what has already been. It needs to point toward new alternatives. My attempts to find other outcomes for this play were met with rigorous resistance. If my characters made a plea out of their suffering, they were mocked, told, "Good, I want you to suffer." If they tried to rise up and fight the injustice, they were made impotent. There were times when the destructive play became so addictive that I felt it required limits. I would say: "I think we've already played this and now you're not using the string to tell me a story but to practice how to be the tyrant. I think you feel that if someone is going to be the tyrant, you want that job, rather than the job of the one who gets tyrannized. But I think there are other stories where no one is tyrannized."

In moments like these, I began to ask Ellen to go beyond projecting her hate and begin taking responsibility for it. I told her that while I thought she had really good reasons to be angry and that I admired her ferocious will, I didn't think hate was going to get her what she really wanted. I began trying to show her how these attacks left her confidence undermined, worried about retribution, and unsure in her friendships. At one point, Ellen brought in a picture of an orc from the *Lord of the rings* trilogy. Her older sister had seen the movie and Ellen wanted to watch it as well, but was worried that she would find it too scary. We spoke about how she had lived with orc-like moments in the world, how she had brought some of this inside, and that knowing where this really came from would help her be less scared watching the movie. In this phase of the work, I deliberately evoked affective-relational skills that I felt were key for Ellen to unravel the developmental knots left from her early attachment history.

***

I will share a final story about working with children from this expanded view of analytic technique. It is a case where I brought in new modes of play to point toward more adaptive affective-relational skills. Robert came to see me after his father died from cancer and his mother returned from residential treatment for alcoholism. From an early age he had been obstinate, avoidant, and verbally gifted. He was now 13 and at great odds with his two younger brothers. Though smart and a gifted writer, he felt school was of no great value because it mostly taught things that "you would never need in your real life." While Robert was close with his mother, she felt at a loss for how to respond to what she saw as his constant provocations toward his brothers. While her drinking had not been deeply out of control, she knew that it had left her unavailable to Robert at times when he was quite young. I began seeing Robert twice a week. He was happy to come in and talk about what happened in his family. Despite his relative youth, he had no interest in playing games and was content to talk thoughtfully about his father's death, his mother's treatment, and his ongoing struggles with his brothers. Robert had loved his father and felt that he had shown Robert real respect in their debates. If Robert made a good point about what was happening in the family, his dad could acknowledge it and make changes. At other points, the father had set limits with resolve.

Despite the open bravery he showed in coming to therapy, Robert avoided many things and justified his retreat with a long list of criticisms. He wittily detailed the limits of poor teachers, bad television shows, his brothers' peculiarities, and his mother's failure to be even-handed in cases of conflict between the siblings. While he was well liked at school, he avoided most activities that would take him out of the house. Part of the work was locating and giving voice to the anxiety that underlay his critical, avoidant stance.

During our work together, I worked hard to understand the logic of his complaints. Robert prided himself on being a fair observer and self-aware in his interactions. While he knew he could taunt his brothers, he felt it was within the ordinary range for siblings and was deeply convinced that his mother saw him unfairly as the origin of the difficulties in the house. He was relieved that I could take in his view of the interactions and empathize with his sense of injustice and wounded esteem at being seen so steadily as the culprit. I held a series of sessions with Robert and his mother, as well as with Robert and his brothers, and these were of some use. My best sense of the situation was that both Robert and his mother bore some responsibility. Robert was more cutting and sarcastic with his brothers than he realized; it was hard for him to understand that his position as the eldest lent his comments more stinging authority than his brothers' retorts. I talked to him about this and he was able to accept my comments.

His mother, though, somewhat overwhelmed as a widow early in her recovery, could not adjust her way of responding to the sibling altercations sufficiently to help Robert feel understood. This kept a destructive cycle going. Robert and his brothers would get into a conflict and his mother would intervene, holding Robert accountable. But this response only reinforced his conviction that the discipline was unfair, deepened his resentment of his brothers, and fortified his wish to get revenge. Robert experienced me as a good ally and wanted to take in my thoughts about the impasse. He could see that he played a role in this cycle and saw that, by changing his behavior, he could try to break it. But this insight was not enough to support him in the crucible of irritation at his brothers and disappointment with his mother.

As we began our second year of working together, Robert returned to therapy after an extended trip to Disneyland with his family. He had genuinely liked Disneyland when they had last visited, but this time the logic of complaint had taken hold. He found his middle brother, a boy immersed in the world of Doctor Who, to be self-centered and unwilling to think about the needs of the grandmother or to compromise on family activities. He had gotten into an argument with his youngest brother when they had visited a rainforest-themed cafe. Robert had found the theme ponderous and declared, sardonically, it was "lame." At this, his youngest brother had hit him and his mother had reprimanded him. It was a bitter pill for Robert that the seemingly larger offense of punching had gone unchecked, while the milder offense – to his mind – of an offhand slight had been taken as central.

My office is in the Presidio National Park in San Francisco. It is a setting that lets me take walks with my child patients. As Robert told me about this too familiar wounding interaction, we came to a grove where a natural spring has been reclaimed from the ivy and cement. It's quite beautiful. I told Robert that I knew how painful these moments were to him. I said that I couldn't know for sure about how best to view these moments, as I wasn't there. I knew his mother believed in her point of view as he believed in his. I told him that I felt this cycle in the family was hard on him and that I understood his hope that his mother would change. I also said that I wasn't sure that she would be able to and that since I was his therapist, rather than hers, I wanted to help him find a way out. I then began talking to him about the foundational generosity of the world. I talked to him about oxygen and its unnoticed availability, about the lavish beauty of the spot, about the logic of flowers and how, through manifesting beauty, they draw bees toward pollen in a multiplying exchange. In all of this, I was trying to help him locate a way of being, an affective-relational skill, that Buddhism knows well.

When Robert came for his next session, I invited him to walk to another spot in the Presidio, an empty lot behind the YMCA that the landscapers had not yet reclaimed. It was compacted dirt, cyclone fence, and spare concrete barriers. I told him that I thought this might be the ugliest spot in the Presidio – a rainforest cafe of sorts. I pointed out the obvious bad features and he readily agreed. I asked him what else was bad about it and he easily saw further fault. I said our task, like his task in his family, was to look through the trouble to see beauty. I pointed out a tangle of dried thistle that was burnt orange and dense. I gave him my cell phone camera and invited him to take a picture of something beautiful in the space. He found a tree wrapped densely in ivy. We took turns looking closely and taking pictures of what caught our eye. I do not want to claim that any of these moments constituted a remarkable breakthrough. The gravity of Robert's character and his family system was strong. I do think, however, that the alternate ways of viewing and behaving in the world that I presented him helped him change over time.

***

We have to find ways of playing that help uncover the experiences that have helped shape each child, that bring to light the ways they construct the intrapsychic and interpersonal universe. But we must also be willing to play, I argue, to help sponsor new ways of meeting the challenges of development. An analytic child therapist must be prepared to encounter moments of real difficulty over the course of a deep treatment. The play may give expression to quite tortured relationships, to long moments of trauma and sadism. Before change can be radiant, the analyst must be willing to live at the center of the child's subjectivity and suffering. But if we are to avoid the danger of the merely repetitive, we must realize when the play has become stuck. If the therapist is feeling tortured, bored, or caught in circular enactments and this does not change despite empathy and sustained interpretive work, new forms of play may be required. I argue that we need to play in ways that help children fashion new affective-relational skills that are personal, that emerge from a strong understanding of their situation. These are not prefabricated techniques or skills – those can only be used as a veneer. It is this effort to help children become authors in their own lives, to respond from their subjective cores, that keeps the work psychoanalytic. Play therapy, when it goes well, moves in the direction of greater fun for both the child and the therapist.

Note

1 The term "skill" is something that follows from my exposure to the work of Kurt Fischer (1980, 1990). Fischer, a neo-Piagetian, has developed a model of development that he calls "Skill Theory". Through an extensive research program, he has detailed how development progresses from birth through a series of four pyramidal tiers: Reflex, Sensorimotor, Representation, and Abstractions. Each tier is founded on the culmination of the skill development of the previous tier: an integrated system of reflexive systems results in a single volitional sensorimotor action; a system of sensorimotor systems results in a single representation. When I speak of psychoanalytic therapy as necessarily concerned with the affective-relational skills of development, I am indebted to Fischer's work.

References

Carnochan, P. (2001). *Looking for ground: Countertransference and the problem of value in psychoanalysis.* Hillsdale, NJ: The Analytic Press.

Ferro, A. (1999). *The bi-personal field: Experiences in child analysis.* New York, NY: Routledge.

Fischer, K.W. (1980). A theory of cognitive development: The control and construction of hierarchies of skills. *Psychological Review*, 87:477–531.

Fischer, K.W., Shaver, P., & Carnochan, P. (1990). How emotions develop and how they organize development. *Cognition and Emotion*, 4:81–127.

Winnicott, D.W. (1971). *Playing and reality.* London, UK: Tavistock Publications.

Winnicott, D.W. (1977). *The Piggle: An account of the psychoanalytic treatment of a little girl.* New York, NY: International University Press.

Chapter 6

The analyst as dreaming filmmaker

Antonio Ferro, M.D. and Elena Molinari, M.D.

Intersubjective theory has profoundly transformed our hypotheses about healthy development and, accordingly, our theory of therapeutic technique as well. Interpretation, which has long occupied a central role, is now part of a toolbox that is gradually being enriched with new implements. To promote development or foster its resumption means moving together toward a goal that is not pre-established, where the analyst does not know the other's difficulties *a priori*. This means that, even given the asymmetry of roles and responsibilities in undertaking the process, analytic therapy involves and transforms both subjects. Just as a mother becomes a mother with the active contribution of her child, so a therapist becomes a person capable of meeting a child patient's subjectivity and of participating and sustaining his development with the indispensable contribution of that particular child.

Many tools have emerged in clinical practice because therapists have been dragged into new practices by the children themselves. For example, for analysts to be able to hear the invitation "Don't talk – play!" without thinking that children are reacting defensively to interpretations has been a long learning process. When we accepted the idea of elaborating the game without the need to decode its content, instead participating as "assistant director" to the construction of the game – as though it were a movie, a daydreaming film in progress – we signaled a turning point in the theory of technique.

Relinquishing the idea that interpreting is necessary in order to unveil the unconscious desire contained in a game or a story and that an interpretation is much more effective to the degree that it is early, penetrating, and explicit has been difficult. It is necessary to point out, however, that the tenaciousness that distinguishes children has meant that, in this instance, child psychoanalysis has anticipated some aspects of the more general transformation of analytic technique (Stern et al., 1998).

When the development of the relationship is placed at center stage, the therapeutic paradigm is radically altered and the relationship becomes able to cure in that it creates an area within which nurturing exchanges can take place. For Winnicott, this area is that of play, while for Bion, it is that of truth.

Winnicott found in the experience between mother and child the idea that development coincides with the capacity to expand the field of play. For Winnicott, play was no longer merely a channel for unconscious representation, as it was for Melanie Klein, but a category of the possible that places both parties – psychoanalyst and child – in the moment at which "things" begin to be constructed. This moment is a sort of Logos in developing the ability to transpose the analytic couple into the generative moment of a representation. Thus, Winnicott (1971a) overturned the established theoretical framework, transforming play from a children's instrument in the psychoanalytic process to a fundamental element in the analysis of anyone, to the point of defining the psychoanalytic process as having been "developed as a highly specialized form of playing in the service of communication with oneself and others" (p. 41).

When he illustrated his way of interacting with the child through squiggles (Winnicott, 1971b), he showed us an analyst capable of actively participating in the creation of graphic representations and, at the same time, one who is available to actively reveal something of himself in relation to the process that is taking place. A pair of subjects works not to uncover something buried in the depths of the unconscious, but rather to create together something that has never existed. The view that playing may be a therapeutic process in itself and not a process by which to activate other therapeutic processes has come to be shared by many analysts today (Frankel, 1998; Bellinson, 2000; Molinari, 2011).

Psychoanalysts managed to relativize the use of interpretations when they were able to shift their attention more onto the act of playing than onto its meaning (Winnicott, 1971b) and when they began to hypothesize about the close relationship between dreaming and playing (Ogden, 2007; Ferro, 2009; Grotstein, 2009). Melanie Klein first theorized that play could be viewed as a dream and therefore as a product of the unconscious. Bion markedly extended this intuition, forming hypotheses on the functioning of the mind that distanced him from drive theory and that promoted an equally radical change in technique.

Bion (1965) described unconscious truth as a necessary ingredient for the mind's growth, comparable to food for the body: "Falling back on analytic experience for a clue, I am reminded that healthy mental growth seems to depend on truth as the living organism depends on food. If it is lacking or deficient the personality deteriorates" (p. 38). Truth needs to be taken in; it requires contact with one's internal world and with one's emotional experience as the source of meaning.

The analytic couple's tension then becomes that of reaching an emotional harmony and learning to dream unconscious emotions together. It is the experience of harmony that permits the patient – particularly the child patient – to develop his own mental container and alpha function, a transformative function capable of converting sensorial data and raw emotions into images. These images, like pictograms, are then put together to bring about an oneiric sequence. Bion suggested that dream work is active both by day and by night, but it is more easily perceptible by the conscious mind at night, just as it happens that the moon and stars are rendered invisible by solar light during the day. In the same way, the daytime mental activities that characterize consciousness obscure the oneiric activity that remains active but is imperceptible.

In the elaboration of Bionian thinking, it has been hypothesized that, during wakefulness as well, we can observe "narrative derivatives" – that is, products that have a relationship with the images that make up the dream (Ferro, 2005, 2008). In the context of the analytic setting, narrations or play – and also sensations and sounds – can be viewed as products that maintain a relationship with the patient's working through of conscious and unconscious emotions that are continually generated. What the analyst in turn does or says in response maintains a close relationship to the dream that the analyst is about to have of his own emotions and those of his patient, together. In the Bionian perspective, the result is that an analytic session is an exercise in shared dreaming. If one hypothesizes that the analyst may be more expert in the process that promotes the capacity to dream, it follows that the patient can gradually experience a form of learning that proceeds through experience.

Fostering development

Children use the characters of their play and their stories to explore their own internal world, to create a form of representation of unconscious emotions, and to give form to the emotions that are gradually generated in relation to the therapist. Often an adult tells stories inspired by something that happened or was dreamed or remembered; children rarely tell stories about what has happened to them. Most of the time, in the analytic consulting room, they invent stories such that, while one shares the experience of play with a child, one has the perception of being immersed in the moment in which things are created. It is as though by magic we are on the set, in the place where dreams are formed, and not in the audience at a movie theater where one can have a dream about a dream.

If we analogize dreaming to making a film in the mind, we can think that when a child lives a situation that stimulates him with a quantity of emotions greater than his capacity to dream and to play, some raw emotional elements will be expelled and will reveal themselves as symptoms. We can imagine the symptom as the "dehydrated" manifestation of a dream that it is not possible to have (Ogden, 2007; Ferro, 2009). Figure 1 illustrates the improving transformation of emotions from raw feeling to narration.

Continuing the film metaphor, it is as though, along a spectrum of growing importance, playing, or a dream that is more or less developed, may correspond to:

- A film segment
- A few disconnected pictures
- Raw film
- Film that has deteriorated through an excess of trauma

If we can say, then, that in starting from any of a variety of different points, the task is that of encouraging the development of the

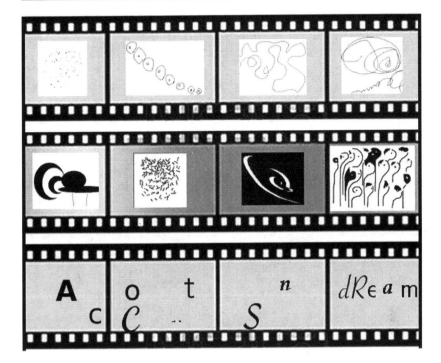

Figure 1 Improving transformation of emotions from raw feeling to narration

Figure 2 Development of the container

container (Figure 2) and the alpha function, we can also imagine that the specific departure point at which we begin will involve an adjustment of technique.

In fact, the situation is very different if we are dealing with a child endowed with an extremely tiny container – a tenuous, fragmented, brittle one.

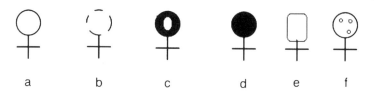

a) Normal container

b) Fragmented container

c) Impermeable container

d) Occluded container

e) Deformed container

f) Container with split, non accessible areas

Figure 3 Different functional situations of containers

The pictures shown in Figure 3 are static images that represent a way to formalize an aspect of the analytic relationship. Containment is a function, not a thing, and so it is always varied and fluctuating in time. However, formalizing the different situations of the patient's container can be useful in describing the style of interaction that the analyst must choose in order to be effective. In our opinion, efficacy is linked to the capacity to build the dream in the session and in life. In other words, each of these situations requires different interventions and timing in the treatment, and we try to show them in the clinical cases.

Children who display symptoms that are not very serious need support from the therapist in editing the waking film/dream. That is, intervention is limited to taking account of the points at which the dream is interrupted and the work of developing the story is done together. For children who do not know how to play, in contrast, what is needed is to construct together a place in the mind where dreams are given life.

In providing examples of different clinical situations, we will discuss aspects that pertain to technique and also address more general questions, such as the weight of historical reality versus emotional reality and the psychoanalytic fact that characters will appear during the session. In addition, we will demonstrate that development within the session – its progress – may be influenced by the analytic couple's capacity to establish, or not, an emotional relationship, and that what the child does or says after an intervention by the analyst may also be a response to the particular emotion that is aroused.

Martina: A zoo of caged and free-ranging emotions in search of editing

Martina's mother had given birth to her sister five months previously. Since that time, according to her parents, Martina had become unmanageable. Recently, she had begun to hold back her feces and suffered from a sleep disturbance. This symptom tells us that, through hyper-containment, Martina was trying to hold her rage inside; if it were to be evacuated, it could, in fantasy, destroy the loved object. The continual awakenings, by contrast, tell us that an excessive amount of anxiety impedes her nighttime dreaming from fulfilling its metabolic function.

At our third meeting, Martina asked to draw a picture (Figure 4).

When she finished, she proudly showed me her drawing and I (all clinical situations in this chapter are Dr. Molinari's) asked her if it was

Figure 4 Martina's bull

a cow. Seeing a cow was influenced by my idea of how much she might miss her mommy who was nursing her little sister.

Martina told me that I was mistaken: she had drawn a bull! Maybe, she told me – in order to give me another chance – I thought it was a cow because I hadn't seen the horns that, as she showed me, were actually very much in evidence.

As a matter of fact, she observed that this apparently smiling quadruped did not have teats, but horns, powerful hooves, and sensitive ears. In this way, the bull came onto the scene – the fury and rage that must be forcefully held back and that my incapacity to see had rendered even more present.

Martina then drew herself on the back of a horse, as though she had succeeded in capturing live what was happening inside herself and in her relationship with me. And, as though to more explicitly show me what she needed – that is, a more secure containment – she sketched a circle around the drawing (Figure 5).

Figure 5 Martina on the back of a horse

I told her that sometimes it is good to feel oneself to be strong and capable of being on horseback. In this way, I decided to support her capacities to cope within the turbulence, waiting for Martina herself to be able to better explore it.

She then drew a pair of animals – a reindeer that repeated the theme of horns and a giraffe that I think may speak to the feeling of being the older daughter (Figure 6).

Immediately afterward, she drew a dog and a cat (Figure 7).

I commented that there are animals that get along well together, while others have difficulty and often fight. She said, "The cat seems a little afraid of this dog, who smiles but may have just teased the cat." Martina smiled as though she had finally begun to feel accompanied in exploring her feeling of being disoriented by an emotion: the jealousy that put her at the mercy of unspeakable desires toward herself and toward others.

I had the impression that the atmosphere of trust that had been created widened the field. Martina then drew a picture that, like a zoom lens,

Figure 6 Martina's reindeer and giraffe

Figure 7 Martina's cat and dog

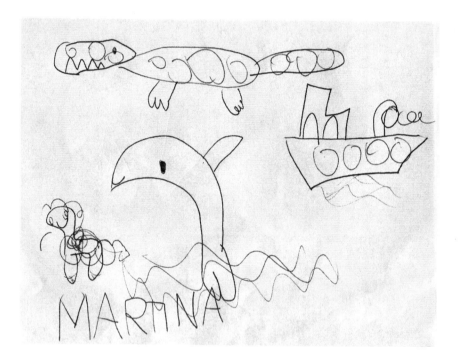

Figure 8 Martina's different sea characters

enlarged our view and seemed to capture the various emotions present in the field: the turbulence of the waves, she who swims nearly underwater, the agility of the dolphin, and the secure container of a ship (Figure 8).

After drawing this picture, Martina asked to play with the little house and the family characters. Through this play, the emotional elements

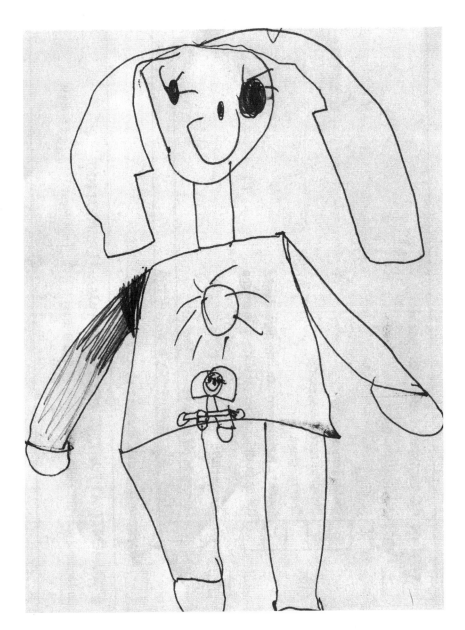

Figure 9 Martina inside her mommy's tummy

graphically portrayed in her drawings were more extensively but less directly developed. The playing allowed us to have some time in which action permitted the digestion of emotions.

Before the end of the session, Martina decided to draw a final picture, with which she demonstrated her uncommon capacity to see inside herself – or, more accurately, to see the dream that we had become able to dream (Frosch, 2007; Ferro, 2009).

The drawing (Figure 9), like a real work of art, contained various levels of meaning. "A work of art is good if it has arisen out of necessity. That is the only way one can judge it" (Rilke, 1903). Martina had a compelling need to feel that she was contained in a secure way, physically, as though inside her mommy's tummy.

She said that this drawing was for me. I think that it may also contain traces of the experience of this session, where through playing and drawing Martina could have the experience of being able to recreate on her own a capacity to feel that she was safe and to rediscover her creative abilities in telling a story through images.

The container capacity of this little girl was only a little deformed and less permeable. Using the graphemes, one could say that the ability to contain the emotions of this child is a mix of "c" and "e" (Figure 3). The hyper-containment of emotions (grapheme "c") creates an emotional situation that constantly interrupts sleep. The scroll and the composition of mental images are affected by the shape of the container and the processing of the content becomes linked to a deformation that changes the fluidity of the process. We see the fallout of this unconscious difficulty in an overflowing of oppositional attitudes in daily life.

Martina's alpha function was not too damaged and, during analysis, she was able to produce oneiric photograms that, with the help of the analyst, became a real daydream. The last drawing would become an interiorized container during the therapy; however, it could also be seen as a trailer of this dream.

Giacomo and the necessary lie

Giacomo had purposely thrown his breakfast, consisting of hot chocolate, out the window. The liquid had landed on the neighbor's white deckchair and valuable wooden table on the balcony underneath. The neighbor's violent reaction in turn produced another disaster: Giacomo's father argued with him and then with Giacomo. Feeling himself to be at the limits of his tolerance for the provocations that Giacomo came up with on a daily basis, the father decided to bring him to therapy.

At the first meeting, and at his initiative, nine-year-old Giacomo gave his version of the event: "I was near the window and I tripped. The hot chocolate flew downward. Tiziano got very mad, but – fortunately – I rescued the cup!"

I was unable to suppress an outbreak of laughter. Giacomo looked at me and laughed, perhaps somewhat surprised that he had not made me angry, as often happened to him with adults.

This child had lived through the separation of his parents with difficulty and could not accept his father's new girlfriend. With his throwing the hot chocolate out the window, his contrariness reached the point of finally expressing to the world that certain things, even though they nourish him and he likes them, are at the same time things he would like to eliminate.

What actually amused me was his capacity to transform reality, because in this apparently manipulative act, the seed of a special creativity is hidden, one that can be used to renew his capacity to cope with a difficult environmental situation. Giacomo told a story in which the character of a cup represents his capacity to contain intolerable emotions that he overturned in actuality in the environment around him.

In his manipulation of what really happened – that is, with the addition of his having fortuitously prevented the cup from breaking – there is obviously a desire to mitigate his own responsibility with respect to the event, but also a desire to protect the relationship with his father who is indispensable to his life.

With this example, I also want to demonstrate that maintaining a focus on emotional truth not only protects against moralistic interventions, but also permits one to grasp a creative aspect, and especially makes one capable of participating in the joint construction of the story that is being created. Like any writer or artist, the child recounted through a story something of himself, even though, as Amos Oz (2002) reminds us in an admirably concise way, "Every story is autobiographical. Not everything is a confession" (p. 163). It is undeniable that sometimes listening to a patient who tells us something improbable can cause a question to arise in the analyst's mind: "But how true can this story be? Isn't this person inventing some parts or exaggerating others with the aim of astonishing us, or of moving us, or even of seducing us?"

If the analyst remains anchored to the idea of reality and probability, he risks distancing himself from what makes up the heart of the analysis: to be amazed, moved, and seduced are the true ingredients with which we are able to work.

It is therefore essential to maintain an interest in the creativity with which children invent play and drawings. It is in the oscillation between freedom of invention and the compelling necessity to give form to intolerable emotions that the analytic therapist reaches a space in which mental development is supported.

We can imagine that Giacomo's container capacity could be a mix of "b" and "d" (Figure 3). The fragmentation of the container can be inferred from his continuous acting out. Giacomo's ability to process unconscious emotions is smaller than that of the previous case, as if his psychic container were occluded by a tremendous amount of undigested emotional residue.

For this case, more time was needed in which to repair alpha function, to transform acting and raw emotions into play and symbolic expressions. Patient and analyst needed time to build the tools. In the metaphor of film, they had to obtain the film itself, to write the screenplay, and to learn to use the camera.

Isabella and the deteriorated film

Isabella was a child of 11 years with eating disturbances of the anorexic type, as well as crises of withdrawal and rage that were serious enough to lead her to suicidal fantasies and an eventual hospitalization. Her symptoms emerged forcefully on the threshold of adolescence, but they were a product of a difficult childhood and a mental container that had struggled to develop substance within a relationship with parents who were almost never present.

Utilizing the Bionian symbols, we can imagine her container function swinging between "b", "d", and "f" (Figure 3). In this unstable functioning, different types of dysfunction prevailed at different times.

Drawing on the film metaphor, we can imagine that Isabella may have developed her capacity to work through emotions, to transform them in oneiric sequences, but the excess of trauma and the lack of another mind that could help in her development produced the emergence of symptoms that represent a tear in the film. We can imagine that the container, damaged by the trauma, is represented by the grapheme "b" and the ripping by the grapheme "d" – a container completely occluded and not working.

By contrast, there may have been moments of functioning that were relatively good, but in which the elements that could not be processed remained excluded, integrated into the content as spots within a frame (grapheme "f"). Despite what may seem to have been the case at first sight, the presence of different types of failure made the relationship with my mind even more problematic.

In a movie, if the director uses an unusual type of shot, the viewer may initially experience some difficulty, but the time necessary to adapt to a new kind of vision is relatively short. In other situations, in addition to the peculiarity of framing, there may be constant interruptions in the film due to tearing, stains, or deformations of the image. This makes it more difficult to establish a creative relationship between patient and analyst in which there can be active co-participation in the shared game. The form in which this is expressed requires rapid adjustments in different ways and is problematic in terms of processing the unconscious emotional experience.

Several of Isabella's drawings that she completed during the first year of analysis were extremely meaningful. With her first drawing, she wished to show me how she would like to clothe herself (Figure 10).

A feature that struck me was that Isabella drew only the outlines, as though by doing so she could better succeed at identifying the object to be represented. She needed to create psychic borders, and through sensoriality she tried to produce distinction in the indistinct. The outline permitted a closure of the shape, an establishment of an "inside" and an "outside". Furthermore, the decision to draw clothing – a sort of second skin – was significant. Women's clothing and accessories are signs of impending femininity, both desired and feared.

When the analytic relationship had created sufficient fabric with which to face these painful elements, Isabella drew her family

Figure 10 Isabella's clothes

(Figure 11). She began to draw her mom, starting with her hair, but interrupted herself, saying that she would color it at the end. Then she took the pink marker in order to outline her face, then rapidly drew her arm, but again stopped, laughing, and told me that she had made a mistake. She wanted to redo it because another action that her mom does, a prettier one, had come to her mind. She was about to take out another sheet of paper, but then decided instead to redo the drawing under the one she had just begun but not completed (she didn't tell me what the action was that she had in mind at the beginning, the one that for her was a "mistake").

I thought that the possibility of considering her parents in terms of mistakes or criticisms could not yet be faced up to mentally; ambivalence was not thinkable, nor was conflict manageable. Perhaps the drawing also represented a growing familiarity with me. I thought that Isabella might have been able to probe the painful history that she had experienced and I chose to let her work.

Figure 11 Isabella's family

Thus, she began the drawing for the second time in the same sequence, but before doing the face, she drew a book that hid her mother's mouth. She told me that she would not do the "parts underneath" (the legs and feet) to make it understood that her mom was in bed. It was only at this moment that she added the eyes to the face: two small, blue dots.

The drawing may have been her first attempt to look – with small, bright eyes – at her mother and herself. In the book and in the bed, intellectualization emerged with which Isabella healed herself of the pain and of leftover traces of the hospitalization to which she was subjected after her suicide attempt.

Next to her mom, she began to draw her dad. I noticed that, in doing the drawing, it was as though she had subdivided the paper into four parts, with each family member corresponding to a "square". In this way, Isabella reproduced the isolation in which each family member lived, but it was also her way of protecting herself from a meeting with the other who greatly frightened her. Furthermore, this orderly composition may have been an indication to stay in her place for now.

"I'll draw my dad with his paintbrush – he's painting, it's his work." She took the black marker and made four decisive lines that sketched out a wall in perspective.

She was about to draw her brother, but she stopped as though she had suddenly remembered something. She gave her forehead a little slap, saying, "What am I doing?! I haven't finished!" So she completed the drawing of her dad, giving him an eye (a small, black dot).

She then began to draw her brother in the square below. She waited a moment, then told me that before drawing him she needed to think carefully about how to do it, since he never did anything. Suddenly, she had an idea: "I'll draw him with his computer – he's always playing video games!" She began to draw his hair, saying that she didn't know how to do his curls. Then she said, "They're disgusting. He seems like a grandma!" She colored his hair and tried to hide the outline drawn earlier. Finally, she drew a dark blue eye – "I'm making the eye its real color," she said, smiling – and drew the mouth, half open and smiling. At this point, she told me she was finished; over each figure, she wrote the "family roles" (mom, dad, and brother). She did not drawn herself, leaving her square empty.

One might observe that Isabella's drawings seem orderly and clean. The turbulence of her emotional difficulties disappears from the labels and contents of the drawings, but begins to reveal itself in some of the details. Her brother's curly hair, as though it were composed of disordered thoughts, "is disgusting," but can reach momentary acceptance through a reference to the grandmother who cared for the little girl and laid the foundation for her partial capacity to contain and work through her pain. The missing legs seem to again take up the wish that the people whom she loves will not run away. It strikes me that several times Isabella made comments about her family members' eyes, and I think that the eye may be our capacity to look inside family relationships together, but also to look inside and among ourselves.

I decided not to interpret Isabella's own absence too directly, nor her difficult identification with her mother, for fear that Isabella could not yet bear such an open dialogue. Instead, I spoke to her of Velásquez and his mysterious painting *Las Meninas*, as well as of the inclusion of the artist in the picture. Perhaps this painting came to my mind because Isabella herself would like to hold a place in the foreground, as though she were the daughter of the King of Spain, and because the painting by Velásquez appears to be a portrait of the future heir to the throne.

Isabella became curious about the painting and I showed her a reproduction. We were apparently conversing about her drawings and the painting by Velásquez, but through the composition and the roles under discussion, we were talking about Isabella herself, about the two of us together, and about the place she would like to occupy in her family. The painting by Velásquez brought other characters on stage: the dwarfs, the dog that is teased by one of the two, the parents in the background, and the palace official who allowed us to introduce aspects of control. Through these characters, we greatly broadened our internal dialogue about Isabella's psychic difficulties, but we could only do this indirectly, maintaining a focus on the characters and not on real people, which allowed us to dream together the difficult emotions that dwelled within her.

At the next session, Isabella began with: "Today, I really want to devour a sheet of paper!" The transformation encouraged by the preceding session made itself evident in this peculiar shift: the desire to devour, earlier held fiercely in check through anorexic behaviors, was transferred to a piece of paper, to a symbolic activity.

She also wanted to change her drawing implements. She told me that she intended to use the pastels with which her mom used to draw when she was young. With pastels, one can make a useful powder for shading. "I'm good at drawing flowers, and I can also invent flowers that don't exist," she said (Figure 12).

Isabella drew the first flower, which she called "Kesket". She explained that its stalk was covered with thorns that protect it and did not permit anyone to handle or pick the flower, which grew along the edges of waterfalls. It was a rare flower, unreachable, which cannot be touched.

"Snow Elf" was the second flower. While she drew this one, she told me that it blooms and grows on the tops of the tallest mountains, near a dangerous waterfall. This flower had no thorns, but it had very strong roots; for this reason, "Snow Elf", too, could not be picked.

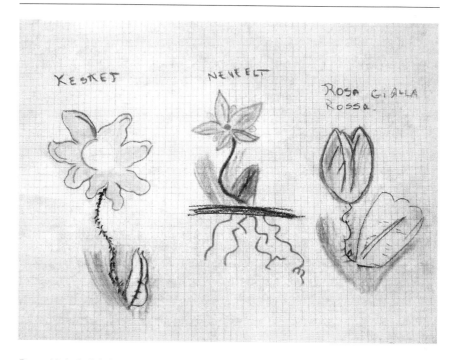

Figure 12 Isabella's flowers

I asked her if she would draw these strong roots that kept the flower anchored to the soil. She said no, she would not draw them, because they're not visible; they're underground. But contrary to what she had just said, before finishing the drawing, she added the roots, sketching them with an orange pastel. Composed of curved lines and broken lines, the roots gave a sense of tension; they seem to be flashes of lightening, thunderbolts, and they branched out underneath the flower – from which, however, they were separate.

The third flower, the last to be represented, was the one Isabella called "Pinkish–Yellow Rose". She began by drawing the petals, and rather than a rose, it seemed to be a tulip – a flower with petals closed almost as protectors of a delicate and precious center. Continuing the story, she said that this flower blooms when there is a rainbow, and so it has all these colors, which she tried to shade a little with her fingers. The stalk of this flower was slender and recalled a string tied to a balloon, her attempt to lighten the load of emotions through an extreme thinning of the body.

It was a very moving session in which we can imagine that Isabella was attempting a complex representation of herself. It is not by chance that she chose to represent protected flowers that cannot be picked – rare flowers with numerous thorns and strong roots that keep them anchored to the ground when they happen to grow near a dangerous waterfall. There are hidden roots that she does not have and must create by herself.

Two of the flowers that she drew had protective thorns that injure anyone who comes close. In addition to referring to an early awareness of herself as prickly, the thorns may also have represented an indication to me not to snatch away her growth and to continue to approach with caution.

It is a drawing where fear still exists, but also where the colored powder of emotions can be touched more directly, mixed and shaded. The invention of exotic and imaginative names for the first two flowers and a composite and common name for the third one tell of a parallel, transformative effort of verbal representation.

Conclusions

Legend has it that the Lumière brothers may have discovered the principle of animated film by observing their mother using a sewing machine. Then, in finding the right speed at which to project the film, they also discovered that the gaps between images cease to be perceived, creating the idea of continuity and movement.

In just this way, the child analyst can again set in motion the development of that private place in the mind in which dream images are formed, learning from what mothers do to help their children grow, inventing with children the stories that they sew together, continuously and discontinuously, in movement and in immobility, and in some cases restoring film that has been damaged by sudden emotional wildfires.

References

Bellinson, J. (2000). Shut up and move: The uses of board games in child psychology. *Journal of Infant, Child, and Adolescent Psychotherapy*, 1:23–41.

Bion, W. R. (1965). *Transformations: Change from learning to growth*. London, UK: Tavistock.

Ferro, A. (2005). Bion: Theoretical and clinical observations. *International Journal of Psychoanalysis*, 86:1535–1542.

Ferro, A. (2009). Transformations in dreaming and characters in the psycho-analytic field. *International Journal of Psychoanalysis*, 90:209–230.

Ferro, A. (2008). The patient as the analyst's best colleague: Transformation into a dream. *Italian Psychoanalytic Annual*, 2:199–205.

Frankel, J.B. (1998). The play's the thing: How the essential processes of therapy are seen. *Psychoanalytic Dialogues*, 8:149–182.

Frosch, T.R. (2007). The missing child in *A Midsummer Night's Dream*. *American Imago*, 64:485–511.

Grotstein, J.S. (2009). Dreaming as a "curtain of illusion": Revisiting the "royal road." *International Journal of Psychoanalysis*, 90:733–752.

Molinari, E. (2011). From one room to the other: A story of contamination. The relationship between child and adult analysis. *International Journal of Psychoanalysis*, 92:791–810.

Ogden, T.H. (2007). On talking-as-dreaming. *International Journal of Psychoanalysis*, 88:575–589.

Oz, A. (2002). Amos Oz talks about Amos O: Being I plus being myself – an interview with Hillit Yeshourun. In: *Somber lust: The art of Amos Oz*. (p. 163) Albany, NY: State University of New York Press.

Rilke, R.M. (1903). Letters to a young poet. F.X. Kappus (Ed.). New York, NY: W. W. Norton & Co.

Stern, D.N., Sander, L.W., Nahum, J.P., Harrison, A.M., Lyons-Ruth, K., Morgan, A. C., Bruschweiler-Stern, N., & Tronick, E.Z. (1998). Non-interpretive mechanisms in psychoanalytic therapy: The "something more" than interpretation. *International Journal of Psychoanalysis*, 79:903–921.

Winnicott, D.W. (1971a). Playing: A theoretical statement. In: *Playing and reality* (pp. 38–52). London, UK: Tavistock.

Winnicott, D.W. (1971b). *Therapeutic consultations in child psychiatry*. London, UK: The Hogarth Press and the Institute of Psycho-Analysis.

Chapter 7

The emergence of the analyst's childhood

Embodied history and its influence on the dyadic system

Christopher Bonovitz, Psy.D.

"No way!" ten-year-old Peter shouted. "Lucky seven works again." Donning a huge grin with raised eyebrows as though he could not believe it himself, he slowly drove his automobile onto the "Free Parking" space and collected the pile of money that sat in the middle of the *Monopoly* board. He snatched the 20-, 50-, and 100-dollar bills, glowing as he held them up and counting every last one in front of me. "I'm buyin' me some houses and hotels," he announced in his adopted slang that he customarily pulled out in such exhilarating moments. Not only was he now on top with his lucky seven roll, but he also made it clear that I was now the "poor" one, dependent on him for loans and "free handouts" from what he had previously named the "free box." The "free box" was not a box per se, but rather money set aside by the person with more (in this case him) that could be used by the one who had less (me) when in need of money to "get by," especially in the event of landing on property that contained houses or a hotel.

"You know what you'll be asking me for soon," Peter joked.

"What?" I said, playing my complementary role to his.

"Free box, free box..." he sang as a jingle, "when you need a helping hand." He ended the tune with a loud, "Yeah boy!" and then proceeded to carefully sort his winnings. Though in the process of heading toward bankruptcy at that moment, I enjoyed witnessing his sheer joy and the playful boasting.

While much was at play here on multiple levels that I will expand on later, the themes of money, power, and the "free box" song brought to mind an older cousin of mine, Tom, who spent time with my younger brother and me from the age of 8 to 11. He was in his early 20s then and lived close to my family growing up, frequently stopping by to hang out with us and play ball on the street, or to take us to collect autographs of the various professional athletes (often basketball or baseball players) that were in town to play against our home team. As Tom passed through my mind, accompanied by a few scattered memories I had not thought of in years, I was unsure what to do with his arrival in my mental space, whether to see him off or to reflect more on his presence at that moment in relation to this game of *Monopoly* with Peter. Why had he arrived now? What significance could be attributed to him? How was he related to the theme of money and Peter's dealings with competition and a recent family divorce?

In this chapter, I will explore a theory of change in child psychotherapy that rests with the emergence of the analyst's childhood and the internal struggle to grasp and make sense of the memories, fleeting images, and reminiscences newly contextualized and reconfigured by the dyadic system within the analytic situation. By emergence, I am referring to the materialization in consciousness of memory, affect, and desire as the result of participation in a particular dyadic (or intersubjective) field. Newly emergent material potentiates a new level of organization (Seligman, 2005; Cambray, 2006; Stern, 2009). As compared with remembering an isolated incident, emergent memories and the sensory elements within them are shaped by the dyadic context that partially gives rise to the memory itself – the recollection that emerges is not frozen in time, but newly reconfigured by the interaction such that it may arrive looking different from before.

I believe these unbidden yet evolving memories that emerge in the context of action-oriented play are critically important to the treatment and to the child's development. In the current age of nonlinear dynamic systems theory, cause and effect have linear as well as nonlinear effects, a system composed of unpredictable shifts and elusive complexity. Change in the system takes place on the "edge of chaos" (Harris, 2005), the moment when the system is poised between disorganization and stasis, moments of disequilibrium arising out of some combination of heightened moments and the slower-moving, ongoing struggle that is part of any patient–therapist dyad.

The main thrust of this chapter is concerned with the state changes and shifting patterns across the therapist–child patient dyad that involve the therapist coming to know aspects of his own childhood within the context of the various transference and countertransference configurations. The extent to which the therapist develops the mental space to house and make sense of his childhood fragments has bearing on the shifts that take place within the system (Ogden, 1997; Jacobs, 2002). More specifically, the therapist's internal struggle to articulate and symbolize aspects of his own self as a child as they emerge hold the potential to make links with dissociated aspects of the child patient's mental life. It is these links that potentially disrupt the system, setting in motion abrupt transitions that open up new and different patterns within the system.

By *embodied histories*, referred to in the title of this chapter, I have in mind the ways in which our histories live inside of our bodies. Only by continuing to emotionally and mentally process our histories can they become more integrated into our lives. Conversely, histories that are unprocessed and unrepresented are more likely to intrude, to disrupt our lives and promote rigid relationship patterns that constrict and confine. In the analyst–patient system composed of their respective unconscious fantasies and projections that circulate throughout (Baranger & Baranger, 2008), the patient and analyst's histories forge links and become more symbolized during the course of treatment (Bonovitz, 2016). The unspoken connections between these embodied histories may then disrupt the rigidity within the system, creating a kind of disequilibrium that further opens up the system for change. As some of the leading theorists in this area have pointed out (Beebe & Lachmann, 2002; Galatzer-Levy, 2009; Gallese, 2009; Harris, 2005; Piers, 2005; Stern, 2009), these pockets of disruptions lead to a progressive integration that facilitates the developmental capacities in the child. From this point of view, the child experiences both internal and dyadic shifts, a reorganization of mental processes and further developed interpersonal capacities that the child may carry into his relations with the surrounding world.

While of course the therapist's childhood recollections are not the only potential catalyst for change, I do believe that the kind of physical action that goes on in child therapy as compared with adult therapy provides a unique context to the analyst's memories, one that inevitably shapes the choreography of the interaction – the arousal, regulation, tempo, sequencing, activation of sensory registers, and general patterns that settle in across the dyad. For instance, in the case of Peter (mentioned at the outset of the chapter) and the movement of our game pieces, the whooping and yelling, and the theme of money that led to the creation of the "free box" song are all forms of action that engage the senses and the body. The physicality of language extends far beyond the verbal exchange. These kinds of actions are not only moving pieces of the dyadic system; they are also the floor from which the therapist makes contact with his own embodied child states and representations. And the degree to which the therapist can apprehend these fleeting childhood self states has an influence on his receptivity to the child's communications, as well as creating opportunity for changes within the system (Bromberg, 1998).

For the purposes of this chapter, I am interested in the nonverbal and procedural levels of communication between therapist and child, the motor movements, sounds, and visual images that accompany the verbal content and are adapted in the service of establishing a rhythmic dialogue taking place in and out of awareness to regulate and communicate emotional states (Trevarthen, 2009). Part of this dialogue in the analytic situation is the therapist's regulation of her own childhood memories elicited by this dialogue. These remembrances then become part of the therapist's self-regulation, and in turn the mutual regulation with the child, an unspoken influence that shapes the nonverbal domain and aids in grasping the child's emotional communication that may not be formulated in words (see Beebe & Lachmann, 2002). The therapist's capacity to host these memories and then use them in receiving and understanding the child's emotional states increases the flexibility of the dyad and allows for a greater synchrony between the subjective states of therapist and child.

The action dialogue with Peter

Peter, scrawny and short for his age, was accustomed to being left alone for long stretches of time ever since his parents divorced when he was six years old. With both his parents steeped in their respective careers, he was forced to become rather independent around the age of nine, walking to and from school himself and cooking meals on his own. His brother, older by four years, was immersed in his social orbit, often spending time with his friends away from home.

Peter was aware that his parents' divorce had something to do with his father "meeting another woman," as well as his overspending to the point of accumulating a hefty debt. Nonetheless, Peter was still confused as to why they had not tried harder to resolve the problems in their marriage. As the tension between his parents mounted due to the mismanagement of money and disputes over their custody arrangement, around the age of ten, Peter began displaying more aggressive behavior toward other children in his school, provoking younger kids, and acting defiantly toward those teachers whom he deemed "unfair" toward either him or his friends in the class.

Though his school had referred him for treatment, his parents were ambivalent about therapy as his mother had not found it helpful for herself in the past. It was Peter's own interest in speaking with someone that moved the referral forward.

When Peter first began treatment on a twice-weekly basis, he let me know that he was a "gamer", which he explained referred to his love of video games and, to my surprise, board games as well. As we settled into a game of *Monopoly* early on, a game that would extend over many sessions together, it came to assume a certain rhythm and pattern. Things usually started out slowly, alternating rolling the dice with Peter impatiently waiting to acquire enough property to begin construction. Peter's movements were initially forced and hurried, with my backing off slightly as he took up more space, trying to will the dice to land on the numbers he desired. I could feel the pressure build along with the uncertainty of how the game would unfold, a heaviness punctuated with releases of energetic excitement and moderate deflation. The decibel level rose if he moved closer to a monopoly or made money from the "Chance" and "Community Chest" cards: "Here we go, look out!" he'd bellow. We shared in the excitement together even if I was on the losing end, a thrill that rapidly receded when the board was not working in his favor.

Adding to the choreography and texture of the play were our particular styles – Peter played big, took chances, and went for broke, with me on the other hand being relatively more conservative, squirreling away money and cautious in buying up property. I occupied the position of restraint while he ploughed forward without considering the potential consequences of his actions. I was interested in houses, he wanted to build hotels; his highs and lows were sharper and greater, mine closer together. And yet despite our different styles of play and arousal levels, they appeared to be complementary, with both of us interested in stretching the game out as much as possible. It was clear that this board game was going to be the main venue for the treatment.

The free box and body-based memory

Over the course of one game, my money dwindled as Peter accumulated more monopolies and rent payments from me. I was hemorrhaging cash as he was becoming a real estate tycoon. As the significance of money abounded in relation to his father and his debts, Peter came up with the idea of the "free box" (referred to at the beginning of the chapter), financial relief that could possibly save me from declaring bankruptcy and thereby ending the game. Rather than face this kind of ending, he donated money to the "free box" that I could draw on when I needed to. His financial triumph was tinged with guilt and twinges of bad feelings for my demise, as well as possibly the satisfaction in perpetuating my suffering as he rolled along on top. If I could survive and tolerate my despair, he could continue to probe this emotional state of mine in the context of the game, one that he had not been able to get to know and understand through his own father.

As the "free box" became a more central piece of our *Monopoly* theatre, Peter had the idea of writing down words to the "free box" theme song, lyrics to a tune that he had started humming each time I drew money from the box (which was frequent at this stage). As he handed me the paper and pen to jot down some of the words, an image floated through my mind of when I would hand my pen and paper to a professional baseball or basketball player when collecting autographs as a kid around Peter's age – the physical act of handing the paper and pen (the paper either a piece of white paper or a picture of the player on a card or magazine/handbook) to the player and waiting for him to sign his name. This remembrance sprung from the physical, a somatic memory of reaching up, sometimes stretching in the case of the very tall basketball players, and handing the player my wrinkled paper that had been tucked into my pocket.

As I began writing the lyrics, and with this body-based memory wandering through my mental landscape, for a moment I also recalled that these autographs often took place with my older cousin, Tom (referred to at the beginning of the chapter), who took me to the various hotels, stadiums, and parking lots where we could get close to the players. Though collecting autographs with Tom was an important part of my childhood, I had not thought about this formative experience in my life for a very long time. Why now? What did this image have to do with the "free box" and the act of writing? What was it about autographs and sports heroes? What did this communicate about the field between Peter and me (the field referring to the interpersonal field composed of our lived experience and the influence of our conscious and unconscious psychic realities on the interaction) (Stern, 2015)? And where did money fall within all this? It was somewhat fuzzy at this juncture.

"OK, so here's what I got so far," Peter said, referring to the lyrics. "Let's start with this: 'Free box, free box, when you need a backup/ Free box, free box, when your mortgage is high...'"

As Peter sang and I wrote, the word "mortgage" bounced around in my head. While it is not terribly unusual for a New York City kid to bring up the word mortgage in light of how much real estate comes up in adult conversation and considering the context of our game of *Monopoly* (you can mortgage property in the game), it stood out nonetheless and my mind returned to cousin Tom and autographs. Though Tom did not sing, he did whistle quite a bit, usually made-up tunes that he'd tweet after winning the autograph of a sought-out player whose signature was difficult to attain for one reason or another. If he was whistling, I knew we were doing pretty well that day.

As Peter and I sang the lyrics together a few times, I asked him about the word "mortgage" and what else he connected it with. He said he did not know exactly what it meant, but he'd heard it a lot during his parents' separation. He would often hear his parents arguing about money. Reflecting back on Tom and his whistling, I asked Peter if money seemed to affect his mother's mood. He looked down at the ground for a few moments and then said, "She sometimes says bad words when looking at papers, and that's how I could tell if she was worried about money. And she said that we need to start spending less money."

"Bad words?" I queried, to which he said, "Yeah, even some words I never heard of. And then she would usually go into her office at home and stay there for a long time." I could see and hear in his voice that he felt anxious as he spoke, perhaps having to do with telling me about something that he was not sure he was allowed to talk about. He spoke of hearing his mother say words he was unsure he was supposed to hear, exposing him to the darker side of language, emotions, and the adult world that he was looking into.

Sensing Peter's anxiety in speaking about his mother's mood around money and her "bad words" brought to mind my own anxiety in overhearing my cousin Tom's conversations with his friends, friends in their early 20s (like Tom) who accompanied us on our autograph expeditions – the way they disparaged or even cursed out those players (behind their backs) who refused to give us an autograph, or players who in some cases shouted at us to back off. This sometimes led to a verbal lashing on the part of Tom and his friends full of expletives and derogatory comments, lashings that I found intriguing to hear, but which also made me nervous as to whether I should be hearing such comments.

In dialoguing with Tom within my own mind, I noticed that Peter became quieter and I had the sense that his reflections on money and his mother's moods brought up feelings that were confusing and unarticulated. The slightly rowdy ambiance that had been palpable before now bled into a more somber moment, but with the unfinished game between us, Peter looked across the board and asked, "So whose turn is it?"

The sensorimotor mode, the analyst's childhood, and changes in the system

While there was much swirling around with Peter in the exchange described above, I am most interested here in the nonverbal dimensions of the dyadic system – the shifting subjectivities, histories that are being recontextualized, the emergence of presences from the past, all threads that are interwoven within the system.

The act of handing me the pen to write the lyrics for the song not only carried content rife with meaning (money, mortgage, etc.), but also elicited my memory of handing paper and pen to various athletes. Another way of stating this is that my observation of Peter's behavior (handing me the pen) automatically became internally simulated within me, a simulation that then triggered this memory of collecting autographs with Tom. In this reflexive exchange, the emotional tones embedded in the physical act (of handing the pen to a player) that sprang from my childhood memory granted me access to a memory that then may have become a bridge to further experience the intentions behind Peter's wanting me to write the lyrics as he sang them. Framed in terms of more contemporary psychoanalytic terminology, while my countertransference and reveries were amalgams of the verbal and nonverbal content, they initially emerged from the physical realm of experience, from the action within a context composed of unarticulated affect states located in the body (Bucci, 2001).

Along with the action language of the body were the sensory elements of my memory of Tom and collecting autographs. Singing with Peter and Tom's whistling became linked in my mind, a sensory memory that then became a window into the mood or affect state situated alongside of the music – Tom's whistling when we scored a hard-won autograph and then Peter's "free box" tune carrying the crescendo of triumph and the depletion of desperation, which led into thoughts of his mother's mood in relation to money.

Harris's (2005) integration of chaos theory into understanding development points to how the moving contexts and state changes that occur in relation to the play with Peter and its intersection with my childhood recollection potentiated some sort of shift within the system. The unfolding of the "free box" song along with my memories may have shifted the patterning and altered the previously established equilibrium. The analyst's childhood experiences, sometimes automatically triggered, may carry something "alive and disequilibrating" (within the analyst's internal system) that can then disrupt the child's rigidity and become a catalyst for some kind of reorganization within the system, as well as within the patient and therapist (Harris, 2005, p. 81). These memories that arrive unbidden in the context of the play lend themselves to expanding the spoken and unspoken dialogue with the child, an exchange that occurs across the multiple registers of communication – physical, somatic, sensory, behavioral, and verbal. This dialogical expansion produces changes in the multilevel system, opening up pathways and new spaces within a system previously dominated by rigidity and stagnation.

Fallen heroes

With the disparity between our financial holdings increasing in our ongoing game of *Monopoly*, my dependency on Peter for leniency and forgiveness with regard to my debts was intensifying. Would he let me take a pass on the rent I owed him? Could I gradually pay off my debts rather than declare bankruptcy? As I faced mounting debts, it was not lost on me that my role was an opportunity for Peter to probe and witness my financial demise in the transference that may have had ties to his own father and mother's financial worries.

As Peter enjoyed his position of power and my leaning on him for handouts, the "free box" became even more of a fixture in our exchanges. Rather than hand me the money directly (which I relied on to survive in the game), he continued to contribute money to the "free box" from which I could draw when needed. Depending on the state of his own finances, Peter either contributed more money if he was secure with the amount he had or withdrew some of his donations when he deemed that he did not have enough. It was noteworthy to see him struggle with what to do with the box, knowing that if he withdrew money there was then less for me to use. He had to manage his circumstances and mine together, his need for security alongside of my reliance on him for handouts. Guilt, self-preservation, and the wish for the game not to end were charged affects he was internally negotiating in our exchanges.

In observing Peter's reciprocal relationship with the "free box" – either physically putting money into the pot or taking it away – a disturbing memory of mine arrived that concerned my cousin Tom again, one that also collided with my admiration for him growing up. As an 11-year-old boy and with Tom still periodically taking me on autograph pilgrimages, my parents sat me down for what was referred to as a "family meeting." Nervous and unsure what it was about, they told me that they had discovered Tom had been stealing money from the drawer where they kept their cash. Evidently, Tom had been taking money from the drawer whenever he was over at the house or apparently was entering the house when no one was home (he had his own key since he was so involved in our lives).

In learning this, I was shocked and not sure what to think. Seeing my parents clearly distraught, I initially found myself wanting to locate some explanation for what he had been doing, searching their faces for a sign that this was going to lead to some kind of a good ending. All they could say was that Tom was in severe credit card debt and that he may have become desperate. Unable at first to reconcile the person I knew as my childhood hero with this act of betrayal, I had trouble believing that he was capable of something like this.

With my mind hosting this significant event, I thought about the obvious stimulus for this memory, namely Peter's give and take with our "free box" – the physical act of taking and giving money from a so-called box that may have called out this memory of Tom taking money from my parents' money drawer. Of course, the differences were intriguing as well, especially the fact that our box did not involve stealing per se, but determinations based on need, security, and survival.

One of Peter's favorite parts of the game, for reasons I did not entirely understand, was the opportunity to pick a "Chance" or "Community Chest" card – cards that in most cases could bring a player good fortune or impose a monetary demand that required paying money either to the bank or to one's opponent. Peter enjoyed the uncertainty of not knowing what outcome might ensue, as well as the act of unveiling the card first to himself so that I could not see it and then, depending on the result, either pumping his fist with a big, hearty "Yes!" or in a more subdued voice echoing the card's unfavorable news. As he read the card in situations like this, I was often in the position of waiting with some anticipation as to which direction his mood would shift – either a burst of enthusiasm or a fleeting deflation.

However, despite this pattern, on one particular occasion, Peter picked a "Chance" card from the top of the pile as instructed by the space he had landed on, but instead of immediately telling me what it said, he read it to himself and then merely put the card back without saying a word. His eyes peered down at the floor and there was a long, silent pause. I was unsure what had happened and confused by what had prompted the shift.

With his body hunched over and his head slightly bowed toward his lap, I looked over at the "free box" song that had been a work in progress across the most recent string of sessions. The last line he had left off with read, "Free box, when you can't pass 'Go'" (in passing "Go", a player collects $200 from the bank).

In the midst of the prolonged silence between us, I told him that I just watched him read something that might have upset him and did not know what it was (thinking of bearing witness to a disorganizing state in him). I said it felt as if we were stuck and unable to pass "Go" (referring to the lyric from the song).

Peter continued to stare at the floor for a moment, then slowly raised his head up and said, "I read some of Dad's emails and I saw one that he wrote to his woman friend that Mom got so upset about." Seeing that he may have felt that he was breeching his father's privacy not only in reading his email, but also in telling me, I noted that he might feel uncomfortable and unsure how to talk about what he had read.

Peter nodded his head in agreement, and then said, "He wrote that he was unhappy with Mom and that he really liked her [the woman with whom he was having an emotional affair and would later go on to live with], that she made him happy and how he liked talking with her." As Peter said this, he brushed his sleeves over his eyes to quickly wipe away the few tears that had leaked out. I said to him that it must have "hurt" to read this, and he said it hurt his stomach and he did not know why his dad was "doing this." With the window closing, as it usually did when we entered this kind of terrain together, Peter glanced over at the *Monopoly* board, letting me know that this was enough for now. Before returning to the game, I offered a parting comment: "I wonder if you feel confused and have trouble putting together what you read in your dad's email with how you thought you knew your mom and dad."

Reaching for the dice for his next roll, he muttered, "I miss when Mom and Dad lived together. It doesn't seem fair."

As we resumed the game, with "it doesn't seem fair" echoing in the background, I thought of my own identification with Peter in this moment in relation to Tom and the conflict between what I found out from my parents in that family meeting and how I, too, had wanted to preserve Tom, just as some part of Peter struggled to integrate his admiration for his father with his father's betrayal of his mother. He wished his parents could still be together. Whether it was Tom's act of taking money or Peter's first-hand discovery of his father's "emotional affair", reconciling these internal collisions in each of our respective relationships with these significant figures and their reverberations in the analytic relationship between us was part of the landscape that lay ahead (see Bonovitz, 2010).

Development, changes in the system, and therapeutic action

One of the many differences that exist between the treatment of adults and children is the movement and action that often occur with children in the context of play. Whether it be games, a dollhouse, sports, or animal figures, the play often involves a kind of physical movement that is generally less pronounced with adults. Adults sit in a chair or lie on a couch in psychoanalysis; children often move around during the course of the session. With this difference in mind, the body becomes more prominent, as the child's body is often in motion, as is the therapist's. This more continuous movement becomes an important channel of nonverbal communication and shapes the memories and associations that arrive unbidden from the analyst's childhood, recollections contextualized by this action that may be different from what would emerge in an adult treatment. For instance, the act of writing the lyrics for the "free box" song that led to my memory of collecting autographs with Tom may not have arrived with an adult patient in quite the same way, as I typically do not write songs with adults in treatment.

The linguistic exchanges and body language of therapist and child are intertwined. The kinetic, mimetic, and postural channels are vehicles for information on an unconscious level that influence verbal and nonverbal responses (Jacobs, 1994). The rolling of the dice, the act of picking cards or distributing money, or the writing of lyrics such as with Peter are automatic responses in the procedural domain of experience that we are not necessarily thinking about, but rather occur out of our awareness and communicate messages that contextualize shifts in our respective states of mind. It is my belief that the analyst's attention to the childhood memories that arrive in the context of nonverbal communication allows for a further expansion of the system and opens up pathways between the conscious level and the sensory/somatic registers of experience.

My memory of Tom stealing money from my parents (on the heels of Peter giving and taking money from the "free box") and its collision with my prior image of him was then followed by a change in Peter's affect as he recalled reading his father's email. Though one did not necessarily cause the other, the state of my mind in hosting this memory of Tom and the physical act of giving and taking (with money in the game of *Monopoly*) that had contextualized it contributed at least in part to what arrived in Peter's body and mind: I had not specifically asked him about his father's emails and in fact did not know about them until he told me at that moment.

So how can we begin to explain the mutative change that took place in Peter's therapy and its influence on facilitating his development? Using the ideas from nonlinear dynamic systems theory, it is twofold. First, my memories of Tom and collecting autographs produced a shift within me, as well as within the system with Peter. This shift first took place on a sensorimotor level (the act of writing that brings together the "free box" song and my handing a pen to a player for his autograph) and then altered the contexts that Peter and I inhabited, changing the unconscious and nonverbal levels of communication that reorganized what we knew and opened up unexplored areas of the field. For instance, following my sojourn back in time to Tom and his betrayal of my family's trust, Peter found the words to describe his father's email concerning his emotional affair, a discovery that had been a secret up until his telling me about it. The gradual synchrony between my childhood memories of Tom and Peter's current familial experiences occurred within a system that settled into new and different patterns.

The gradual changes that did indeed take place during the string of sessions reported above certainly appear to be significant, examples of therapeutic action-interactional patterns becoming less rigid (as evidenced by the spontaneous shifts that took place during the game). The theme of money in the game and the "free box" song provided a format for Peter to sort out his thoughts and feelings around the negotiation of money in his family and he began to speak about having read his father's email and its effect on him. And though the verbal content and its multiple meanings were ingredients of therapeutic action, I am emphasizing the nonverbal elements of therapeutic action here that unexpectedly gave rise to the analyst's sojourns back to his childhood and its influence on shifts that took place within the dyad.

Further confirmation of these changes in Peter came from my periodic meetings with his mother and father, as well as conversations with his school, where the general consensus was that he was better able to control his aggression, more able to rely on his words to communicate his distress, and was performing at a higher level academically.

I regard the changes that took place with Peter as developmentally based. His ability to reflect on his mental states as evidenced by experiencing and then speaking about reading his father's emails, his making connections between his mother's moods and money, the spontaneous twists and turns that took place during the play that demonstrated an increased interpersonal flexibility, as well as finding a new balance between self and mutual regulation are all changes I would situate within the domain of his development.

My contention is that the respective embodied histories of analyst and patient are discovered and rediscovered in relation to one another, a discovery that requires the experience of recognition for the child (Trevarthen, 2009). This process becomes an important context for movement within a system that is more open than closed and brimming with the potential for change. The conscious and unconscious links between the histories in the analyst and child patient foster an intersubjective dialogue between two separate but entwined subjectivities.

Completing the song

As the *Monopoly* game progressed and the lyrics to the "free box" song evolved with the fluctuations and distribution of property and payments, Peter became less invested in keeping me financially afloat. My dependency on him began to feel different; it had become more burdensome, and he acknowledged this to himself as well as to me. This change in the game coincided with his becoming more involved in his school's activities, running for school government (he was a skilled debater), and playing more team sports than he had in the past.

On one occasion in the midst of this emerging shift, my iron game piece landed on Boardwalk, the most expensive property on the board. Of course, as you might imagine, Peter had a monopoly in his ownership of Park Place and Boardwalk, together with four houses on each property, which meant that he could decide my fate, as I clearly did not have enough money to make the payments. He could contribute money to the "free box" that I could then withdraw or withhold money (which he had not done up to this point), a decision that would effectively end the game.

After a quiet pause with my fate hanging in the balance, Peter handed me the paper and pencil. He sang out in a rather loud but melodic voice, "Free box, yeah, when you run out of lyrics." I was a little taken aback as he said this. It seemed in that moment that he could see the surprise in my face. I asked him what he was trying to tell me with this lyric. He smiled softly and then said, "I think I'm ready to end this game. No more handouts." He uttered these words with a hint of pride and I could appreciate his willingness to announce his intention.

"What am I to do?" I asked half-jokingly, playing along.

"I don't know, you just might have to retire," he said.

With the end of our game and the completion of our song, I could sense that Peter was letting me know that he indeed might be ready to retire from therapy soon, as his life was becoming fuller and there were other opportunities awaiting. He was ready to retire from carrying such a heavy load.

References

Baranger, M. & Baranger, W. (2008). The analytic situation as a dynamic field. *International Journal of Psychoanalysis*, 89:795–826.

Beebe, B. & Lachmann, F. (2002). Organizing principles of interaction from infant research and the lifespan prediction of attachment: Application to adult treatment. *Journal of Infant, Child, and Adolescent Psychotherapy*, 2:61–89.

Bonovitz, C. (2010). The interpersonalization of fantasy: The linking and de-linking of fantasy and reality. *Psychoanalytic Dialogues*, 20:627–641.

Bonovitz, C. (2016). On seeing what is not said: The concrete mode of psychic functioning and the development of symbolization. *Psychoanalytic Dialogues*, 26:280–293.

Bucci, W. (2001). Pathways of emotional communication. *Psychoanalytic Inquiry*, 21:40–70.

Bromberg, P.M. (1998). *Standing in the spaces*. Hillsdale, NJ: The Analytic Press.

Cambray, J. (2006). Towards the feeling of emergence. *Journal of Analytical Psychology*, 51:1–20.

Gallese, V. (2009). Mirror neurons, embodied simulation, and the neural basis of social identification. *Psychoanalytic Dialogues*, 19:519–536.

Galatzer-Levy, R.M. (2009). Good vibrations: Analytic process as coupled oscillations. *International Journal of Psychoanalysis*, 90:983–1007.

Harris, A. (2005). *Gender as soft assembly*. Hillsdale, NJ: The Analytic Press.

Jacobs, T.J. (1994). Nonverbal communications: Some reflections on their role in the psychoanalytic process and psychoanalytic deucation. *Journal of the American Psychoanalytic Association*, 42:741–762.

Jacobs, T.J. (2002). Once more with feeling. *Psychoanalytic Inquiry*, 22:599–616.

Levin, F.M. (1996). *British Journal of Medical Psychology*. LXVII, 1994. *Psychoanalytic Quarterly*, 65:843–845.

Ogden, T.H. (1997). Reverie and interpretation. *Psychoanalytic Quarterly*, 66:567–595.

Piers, C. (2005). The mind's multiplicity and continuity. *Psychoanalytic Dialogues*, 15:229–254.

Seligman, S. (2005). Dynamic systems theories as a metaframework for psychoanalysis. *Psychoanalytic Dialogues*, 15:285–319.

Stern, D.B. (2009). Partners in thought: A clinical process theory of narrative. *Psychoanalytic Quarterly*, 78:701–731.

Stern, D.B. (2015). The interpersonal field: Its place in American psychoanalysis. *Psychoanalyic Dialogues*, 25:388–404.

Trevarthen, C. (2009). The intersubjective psychobiology of human meaning: Learning of culture depends on interest for co-operative practical work – And affection for the joyful art of good company. *Psychoanalytic Dialogues*, 19:507–518.

Winnicott, D.W. (1965). *The maturational processes and the facilitating environment*. New York, NY: International Universities Press.

Chapter 8

Theory of mind and therapeutic action

A contemporary Freudian integration

Neal Vorus, Ph.D.

Introduction

In this chapter, I present a contemporary Freudian model of therapeutic action that aims to bridge a conceptual divide that has long plagued our field: a tendency to view either interpretation *or* the therapeutic relationship as the primary ingredient of change. In my view, the tendency to treat interpretation and the therapeutic relationship as alternative factors is symptomatic of a failure to fully consider the developmental processes that underlie therapeutic action. While psychoanalysis has long featured powerful developmental models, these models initially served to explicate pathogenesis and had little to say about the therapeutic process itself. Therapeutic action in the early days was primarily conceived in terms of insight, with the treatment relationship functioning in a supportive role. During the classical Freudian period, the relationship factor came to be increasingly viewed as a potential contaminant to the "pure gold" of interpretive insight (Friedman, 1978).

Later object relations and self-psychological models, such as those put forth by Winnicott (1955) and Kohut (1968), did offer a developmental view of the therapeutic process, mainly with regard to treating more disturbed patients. In these contributions, the role of the environment in both pathogenesis and treatment is emphasized (e.g. environmental holding leading to integration, parental mirroring facilitating transmuting internalization). This heightened environmental focus on the treatment process itself has, perhaps inadvertently, contributed to a reduced emphasis on the *interpretive* dimension of treatment, as interpretations have come to be seen by some as a secondary or even tertiary component of treatment. For example, it is often stated that, for many patients, interpretations should be held back, as they may prove disruptive to the growth processes taking place within the therapeutic relationship.

From another angle, relational analysts have long criticized Freudians for advancing a "one-person psychology" that fails to recognize the extent to which patients and analysts are embedded in mutually interactive processes (Aron, 1990). The traditional analytic goal of insight is called into question, as it rests on the dubious assumption that the objective analyst can know with some certainty the *individual* mind of the patient (Mitchell, 1997). Rather than viewing insight (and its catalytic agent, interpretation) as a key ingredient of change, relational analysts consider a variety of other interactive processes within the treatment relationship to be the more fundamental therapeutic factors (Hoffman, 1994, 2006).

Perhaps it should be no surprise that a new avenue for understanding the relative roles of interpretation and the therapeutic relationship would arrive from outside of psychoanalytic theory. It is through the work of autism researchers that a new conceptual framework has emerged that allows us to see change processes from a perspective that integrates the interpretive and relational dimensions of treatment. This framework is consistent with the view that, when it is proceeding well, psychoanalytic treatment takes place through the establishment of a *relationship that facilitates meaningfulness* (i.e. a relationship that is intrinsically interpretive, whether or not formal interpretations are actually offered). In this chapter, I will first briefly describe the limitations of the traditional Freudian model of therapeutic action insofar as it neglects the developmental need in the child for establishing the capacity to meaningfully represent experience. I will then discuss the "theory of mind" perspective that has emerged out of research on autism and has recently begun to inform psychoanalytic theorizing. A primary goal of this chapter is to demonstrate the way in which this body of developmental research dovetails with a contemporary Freudian perspective that reconceives the therapeutic process as facilitating not *insight*, but *insightfulness* (Sugarman, 2003); in other words, the functional capacity to process experience reflectively. What the theory of mind perspective illuminates is the extent to which developing the capacity to generate, symbolize, and reflect on the meaning of experience (particularly emotionally intense experience) is the product of a relationship in which experience is reflectively engaged and tolerated, one in which a continuous endeavor to think about the patient's unthinkable experience is provided. It is out of this perspective that an expanded definition of interpretation as an ongoing dimension of treatment, rather than a series of discrete verbal utterances, emerges. In my view, it is the interpretive nature of the therapeutic relationship that constitutes the core of therapeutic action. A clinical example will be presented at the end of the chapter to illustrate this perspective.

The classical model and therapeutic action

Within the Freudian child psychoanalytic tradition, theories of therapeutic action have largely derived from the view that pathology results from a disruption in emotional development, usually as a result of intrapsychic conflict. This disruption has often been thought of in terms of a fixation in a normative developmental sequence, whether conceived in terms of psychosexual stages, ego maturation, or the integration of internalized object relations. Children who seek our help are stuck in maladaptive ways of regulating their emotions and behavior and suffer from concomitant disturbances in relationships. While ways of conceiving of the work of treatment vary widely, there is a common view that child analysts aim to restore development by interpreting the emotional knots that are impeding growth. *I believe that a key to the process of helping our patients lies in our capacity to perceive the largely unspoken story conveyed through a child's actions in the consulting room and finding the means to think about the child's experience and respond in a way that conveys a depth of understanding and acceptance.* Something in the process of being deeply thought about and understood by another restores the process of emotional development.

While the traditional psychoanalytic framework provides conceptual lenses through which to make sense of this process, in my view it fails to adequately capture some of its most essential aspects. For example, it does little to explain why a child begins to show symptomatic improvement even before there has been much interpretation of content. With many children, the beginning phases of treatment consist of the therapist engaging in play and finding (often intuitively) the words and actions that begin to resonate with an underlying story, the meta-narrative running through the play. The initial task of the clinician is to feel his or her way into the story, to express through words one or another aspect of the play – and, typically, not to usher explanatory interpretations.

Throughout this chapter, I will be discussing Billy, a three-year-old boy who came to me several months after the death of his father. Billy began treatment excitedly playing with toy vehicles, repeatedly punctuated by episodes in which one of the trucks mysteriously vanished, followed by the question, "Where did it go?" and shortly thereafter, "I hear a noise – it's back!" Symptomatic improvement occurred relatively quickly as I found ways of echoing the range of feelings associated with these disappearances and reunions. As words were found and provided, the repetitive nature of the play soon expanded to include more elaborate and varied forms of the core experience of someone leaving mysteriously, other people hoping fervently for a return, and (increasingly) feelings of sadness and anger when the hoped-for return failed to materialize. While the theme of the father eventually became explicit, the immediate positive impact of treatment could not be accounted for by way of explanatory interpretations related to the loss of the father. Rather, it seemed that the active ingredient was the therapist's reception and articulation of the child's immediate emotional experience as communicated through the play.

This brief example points to a long-standing obscurity in a theory of therapeutic action that features an intrinsic link between interpretive *insight* and psychic change. What do we mean by "insight" when it comes to the treatment of young children? Traditionally, the Freudian perspective has viewed young children as primarily motivated to gain pleasure and relieve pain. Only with ego maturation does the child attain the necessary controls and motivation to arrive at a reality-oriented perspective. Interpretation aimed at facilitating insight has customarily been viewed as targeting these ego capacities in the interest of bringing about the capacity for self-reflection and thereby more optimal self-regulation. For this reason, some Freudian clinicians have considered psychoanalytic treatment to be only moderately beneficial for children under the age of five due to their developmental limitations (e.g. Kennedy, 1979).

How, then, to explain: (1) the observation that children under the age of five (i.e. prior to the age of objective self-reflection) are often helped by a psychoanalytic mode of play therapy; and (2) the repeated experience that children often improve in the relative absence of explicit interpretive work along *explanatory* lines? As in the above example, children entering treatment often appear stuck in a particular play sequence or scenario, typically organized around a central emotional chord. To use a dated musical metaphor, the child begins as a broken record, endlessly repeating a single thematic element. Through our help, he/she begins composing riffs and eventually a larger symphonic arrangement emerges. Somehow, our ability to listen, to hear the themes, to "hum along", and to convey a welcoming attitude toward new and unexpected developments emboldens and supports the child in leaving behind the previously limited range of notes and keys.

I use this musical metaphor rather than a traditional psychoanalytic explanation because I find that much of our theory fails to adequately convey what it feels like to work with a child psychoanalytically. It does, however, provide a model to conceptualize pathology. For example, the child described above is clearly suffering from conflicts related to the loss of his father and the related emotional family upheaval. One could say that he suffered a painful loss and defended against it with an unspoken fantasy of imminent return, but this fantasy met with repeated disappointment. Because of his mother's traumatic grief, he was unable to find the emotional support necessary to encompass this loss, so was unable to move beyond defensive repudiation.

But what does our received theory have to say about what actually helps in this circumstance? Again, quoting Kennedy (1979), "Our work with children is aimed at fostering self-awareness and self-knowledge ... the analytic work fosters the child's ability to contain and verbalize wishes and feelings, and to reflect" (p. 26). Child analysts tend to think of their work as fostering a process of increasing conscious awareness of unconscious wishes and fears. The ego's capacity to *reflect* on unarticulated experience is thought to be the key and clinicians feel pressure to make interventions to the conscious ego, to make the child aware of previously unconscious mental contents.

While something like this often occurs at certain points in treatment, it is my view that this model does not adequately capture the most essential element of child treatment, which feels more akin to the musical metaphor offered above. Rather than self-observation, it feels more like we begin to *play-think* with the child. A number of child analysts have noted that premature attempts to offer comments aimed at facilitating self-observation can be disruptive of a process that takes place through our participation in the play (e.g. Ritvo, 1978; Neubauer, 1987). However, aside from a few notable exceptions (Mayes & Cohen, 1993; Fonagy & Target, 1996, 1998; Rosegrant, 2001; Sugarman, 2003), the model of therapeutic action informing work with children continues to hold verbal interpretation of unconscious content as the gold standard. While there is increasing recognition that children are often "highly resistant" to such interpretations (Mayes & Cohen, 1993) and that interpretations need to be made "within the metaphor" for a period of time before being offered in a more explanatory mode, clinical writing about the therapeutic role of play itself in the absence of traditional modes of interpretation is treated as an exception (e.g. as operative when treating "ego disturbances" rather than unconscious conflict) (Neubauer, 1987; Cohen & Solnit, 1993). The implication is that one is always ideally aiming at the gold standard of explanatory interpretation, but when this is not tolerated, one can find alternative benefits in therapeutic play (i.e. the notion of "developmental help", as contrasted with "analysis").

However, as noted above, the Freudian tradition in child analysis is not monolithic. More contemporary thinkers have begun to articulate a broadened perspective on the nature and role of insight in the psychoanalytic process (e.g. Fonagy & Target, 1996; Sugarman, 2003; Vorus, 2011). Briefly, these authors all present a view of interpretation as an ongoing dimension of treatment, one not reducible to a particular phrase or spoken exchange, but rather the analyst's sustained endeavor to understand the mind of the patient, whether this is conveyed directly through verbal interpretation or through a variety of indirect verbal and nonverbal interactive modes. As I will discuss below, while this broadened perspective originates in Loewald's (1960) interactional Freudian vision, as well as Bion's (1962) post-Kleinian writings on reverie and containment, it is from the labs of autism researchers that one finds the basis for a more comprehensive developmental framework.

Theory of mind: Autism and beyond

In the past 20 years, a new model for understanding therapeutic action has emerged in the child psychoanalytic literature based on the findings of several prominent autism researchers (e.g. Baron-Cohen, 1995; Gopnik & Wellman, 1992). Briefly, these investigators have identified a deficit in autistic individuals involving their ability to conceive of themselves and of others as operating on the basis of a "theory of mind". These researchers all draw from the work of Daniel Dennett (1987), who posited the idea that humans have evolved the capacity to navigate the social world based on attributions of intentionality (beliefs, desires, and feelings). He named this the "intentional stance," and contrasted it with the "contingency stance" in which one understands the social world on the basis of stereotyped causal sequences (i.e. thinking like a behaviorist). From within the contingency stance, a child seeing a parent's face turn red and brow grow furrowed might lead to the expectation that the latter will begin to shout or even become violent. This is a behavioral sequence and does not involve making attributions of mental states. In the intentional stance, the child automatically attributes agency, emotion, and belief. The advantage of the intentional stance is clear: it offers the capacity to make far more subtle behavioral predictions, as well as pointing a way toward effective recourse (e.g. in the above example, quickly saying, "I'm sorry, I didn't mean to!" might avert escalating states of anger and punitive consequences).

The relevance of Dennett's framework for extreme forms of psychopathology is evident in the empirical finding that children with autism have a profound deficit in their capacity to operate on the basis of the intentional stance (e.g. Leslie & Frith, 1988; Perner et al., 1989). In a word, children on the autistic spectrum suffer from "mindblindness" (Baron-Cohen, 1995). The identification of this core deficit in autism has spawned considerable research on the ontogenesis of the capacity to make intentional attributions. How do children develop the ability to relate to themselves and others on the basis of mental states, to acquire a "theory of mind"? Researchers addressing this question from the perspective of developmental psychopathology have conceived of this capacity as an innate "module" that unfolds over time in the presence of average, expectable environmental inputs (Baron-Cohen, 1995).

Others have emphasized social learning processes whereby a child develops a theory of mind on the basis of experience (the so-called "theory theory" approach) (Gopnick, 1996). A third group assumes that intersubjectivity arises from a child's attribution of their innate knowledge of their own subjective states to the experience of others ("Simulation Theory") (Goldman, 1992). These three dominant perspectives share in common the view that, while the capacity to conceive of the mental state of self and other unfolds over time in the context of normal interactions, the basis of the capacity is inborn and significant disturbances in this capacity are primarily due to innate factors.

Another perspective has emerged from researchers studying not the kind of gross pathology in intersubjectivity found in autism, but rather more subtle variations in this capacity. Peter Fonagy (1991) was among the first to develop a methodology for studying the intentional stance as a continuous variable and to observe differences in this capacity that vary based on differences in quality of parent–child communication. Based on the research of Fonagy et al. (2002), the child acquires a theory of mind dialogically, through a process that begins early in life, mediated by a child's inborn capacity to recognize contingency (see also Gergely & Watson, 1996; Gergely, 2000). Briefly, these researchers have found that, beginning at three months of age, children show a clear preference for close (but not perfect) contingency between their movements, vocalizations, etc., and feedback from the environment. For example, children at three months will look longer at a video monitor showing a temporally delayed image of their legs than at an alternative monitor without a time delay (i.e. perfect contingency) (Gergely, 2000, pp. 1202–1203). These researchers have posited a theory that this preference for *close but imperfect contingency* reflects an innate preparedness for exploration and representation of the social world, particularly insofar as that world provides representational feedback about the self.

In Gergely's (2000) formulation, the young child begins to develop the capacity for emotional self-regulation through what he describes as "social biofeedback," whereby the mother attunes to the child's initially unorganized and unformulated primary affective state and her more organized and formulated responses are sensed by the child as *similar, but differentiated* from his or her own somatosensory experience. This differentiated integration between mother and child provides the basis, through internalization, for the achievement of second-order representations of the child's "constitutional self". Like the traditional biofeedback process whereby patients learn to control formerly autonomic physiological processes through recognition training, the child acquires recognition and the means for representing their emotional states through the attuned, somewhat more elaborated responses of the parent.

According to Gergely (2000) and Fonagy et al. (2002), a key to the social biofeedback process is the parent providing mirroring responses to the child that are characterized by "markedness", that distinctively exaggerated form of response to children that tends to come naturally to parents (i.e. "motherese"; see Trevarthen, 1985). The purpose of markedness is to *decouple* the parent's response from their actual internal state and to signal its non-consequentiality, thereby facilitating its availability as a symbolic expression of the child's own internal state. For example, a child might grow frustrated with a toy and throw it down in anger, then burst into tears. A typical parental response would usually include a brief display of exaggerated sad and angry part-expressions, accompanied by soothing words and then a reassuring smile. In this brief exchange (repeated countless times over the first few years), the child associates his or her upset state with the recognition supplied by the marked facial affect display of the parent, as well as the more complex features of soothing and reassurance. For the slightly older child, such moments will include more elaborately verbalized expressions of the upset, as well as some ideas meant to counter the dominant emotional state (e.g. providing an alternative perspective).

A key to this process is that, while markedness is essential in decoupling the parental emotional expression from their real feelings, it must maintain enough of a contingent relation to the child's emotional experience to remain adequately referential. For this reason, Fonagy et al. (2002) refer to this process as "referential decoupling" (p. 178).

Theory of mind and therapeutic action

So, what does all this have to do with therapeutic action in child treatment? Recall the observation noted above that children begin to improve prior to the delivery of the explanatory interpretations that we so often treat as the "gold standard" of psychoanalysis. It is my view, building on both the body of research briefly outlined above and also the psychoanalytic vision of analysts like Bion (1962) and Loewald (1960), that the psychoanalytic process is fundamentally one in which we make use of our relationship with the patient in order to create the conditions in which more complete "mindedness" becomes a possibility. While with adults explanatory interpretations can provide a useful means for becoming more familiar with the hidden complexity of one's own mind, children are typically at a more beginning stage. Rather than thinking of the psychoanalytic process as overcoming a defense against specific contents ("make the unconscious conscious") or ameliorating a developmental deficit ("provide a holding environment"), it is my view that we are better served by drawing on a model of therapeutic action that integrates these dimensions of the treatment process in the service of facilitating an enhanced capacity to experience the "mentalness of mind" (Alvarez, 1995). The theory of mind or mentalization perspective offers the advantage of helping clinicians move beyond the dichotomization that has long been woven into the psychoanalytic framework. Rather than the forced choice of relationship-based versus interpretive modes of treatment, the mentalization model points toward the continuous variable of becoming *minded*, of developing the capacity for "meaning-space" (Vorus, 2011).

From this perspective, we conceive of therapeutic action in terms of a general process of helping people develop the *capacity* to more completely know their own mind. This functional capacity is developmental and is facilitated by an emotionally attuned relationship wherein the parent/therapist does not merely copy (mirror) our experience, but interacts with us in a way that enhances the capacity to apprehend greater complexity in ourselves and in others. For the very young infant, it is the markedness of maternal mirroring that facilitates the beginning of this capacity. For the somewhat older child, it is the emotionally attuned "thinking about" the child's experience (often conveyed implicitly) that begins to provide the basis for greater depth and elaboration. For the adolescent, it is the experience of talking with an adult who thinks very carefully and reflectively about what the patient is saying without imposing censorship or control. For the adult patient, it is one's capacity to be in any of these positions, as well as to provide more elaborate, explicit interpretations when the patient is ready to discover unseen internal connections when that appears most useful.

As Sugarman (2003) points out, the integration of a theory of mind or "mentalization" perspective of therapeutic action leads to a shift from a content-focused, interpretive stance to a process-focused perspective wherein the clinician aims to help the patient restore a functional capacity, which he refers to as "insightfulness":

> What is essential in the analysis of young children is the facilitation of a mechanism of self-understanding. *To be sure, awareness of repudiated content will usually accompany the development of mentalization. But the point of insightfulness is to regain access to inhibited or repudiated mentalization, not to specific content per se.*
>
> (p. 331, original emphasis)

Theory of mind and defense

As with more traditional approaches, dealing with defenses and resistances is crucial to the therapeutic perspective described in this chapter, although the way they are conceived differs somewhat. Traditionally, defense mechanisms have been conceived largely based on Freud's (1926) late model of anxiety, wherein particular impulses become associated with one or another of the basic danger situations and thereby become anxiogenic. When one of these impulses becomes aroused, the ego responds to the resultant signal anxiety with the activation of a defense that serves the function of suppressing, redirecting, or disguising the impulse sufficiently to avert greater levels of anxiety. Following this model, the role of the adult or child analyst is to recognize and articulate the operation of the defense, thereby exposing the anxiety-generating impulse so that, through therapeutic investigation, defenses are reduced and potential barriers to optimal development are lessened. The goal is expansion of the capacity for self-experience through the investigation of defenses against specific mental contents.

From a theory of mind perspective, defenses are conceived less in terms of specific mental contents and more in terms of the patient's relationship to "mindedness" itself. As in the traditional ego psychological framework, defense is conceived as restricting or inhibiting awareness in order to avert anxiety (Freud, 1936). However, ego restriction or inhibition are here understood as reflecting interference in the child's original ability to make use of the environment to co-regulate emotional states. In Fonagy et al.'s (2002) description, the child develops reflective self-awareness through the process of a mother apprehending the child's emotional state and conveying understanding in a way that simultaneously conveys *difference*. The child's taking in this differentiated connection paves the way for establishing second-order representations of primary (somatosensory-based) emotional experience. Through this process, the child internalizes the parent's attuned but more developed awareness of his or her mind, creating the foundation for reflective self-awareness. The form taken by parental attunement evolves developmentally, in tandem with the growing complexity of the child's mind. Parenting necessarily involves providing an attuned but (tolerably) differentiated perspective on the child's mind, which, via internalization, becomes the foundation for reflective self-awareness. This mode of self-awareness constitutes a more developed method of regulating emotion, whereas most forms of defense reflect limitations in this regard. While some of these limitations may be intrinsic to being human, many others reflect more overt deficits in parental responsiveness. In either case, defense is understood as an alternative to reflective awareness, which is always understood to be the result of an initially dialogical process.

The implication of this perspective for the treatment situation is that defenses are not conceived as solely existing within the child, but instead reflect the child's experience that some feelings or impulses are intrinsically intolerable to the other and have to be managed independently. The choice of managing via defense versus reflective awareness comes down to one's experience of whether the other is willing and able to tolerate and think about the fullness of one's experience. While the patient who is processing emotional experience defensively may not consciously think of the situation in these terms, it is an important perspective for the clinician to bear in mind. In effect, the defensive child has no belief in mutual processing of an emotional experience or has lost that belief. What is needed in treatment is an experience, over time, of re-establishing the possibility of mutual regulation. In my view, this perspective dovetails with Loewald's (1960) well-known description of the analyst as a new object, in the sense of "new discovery of objects":

> I say new discovery of objects, and not discovery of new objects, because the essence of such new object-relationships is the opportunity they offer for rediscovery of early paths of the development of object-relations, leading to a new way of relating to objects as well as of being and relating to oneself.
>
> (p. 18)

As with Loewald's (1952, 1960) groundbreaking reinterpretation of Freudian theory, the theory of mind perspective on therapeutic action posits an important distinction between an "open system" mode of regulating inner life, which rests on an original integration between ego and environment, and a "closed system" mode, wherein such integration is foreclosed and the child relies on defensive processes to manage anxiety. This is an inter-psychic understanding of defense; psychic growth is always conceived of interactively and defense entails an interruption of a dialogical growth process due to a breach or disconnect with the caretaking environment. The child is left to his/her own devices in order to manage, necessarily entailing a less developed or, in Loewald's (1960) terms, a more regressive solution to situations of conflict.

What are the treatment implications of this view of defense? From my perspective, one of the most important implications has to do with the way we conceive of our role as child therapists. Rather than thinking of our job as pointing out defenses as they occur (which can sometimes begin to resemble a game of "gotcha"), we should think in terms of our role as environmental regulators. To what extent is the child using us as a medium of representation of his or her inner life; in other words, to what extent do we and the child make up an *open system* wherein the as-yet unformulated inner reality of the child can begin to emerge? To what extent is the child a *closed system*, relating to us from across the subject–object divide as an external reality that must be contended with or adapted to in some way? Of course, this is not a dichotomous issue. Defensive processes come and go in the course of a session (although for some children this can have a more pervasive quality). The important point for technique is that one keeps at the forefront the understanding that defensive processes signal the perceived inadequacy of the environment to receive and engage helpfully with some aspect of experience. As the embodiment of the (potentially) new environment, we hope to hold ourselves out in a way that offers another chance at ego–environment integration, and when we interpret defense, it is always from this vantage point. We respond to resistance in a way that points toward another possibility, one that involves engagement, acceptance, and understanding.

Theory of mind and contemporary Freudian theory

While the description above might appear to be a relational view of defense and of the treatment process more generally, in my view it is *also* intrinsically Freudian. Why? Because while the relationship is seen as both the vehicle of the psychoanalytic process and the medium of both conscious and unconscious communication, the goal of treatment remains establishing and supporting the truth of the patient's experience *as an individual.* Hans Loewald, whose visionary rearticulation of Freud is considered by many to be the core of the contemporary Freudian perspective, grounded all of his major contributions on the dialectical relation between *two realities.* The first of these is the reality of primary narcissism, of a primal relational embeddedness of the infant and the mother (and, later, the self and the world). The second is the form of reality bound up with the father, of reality as external and fundamentally separate from the self. For Loewald, these forms of reality exist in dialectical relation to one another throughout life and the movement of this dialectic constitutes a core organizer of psychic growth. From this perspective, individuality and relatedness are only conceived as opposite concepts from a defensive standpoint – in Loewald's (1952) words, resulting in a "neurotically impoverished reality" that potentially infects psychoanalytic theorizing itself. Bifurcating these two modes of reality, elevating one and repudiating the other, represents a form of splitting at a conceptual level. We could easily look at our current psychoanalytic political scene, with its bifurcation into "Relational" and "Classical" positions, to see the continued relevance of Loewald's observations. It was in the spirit of a dynamic, dialectical relationship between individuality and relatedness that Loewald (1960) stated what might be considered a guiding principle of treatment: "It requires an objectivity and *neutrality* the essence of which is *love and respect for the individual* and for *individual development*" (p. 229, emphasis added). It is Loewald's vision of individuality, rooted in (and continually enriched by) a fundamental relatedness and openness, that the psychoanalyst aims to support, rather than either a stunted, regressively organized separateness or a mode of being in which everything is viewed *only* in terms of mutuality and relatedness. In my view, it is the continued (albeit broadened) *interpretive* emphasis of the treatment process, in conjunction with the fundamental aim of finding and articulating the patient's inner, individual truth (an individuality rooted in and rediscovered through relational processes), that constitute the distinctive hallmarks of a contemporary Freudian psychoanalytic approach.

To put this in different terms, the contemporary Freudian position does not elevate the relationship (mother principle) over interpretation (father principle), but instead emphasizes the ongoing dialectical relation of these two dimensions of experience. Patients form transferences that are motivated by a desire for unity (primary narcissism, the mother principle). Effective treatment requires that we recognize and respond to this need while also introducing an element of difference or, in Loewald's (1960) terminology, a *differential*. Interpretation, as I define it in this chapter, is the introduction of that differential. However, rather than defining interpretation as a series of verbal statements, I am broadening the term in order to describe an ongoing process generated by the analyst's ability to think about the patient's experience in a way that is both attuned to and at a higher level of organization than the patient's current experience. This may take the form of interpretation in the classical sense, but can also include other kinds of verbal or nonverbal interaction that present an element of difference in relation to the patient's experience that the latter is (hopefully) able to tolerate and utilize. This differs generally from a relational perspective in at least two ways: (1) for Freudians, the primary aim of the treatment process is to explicate the patient's *individual* experience, although the therapeutic relationship is both the medium for expression and the means of addressing that experience; and (2) interpretation is recognized as an *essential* element of treatment, *inseparable* from the treatment relationship. It is not distinct from or of a lesser order than the therapeutic relationship, as some relational writings appear to imply (e.g. Hoffman, 2006).

Contemporary Freudians now recognize that a tremendous amount takes place between patient and analyst; they have come to recognize that we are always embedded in an interactive matrix with our patients, forever engaged in mutually enacted processes (Katz, 2014). In my view, contemporary Freudians owe an enormous debt of gratitude to relational and interpersonal thinkers for illuminating the continuously interactive dimension that was long neglected and ignored by our classical Freudians forebears. In this sense, Freudians have grown more relational and the differences between our traditions have diminished over time. However, one way contemporary Freudians continue to differ from many relational thinkers is in our assertion that a focus on the unique experience of our patients – their developing individuality – remains essential to the outcome of treatment. Contemporary Freudians see patients benefitting from coming to know themselves as both relational participants *and as individuals*. Doing so requires both intimacy *and* space. It is important that not everything be interpreted (or even understood privately) as an expression of the treatment relationship; it is essential that we recognize, validate, and at times protect a sphere of autonomy within the patient. While it is easy to make the philosophical case that individuality is an impossibility, at an experiential level, contemporary Freudians generally feel that a mode of working that supports the potential for individual experience remains essential, similar to the way good parents interact with their developing children. Intuitively, we as parents know something about the importance of protecting the individual experience of our children. I believe we should be equally attuned to protecting the space for individual experience in our patients, both child and adult. It seems to me that commitment to a theoretical system that is fundamentally organized around critiquing the very possibility of a non-relational experience errs on the side of ignoring an important dimension of human experience, mirroring the one-sidedness of the classical Freudians of the past.

As discussed above, the theory of mind perspective that is presented in this chapter is consistent with the contemporary Freudian position first outlined by Loewald, in which treatment is modeled on the dimension of the parent–child interaction by which the mother gives shape to the emotional experience of the child by first joining with it, then articulating it in a way that involves difference, *something more* than the child's experience. By repeatedly engaging in such a relationship, the child takes in a more differentiated and articulated experience of his or her own mind, as well as the parent's (or therapist's) reflective capacity. With the internalization of this capacity, the child develops a higher degree of emotional self-regulation and, with the development of self-reflection, can begin to evolve a more differentiated and individualized sense of self.

Clinical example

Now we will return to Billy, the child mentioned briefly at the start of this chapter. Billy was just under three when his father, a firefighter, passed away following a long illness. Billy was brought to my consulting room nine months later. He was referred by his preschool due to a pervasive preoccupation with the comings and goings of children and adults from the classroom and a sense of anxious preoccupation that prevented him from settling into an activity for any length of time. He remained hypervigilant and at times behaved aggressively toward other children, usually immediately following a transition. While Billy was clearly a very bright boy, he came across as developmentally younger; Billy tended to use single words to express himself ("gone") and his social repertoire was rather limited, with parallel-play the leading mode of interaction with his peers. Billy's language for his emotional life was especially limited. His emotional upheavals were never accompanied by expressions of negative affect, but were instead inexplicable, unpredictable, wordless events.

Billy's mother was unsure how the death of his father had affected him. She felt he had little understanding at the time of his father's passing, but she had done her best to explain. In the months that followed, she periodically brought up the subject with him. She knew Billy had taken some of this in, but idiosyncratically and with no awareness of the permanence of his loss. At around the time of the consultation, he had taken to saying, on occasion, "Daddy's in the clouds?" or, "Daddy's in an airplane!" His mother's repeated attempts to explain, gently, that Billy's father was not coming back seemed to never quite reach him.

When he first visited my consulting room, I was struck by the odd juxtaposition of Billy's sharp, intelligent gaze and oddly monosyllabic way of expressing himself. As he approached the play area, he began naming some of the toys – "Truck!" "Blocks!" – and I found myself echoing and slightly expanding on his words, as I would with a much younger child. Billy's play was stereotyped and repetitive. He took one car and gave me another. My car sat under the patient chair while his circled around slowly. At the same point in the circle, he would say, "A noise!" and I would respond, "What was that?!" His car would once again speed up and I found myself speaking with sadness and disappointment, "Where did it go?" This sequence repeated for many weeks, alternating with Lego play, which Billy referred to as "monster trucks." In that play, we built trucks and ran them around an imaginary semicircular track on the couch. This play had a nearly hypnotic quality in its repetitive monotony, occasionally punctuated by one of the trucks breaking down while the other sped away rapidly. Again, I found myself giving voice to the experience of being left, and of not understanding: "Come back! Now I'm sad, where did you go?"

As described above, my interventions during this early phase consisted largely of my articulating in simple terms my subjective response to situations imposed upon me in the play. To return to my musical metaphor, I responded to the simple melody of Billy's play by "humming along" and gradually introducing a bit of variation, initially just a few grace notes or a bit of harmony. On a theoretical level, I was guided by my understanding that my role was to receive and give voice to Billy's psychic reality and that the repetitive nature of the play reflected Billy's difficulty in thinking beyond the present moment of absence and imagined (but always frustrated) return. As I bore the repetitive, frustratingly tantalizing experience of someone almost but never quite returning, I began to voice other emotional aspects of the experience – "It's so frustrating!" "Now I'm sad *and* mad" – always spoken with playful, "marked" inflection (Gergely, 2000).

Billy's response to this beginning phase of treatment was to begin introducing variation; prompted by my grace notes, he began to riff and the melody of play began to expand. Billy started making use of the play firehouse (something he initially avoided), typically introducing a scenario that involved one fireman being left behind by the others as they went to put out a fire or rescue a cat from a tree. Often, the firehouse dog took off in the helicopter and the firefighters looked out, noticing the noises of the helicopter but never quite seeing the dog. Again, I articulated the feeling, guided by my subjective experience, and as Billy's language and play repertoire expanded, so did the complexity of my interventions. For example, I would say, "I feel sad that the doggy is gone. I don't know if he'll come back," to which Billy responded, "Look, he's back!" followed by another tantalizing near-return and sudden departure.

Over time, the theme of the father explicitly entered the play. This took place not in the firehouse, as I might have expected, but with scenarios involving family members (mother, father, and child) and a doctor. In these scenes, the father is sick or injured and is being helped by the doctor, but the latter is foiled by a robber who steals the medicine. The policeman (or sometimes the mother) gives chase and then endures the familiar sequence of almost but not quite catching the thief and retrieving the medicine. The theme of noises providing an anticipatory cue for the almost-arrival of the longed-for object remains a staple of Billy's play throughout all the variations. In recent sessions, Billy has introduced the theme of the child as the aggressor, pushing the father down and injuring him, then stealing the medicine and running off, with the mother in hot pursuit. Sadness is now more palpable, as are indications of guilt, and I'm finding myself increasingly able to voice conflictual feelings within the metaphor of the play: "You're so angry with Daddy, but also very sad because he's so sick." Billy (as the thief): "That's OK, he'll find the medicine, he'll be better" (then running off with it, looking back toward me expectantly). Me: "You're taking away the medicine again. What will happen to Daddy? Now I'm sad all over again and so frustrated!" (At this point, Billy throws the medicine behind the couch and makes a face that looks both angry and sad.) Me: "Oh, the medicine is gone now. Now it's really angry and sad for Daddy. He can't get better."

Discussion

My general treatment approach with Billy, as with many child patients, is congruent with the theory of mind perspective discussed throughout this chapter. My view of Billy's difficulty is that there are aspects of the loss of his father that were impossible for him to mentally absorb and make sense of at the time, both because of his developmental immaturity and due to his mother's state of acute grief. Instead of finding in her responses an attuned but modulated representation of his own emotional experience, Billy found the overwhelming reality of his mother's grief. Instead of providing containment and understanding, her emotional state amplified his own, which required him to turn away from the intersubjective mode and rely on his own defensive capabilities. Billy found a way of protecting himself from the painful and confusing experience of loss by constructing a fantasy in which his father is gone but will soon return. The regular intrusion of city noises into the apartment may have served as signals of his father's imminent return. The comings and goings of teachers from the classroom were experienced unconsciously as the leaving and return of his father. Billy's inexplicable eruptions of aggression can be understood as reactions to the repeatedly tantalizing and frustrated promise of return.

The therapeutic task with a child such as Billy is to provide a way of giving voice and shape to what had become unthinkable. I'm guided by the metaphor of a mother echoing but also adding verbally to the emotional expression of her child. In Fonagy et al.'s (2002) words:

> The child who looks for a way of managing his distress finds in the response of the caregiver a *representation* of his mental state that he may internalize and use as part of a higher-order strategy of affect regulation. The secure caregiver soothes by combining mirroring with a display that is incompatible with the child's affect (thus perhaps implying coping).
>
> (pp. 42–43, emphasis added)

With Billy (as with many other children), I have typically not found it necessary to make explanatory interpretations or to introduce references to external reality in the play (e.g. the actual death of Billy's father). I believe this is more or less consistent with a theory of mind approach to treatment, wherein the work centers on providing an intersubjective environment that supports an expanded awareness of the child's mind through the mind of another. As Fonagy et al. (2002) describe, the form of interaction needed is one that is explicitly representational, wherein Billy can see, hear, and feel his mind through my attuned but differentiated responses. Unlike the overwhelming experience of grief he encountered within the mind of his mother, it is hoped that Billy finds in my responses resonance with his own felt experience, but in imaginary, playful form. It is hoped that as he begins to trust me to reliably help him scaffold his experience through interactive play, Billy's reliance on defensive restriction will wane and the range of fantasy play expand. In the most recent sessions, painful conflicts involving sadness and anger toward father have come increasingly to the fore, allowing for their more direct articulation in the play.

Interestingly, while I have so far refrained from introducing factual reality into the play, Billy's mother has described several recent episodes in which he spontaneously brought up the death of his father in ways that demonstrated his newfound ability to grapple directly with that important piece of reality. On one occasion, Billy lay on his mother's bed and said, "This is Daddy's side of the bed." When she acknowledged that this was true, Billy said, "I'll just stay here until he gets back," to which his mother informed him, yet again, that his daddy wasn't coming back. Billy listened very thoughtfully as his mother explained again what had happened to his daddy. Billy then asked his mother if she felt sad. When she said she did (in fact, she was in tears at that moment), Billy said he felt sad, too, but "we still have our family." The next day at school, Billy spontaneously told the children in his preschool class that his father was dead. When one of the children protested, insisting, "I think that's pretend," Billy replied firmly, "No, it's not pretend. It's real." There then followed a discussion between the teacher and children about death and each child, in turn, gave Billy a hug. According to his teacher, this was the first time Billy had discussed his father in the classroom. She described it as a very heartfelt moment. She said she was especially impressed with Billy's ability to bear the obvious pain of what he was sharing without shutting down, a clear advance from his mode of relating in the previous year.

References

Alvarez, A. (1995). *Live company: Psychoanalytic psychotherapy with autistic, borderline, deprived, and abused children.* London, UK: Routledge.

Aron, L. (1990). One person and two person psychologies and the method of psychoanalysis. *Psychoanalytic Psychology*, 7:475–485.

Baron-Cohen, S. (1995). *Mindblindness: An essay on autism and theory of mind.* Cambridge, MA: MIT Press.

Bion, W. (1962). The psychoanalytic study of thinking. *International Journal of Psychoanalysis*, 43:306–310.

Cohen, P.M. & Solnit, A. (1993). Play and therapeutic action. *Psychoanalytic Study of the Child*, 48:49–63.

Dennett, D. (1987). *The intentional stance*. Cambridge, MA: MIT Press.

Fonagy, P. (1991). Thinking about thinking: Some theoretical and clinical considerations in the treatment of the borderline patients. *International Journal of Psychoanalysis*, 72:1–18.

Fonagy, P., Gergely, G., Jurist, E., & Target, M. (2002). *Affect regulation, mentalization, and the development of the self.* New York, NY: Other Press.

Fonagy, P. & Target, M. (1996). Playing with reality: I. Theory of mind and the normal development of psychic reality. *International Journal of Psychoanalysis*, 77:217–233.

Fonagy, P. & Target, M. (1998). Mentalization and the changing aims of child psychoanalysis. *Psychoanalytic Dialogues*, 8:87–114.

Freud, A. (1936). *The ego and the mechanisms of defense.* New York, NY: International Universities Press.

Freud, S. (1926). Inhibitions, symptoms, and anxiety. In: *The standard edition of the complete psychological works of Sigmund Freud* (pp. 77–172). London, UK: Hogarth Press.

Friedman, L. (1978). Trends in the psychoanalytic theory of treatment. *Psychoanalytic Quarterly*, 47:524–567.

Gergely, G. (2000). Reapproaching Mahler: New perspectives on normal autism, normal symbiosis, splitting, and libidinal object constancy from cognitive developmental theory. *Journal of the American Psychoanalytic Association*, 48:1197–1228.

Gergely, G. & Watson, J. (1996). The social biofeedback model of parental affect-mirroring. *International Journal of Psychoanalysis*, 77:1181–1212.

Goldman, A. (1992). In defense of simulation theory. *Mind and Language*, 7:104–119.

Gopnik, A. & Wellman, H.M. (1992). Why the child's theory of mind really is a theory. *Mind and Language*, 7:145–171.

Gopnik, A. (1996). Theories and modules: Creation myths, developmental realities, and Neurath's boat. In: P. Carruthers & P. K. Smith (Eds.), *Theories of theories of mind* (pp. 169–183). Cambridge, UK: Cambridge University Press.

Hoffman, I.Z. (1994). Dialectic thinking and therapeutic action in the psychoanalytic process. *Psychoanalytic Quarterly*, 63:187–218.

Hoffman, I.Z. (2006). Forging difference out of similarity: The multiplicity of corrective experience. *Psychoanalytic Quarterly*, 75:715–751.

Katz, G. (2014). *The play within the play*. New York, NY: Routledge.

Kennedy, H. (1979). The role of insight in child analysis: A developmental viewpoint. *Journal of the American Psychoanalytic Association*, 27:9–28.

Kohut, H. (1968). The psychoanalytic treatment of narcissistic personality disorders: Outline of a systematic approach. *Psychoanalytic Study of the Child*, 23:86–113.

Leslie, A. & Frith, U. (1988). Autistic children's understanding of seeing, knowing, and believing. *British Journal of Developmental Psychology*, 6:315–324.

Loewald, H. (1952). The problem of defense and the neurotic interpretation of reality. *International Journal of Psychoanalysis*, 33:442–449.

Loewald, H. (1960). On the therapeutic action of psychoanalysis. *International Journal of Psychoanalysis*, 41:16–33.

Mayes, L.C. & Cohen, D.J. (1993). Playing and therapeutic action in child analysis. *International Journal of Psychoanalysis*, 74:1235–1244.

Mitchell, S. (1997). *Influence and autonomy in psychoanalysis*. New York, NY: Routledge.

Neubauer, P. (1987). The many meanings of play – Introduction. *Psychoanalytic Study of the Child*, 42:3–9.

Perner, J., Frith, U., Leslie, A., & Leekham, S. (1989). Exploration of the autistic child's theory of mind: Knowledge, belief, and communication. *Child Development*, 60:689–700.

Ritvo, S. (1978). The psychoanalytic process in childhood. *Psychoanalytic Study of the Child*, 33: 295–305.

Rosegrant, J. (2001). The psychoanalytic play state. *Journal of Clinical Psychoanalysis*, 10:323–343.

Sugarman, A. (2003). A new model for conceptualizing insightfulness of young children. *Psychoanalytic Quarterly*, 72:325–355.

Trevarthen, C. (1985). Facial expressions of emotion in mother–infant interaction. *Human Neurobiology*, 4:21–32.

Vorus, N. (2011). Cultivating meaning space: Freudian and neo-Kleinian conceptions of therapeutic action. In: A. Druck, C. Ellman, N. Freedman, & A. Thaler (Eds.), *A new Freudian synthesis: Clinical process in the next generation* (pp. 219–238). London, UK: Karnac.

Winnicott, D.W. (1955). Metapsychological and clinical aspects of regression within the psychoanalytic set-up. *International Journal of Psychoanalysis*, 36:16–26.

Mutuality and the self in relation

Chapter 9

A child therapist at work

Playing, talking, and the therapist's inner dialogue[1]

Christopher Bonovitz, Psy.D.

The beginning

Jason, eight years old, walked into my office and scanned the room, appearing to check if anything might catch his interest. He was used to being dragged to many different types of professionals – occupational therapists, pediatricians, psychotherapists, tutors, psychiatrists, and so on – and I had the feeling that, for him, we were all interchangeable. He asked me to show him the various toys and games that I had and seemed willing to give me the opportunity to engage him. He was eager to find something that might capture his attention and I felt the pressure to come up with the necessary entertainment. He was rather chatty, asking me questions about my office and how things work and telling me about some of his animals. In fact, he loved animals. His guinea pigs, hamsters, dogs, and cat were his "friends," and he proudly took good care of them.

Throughout the first few sessions, Jason set up farm scenes with the toy animals, careful to lay out the perimeter of the farm with a sturdy fence. While the interactions with the animals were fairly benign, it was the fence that caught my attention. It did indeed look sturdy and I wondered about its place in our nascent treatment. In response to my asking him about the fence, he told me it was so the animals "do not walk away or get lost."

"What might happen if they do?" I queried.

"Then their owners might never find them again," he replied. He seemed very serious as he said this, conveying it as though he knew what this felt like. It seemed he was letting me know that it was going to be most critical that I help to maintain this fence, otherwise Jason might "walk away and get lost."

During the first several months of treatment, Jason seemed eager to dive in and get to know this situation and me as a new person, one who held the potential to be different from the other "boring people" he was "forced" to see. And, in turn, I felt the pressure to keep it going and the hope to distinguish myself from these other professionals. In his play, he often jumped from one thing to the next, disrupting narratives or games after beginning the story or setting them up. It felt as if he were conflicted in learning more about what might unfold.

Farm scenes such as the one mentioned above customarily ended with him randomly throwing the animals up in the air, scattering them across the rug. Games of *Connect Four* were abandoned regardless of whether or not he was winning. He interrupted any momentum or rhythm at the same time as he was desperately trying to form a connection. These kinds of disruptions sometimes came across as forced, pre-empting what might have been felt to be an inevitable and more terminal interruption.

With the disruption in play came the persistent question: "What else is there to do?" As long as I could come up with something that might hold Jason's attention, he looked forward to his visits, even mentioning on a few occasions, "I like it here." But I felt that my time was running out and the tension was building. I could sense my own anxiety with what might happen if I could not hold his attention, if the novelty and intrigue that were there in the beginning faded.

In this chapter, I explore my own thinking and ways of working with Jason, looking back on a treatment that has since ended. One implicit focus in revisiting this work is what my thought processes, imaginings, and associations were in relation to what I actually said and did with him. Across the various schools of thought, there is an interest in the relationship between the unspoken and spoken, how each influences the other. How do we negotiate these two interconnected yet separate realms? How much do we speak from what we are thinking or feeling in a given moment? To what extent is there a gap between what we are experiencing internally and what we say or do with the patient? And how does the dyad negotiate the anxieties and unarticulated affect states that move back and forth, the undercurrents of the exchange that are difficult to translate into words?

In the analyst's internal pool of thoughts and feelings are the threads to theory, metaphors that become an aid in organizing the clinical material as the analyst wades through the thicket of transference and countertransference, projections and introjections, and the interpenetration of the inner and outer worlds. The theory in this paper does not appear so much in the language of metapsychology or even theoretically based formulations, but more in the language and words I use to describe to myself what might be happening that have the ring of the theoretical influences on my thinking. My use of theory and the construction of metaphors within my own mind are shaped by the unfolding process between me and Jason and my attempt to navigate the lived experience of his internal objects along with the interpersonal exchanges that extend and move beyond the confines of these objects.

While any retrospective analysis of clinical material is at least in part influenced by the fact that it is taking place at a distance and away from the field of action, I have tried to flesh out as much as possible what was occurring in my internal dialogue, as well as step back at moments to describe how I was thinking and understanding some of my own affective experience in relation to Jason's. Though I regard this chapter as primarily clinical, my hope is that this segment of analytic work may be used to generate ideas around clinical theory in the treatment of children as well as adults.

Brief history

Jason was adopted from birth following an unwanted pregnancy. Born six weeks premature, underdeveloped, and with medical complications, he spent the first two months of his life in an incubator while in a neonatal intensive care unit (NICU). During that time, his newly adoptive mother and father visited him almost every day, spending long hours at the hospital, watching him but unable to hold him for any extended period of time. To this day, Jason has a tic in which he lifts his mouth up into the air as if reaching for something to put in it. He later developed the story that he "caught" his tic from the intensive care unit.

Jason's adoptive parents were well-meaning people who tried to conceive over a span of eight years, a time fraught with numerous miscarriages, unsuccessful in vitro fertilization treatments, and severe marital tension that accompanied this process. Jason's development was mildly delayed through the first years of his life, with delays in speech and fine motor coordination due to low muscle tone. He had a two-years-older brother who had been adopted as well from different birth parents and who did not have any developmental delays. From the parents' report, his brother was much "easier" and more "independent" than Jason.

Jason experienced tremendous difficulty in school and at home. He was easily frustrated and had frequent tantrums that consisted of yelling, throwing and breaking objects, and occasionally slamming his head against the wall. His parents described him as "never satisfied," inevitably becoming "bored" with everything around him. No one person or thing had any lasting value. From the time when he was about four years old, he was told about his adoption and given a version of the "facts" that helped to explain why he was given up by his birth mother. Though Jason had not asked his parents many questions, in the throes of his tantrums he often screamed out that he "hated" his adoptive mother and father and wished that he could live with his "real" mother who was "nicer" and would give him what he wanted. He could be denigrating toward his adoptive mother in particular, and did not allow her to comfort him when he was upset.[2]

Witnessing Jason's internal battle

As time moved forward in the treatment, Jason's initial intrigue eroded as he eventually grew tired of me, perhaps as a response to the possibility that something meaningful could take place between us. He was uninterested in my room and its toys and complained of feeling "bored" with "nothing to do." Akin to what his adoptive parents often mentioned, I felt as though I was not good enough, an incapable parent who was unable to establish a meaningful connection with him. And though some part of me had the sense that this change was our destiny from the beginning, I also experienced my own version of the disappointment that Jason felt; namely, that I had not fulfilled some wish of his that I could be different from the other professionals who had tried to help him.

The shift was precipitated by his family's vacation (the first one in the treatment), which resulted in our not meeting for two weeks. This disruption, along with my inability to keep up with his desperate hunger for novelty and my failed search to find something that had lasting value to him, gave rise to an intense futility and an agonizing frustration. The fence around the farm animals that he had constructed in our first session was metaphorically collapsing, which raised the question of whether I could now create a fence with him in the face of his emerging turbulence. I questioned to what extent I would be able to contain his affective surges and wondered how our own dyadic system and the shifts within it might form a fence of some kind.

In one session that took place after the vacation and around the time of Jason's increasing "boredom", I greeted him only to be met by his downcast eyes as he ploddingly followed me into the office. His pout and slump demonstrated that I was the last person in the world he wanted to see. I could not tell how much he was exaggerating his dislike of me so as to convince himself and me that it was all not worth it anymore. He walked as though he were being dragged, his head hanging, but from under his downcast eyelashes he snuck looks around the play area. Picking up a dinosaur with his fingertips, his expression suggesting he was holding a piece of rotten carrion, he screamed, "I hate being here. You made me miss my favorite television show. This is so boring!"

"What show?" I asked.

"Ghostbusters," he growled. This was not a bad nickname for a therapist. But who was the ghost that Jason and I were trying to "bust"? Were the ghosts of his birth mother or father lurking around? Was there the incarnation of the ghost in me? I could feel myself beginning to walk on eggshells, concerned that if I said the wrong thing he might explode. My thoughts were slowing down in the face of his disparagement and the ability to imagine and make associative connections in my mind felt impeded. I could feel my speech becoming slightly more forced and distant, not as much of a direct extension of my reflections.

Feeling unsure, and in a slightly dampened tone, I said, "It feels like I took something away from you that you like and now there is nothing to replace it."

Jason paused, then said, "You're stupid," and proceeded to wrap a boy figure in pipe cleaners until he was completely covered from head to toe – a mummified boy. For a fleeting moment, I had the picture of the neonatal intensive care unit and the incubator in which Jason had spent the first two months of his life. This image quickly evaporated when Jason looked at me with a steely gleam in his eyes. With the mummified boy clutched in his hand, he fiercely declared, "This is my brother."

With these words, Jason tied a string to his wrapped "brother" – the older brother who had an easier time of it and was the preferred sibling in Jason's eyes – and proceeded to swing him around the room, flinging him into walls and stomping on him. There was ferocity in Jason's play, a sadistic glee tinged with a feeling of righteousness for all the teasing and humiliation his brother had wreaked on him. "This is what you get for making fun of me and taking my stuff!" Jason yelled as he whipped his "brother" across the floor. Witnessing this, I was imagining his "brother" getting flung around and then lying on the floor. I was imagining the kind of humiliation Jason may have felt in relation to his brother, envious of his ease as well as humiliated by the ways in which Jason fell short of him. I could sense the depth of Jason's rage and the presence of my own anxiety that crept in as I contemplated what I might be faced with if I did not give him what he wanted or if what I had to give was inadequate. For a moment, I wondered if he was also communicating to me what I may have to endure with him; was I going to be receptive to this same kind of treatment? A fleeting image of my own brother arrived, as well as my identification with Jason at his age in relation to a brother who could do no wrong.

Life for his older brother was free of the complications that came with the developmental delays and temperamental vulnerabilities with which Jason had to contend. His envy was palpable in relation to his brother, and perhaps toward me as well for seemingly having more. Jason's envious attacks were of the pernicious kind, the kind of envy that resided in an enclosed inner world where I existed as more of an object. He appeared to be in the throes of making a desperate attempt to "kill off" his brother. If he could psychically kill his brother, then he would not have to feel the agonizing pain his envy brought with it. The chaotic nature of his play felt as though he were enacting a trauma of sorts, or perhaps a disorganized attachment style that pervaded his relationships.

In his fury, I sensed how the play could come to feel less symbolic, with objects drained of psychic representation and multiple meanings. My reflective mental space closed up alongside Jason's attacks; there was just his physicality to respond to, as I was unable to see beyond his behavior. I could no longer play in my mind and was unable to create meaning from what was transpiring between us.

In the midst of torturing his "brother", and with more time left in the session, Jason stopped midstream to ask, "Can I just go now?" It was another sudden stop and I felt taken aback. My thoughts at a standstill, with the feeling of being one step behind and unable to catch up, I wondered whether he wanted to leave before even more destruction took place. Had he become frightened of this surge of rage? Was this his way of trying to put on the brakes? Or was there some part of me that wanted him to leave and to what extent was he reacting to that feeling in me?

Jason continued in an accusatory tone of voice, "You make me think of all these sad memories – like my pet frog dying – and I just want them to get out of my head." In that moment, I could feel the sadness as the climate in the room quietly shifted. The word "dying" lingered. Who was dying? Who had already died? If he became more attached to me, could I die or go away as his birth mother had? What was the nature of these "sad memories"? I felt as if my presence and desire to know were inflicting these memories onto him, a retraumatization of sorts. Memories and the past pained him and if I were to embody pieces of his history I was also going to come into conflict with the part of him that wanted to attack its presence in me.

As I wondered if he was angry with me for making him think about the things he did not want to remember, he interrupted to ask, "Can I take something home with me?" This was a demand masquerading as a question. I felt both a sense of urgency in the question and the pressure to acquiesce, as denying his request might further incite him. Before I could even respond, he retrieved a stuffed salamander from the shelf and held it up. As he did this, I commented that it seemed he was determined to take the salamander before I had a chance to answer his question about whether or not he could take it. He bellowed in a commanding voice, "I need it!" It seemed that his intense need here trumped the process of giving and receiving, a process that would give rise to the possibility of rejection and exclusion. With his demand making it difficult for me to process the exchange, I commented about his wish to make the sad memories go away, to which he pleaded once again, "Can I please just take it home?" The request felt desperate, as though something of great consequence was at stake.

With time winding down and my next appointment waiting, formulating anything of substance seemed futile. I felt stuck, trapped in the face of his urgent request. In the end, I said, "You can borrow it as long as you bring it back next time." As I told him this (in what sounded even to my ears as school-marmish tones), I had the sinking feeling that this could very well be the last time I ever saw my salamander. As Jason clutched the salamander in his hand and I bid farewell to both of them, there emerged a hint of scorn on Jason's face. I felt I had given in and perhaps he was in conflict as to whether he really did want me to allow him to take the salamander with him.

I had acquiesced and in doing so I took the easier route rather than be faced with Jason's aggression for denying him what felt so critical at that moment. But what was the sense of urgency about in that moment? Jason had more toys than anyone I knew, with objects repeatedly losing their value after a day or two, replaced by something new and better, only then to be disposed of shortly thereafter – possibly a cycle designed to avoid the experience of absence. Had I colluded with this avoidance in allowing him to take the salamander home?

An attack on linking and a search for connection

As the door shut and Jason departed my office clutching my amphibian friend, I felt as though I had been coerced, allowing him to take something of mine without my having fully given it to him. Though of course I had said he could take the salamander with him, I was unable to sift through my thoughts at the time as to whether I had wanted to give it to him or not. I had submitted to the pressure and weight of his desperate plea and, in the process, compromised my own conflicting feelings about it. I was unable to contain the conflict. It was as if I could only comply with the demand. And, yet, to say "no" in retrospect may have felt like I was reinflicting the experience of making him feel his own unfulfilled need in that moment, imposing the feeling of hunger and absence without the temporary and fleeting sense of satisfaction.

Following Jason's departure, I wondered if I would ever see my salamander again. Was Jason giving me the experience of what it felt like to have something that felt rightfully mine taken away (possibly a reference to his birth mother), not knowing if I would ever get it back? And yet I had allowed him to take the salamander, so was I in some way to blame for being without? And was it the case that my salamander, once in his grasp, no longer carried any meaning or value, that it would become yet another meaningless object? Our interaction around the salamander had turned the exchange of giving and receiving into my feeling that it had been "taken" from me. For him to feel that it was being given to him would change the whole scenario and its meaning, as for him to acknowledge receiving an object not only might incite more intense need in relation to me, but also might imbue the object with more value and therefore make him feel more of his own dependency and attachment to me.

On the one hand, throughout the session reported above, Jason was attacking the connection he was forming with me by disrupting the momentum of a play scene or game. His sudden stops stymied my own thought process and his attacks on linking (Bion, 1959) made it difficult for me to think and imagine when with him. I was unable to contain the projections in his communication, unable to hold on to the various pieces of unprocessed emotional experience that were in need of a receptor site within me. His actions had not yet found a home in our interactive minds as a "thinking couple" (Brown, 2009, 2010).

On the other hand, Jason's actions embodied perseverance, a relentless search not just for more or to fill an internal void, but for meaning and understanding, to establish a link or connection that he could hold on to and preserve. There was something hopeful in his relentlessness. Jason was desperately trying to find ways to communicate his inner experience to me and only by doing so could he begin to mend the disrepair with which he lived. The request for the salamander might even be regarded as a creative attempt in communicating an experience he did not yet have the words for, to convey the sense of urgency and the feeling of having something taken away with the uncertainty of whether or not it would ever return.

While there certainly appeared to be intense envy of his brother, I wondered about Jason's relationship to his adoption as well. Was his desperate need to fend off absence and loss somehow connected to his birth mother whom he had never met? Was she the idealized object that he clung to, not settling for anything less? Might there be a hopefulness embedded in his envy and the tenacious search for this lost object?

The emergence of the baby and the birth mother

As expected, in the session following its departure from my office, the salamander did not make it back. Jason shrugged his shoulders in telling me that he had no idea where it was. In hearing this, I felt a little silly having even asked about it. From his lackluster response, he convincingly conveyed that the salamander was the furthest thing from his mind, as though he had no idea what I was talking about. What had felt so urgent at the end of the prior session now had the appearance of being forgotten. I was aware that the feeling of the salamander being missing and the uncertainty of whether it would ever return was located in me, with Jason seemingly detached from it. I felt absence, but he had moved on.

"What do you care anyway? There's other stuff here," Jason asserted.

Then, as if to show me how destructive he could be, he randomly grabbed toys out of the chest, one by one, held them up to his face for a closer inspection, and then proceeded to hurl each one across the room. Superheroes, race cars, and wrestlers went whizzing along the rug or catapulted through the air, landing on the floor and skidding into the wall. With each throw, he yelled in an angry, aching voice how much he hated my "stupid toys!" Jason's angry pain and sadness were palpable and left me with the feeling that my presence was a constant reminder of what was missing. It was as if he were recreating a traumatic scene, with me as witness to the chaos and aggression that accompanied it.

With words unable to capture the depth and charge of affect flying around, I struggled to find a verbal medium. In calling attention to his attempt to mess everything up so there would be nothing left that he wanted, he responded by grabbing one of the wrestler action figures and breaking its arm off. The one-armed wrestler lay on the ground with his dismembered arm a few yards away. I was thrown off balance by Jason's outburst, anxious about how far this could go, and controlled by the power in it. I reiterated the parameters in order for him to feel safe with his own aggressive impulses, as well as for me to feel that there were limits as to what he could do. Glancing over at the wrestler who had just lost his arm, I had the fleeting thought as to whether Jason felt handicapped in some way, without full mobility and constrained by his limitations. Accompanying this thought was my identification with the wrestler's broken arm in that moment, as the arm captured my struggle in holding on to my thoughts – as though some of my thinking had been severed just as the wrestler's arm had been.

When I remarked on the change in him since returning from his vacation – how he had gone from wanting to see me to finding it so incredibly boring – he at first pretended not to hear me. In prodding him more, he told me that he was "bothered" by my "voice" and that I spoke to him as if he were a "baby." The word "baby" had gravity to it. "Your voice sounds like this—" and he then proceeded to raise his voice a few octaves that did indeed make it sound as though I were speaking to a two-year-old. I considered what it was in me and the situation that transported him to this self-state. Was there some unconscious wish in him to be my baby, perhaps to revisit being a baby?

I cringed a bit in hearing Jason's imitation of me and wondered if my "baby voice" was an attempt on my part to diminish his power, to make him more of a baby in the face of his eruption. I was also aware upon hearing his imitation of me that this was the first time he had made a specific reference to some quality about my person. He went on to say, "I sometimes wish I could be with my first mom … I miss her. I want to see what she looks like." There was a wistful tone in his voice. A moment later, he added that his adoptive parents (whom he referred to as his "mom" and "dad") sometimes were not as "nice" to him as his "first mom" would be. "I wish I could see her," he said quietly. When I asked him what he imagined she looked like, he paused and then said, "She is really pretty and has long hair."

Though I was aware through the various accounts and in my meeting with his adoptive parents that in fact they were quite loving and well meaning, I could begin to see how he harbored this image of his birth mother as someone who was somehow "better". And though he had had no contact with her since his birth (and had not seen any photographs of her), he had nevertheless developed a picture of her in his imagination. She came "first" in his mind, and her ambiguousness lent itself to a fantasy that he carried around with him. This was one of the few occasions when he made this fantasy explicit, as I had the sense that this conception of his "first" mother existed in a private place in his mind and yet fueled his rejection of those who loved and cared for him. Whatever bad feelings he had regarding being given up, the splitting he employed allowed him to preserve his birth mother as an idealized fantasy object, and to denigrate his adoptive parents as well as me in the transference.

In the following session, there was more continuity as Jason continued with the theme of babies. "I didn't like it when I was a baby," he announced shortly after the session began. When I asked him what he thought (imagined), he told me that it was "cold" in the room where he was born. As he said this, an image arrived in my mind of a room full of babies in incubators, surrounded by glass walls with adults peering in, looking but unable to touch – a cold, sterile room. The sensory surround made the image feel more three-dimensional. I echoed the word "cold" as the temperature settled into the image, to which he said, "I think my first mom was watching me, but then I never saw her again."

As Jason said this, he sat very still, the stillest I had ever seen him, and looked at me with his sunken eyes. A heavy sadness moved in. Then, turning away from me, he said, "I was a broken baby," and he started to tear up. I felt heartbroken and pained by his words.

The shame of being given up

Across the next string of sessions, Jason ushered out the "pretty," "nice," "first" mother of his, the one preserved as the imagined good object, as a way to possibly manage this ambiguous loss. Everyone else fell short as compared with her. Along with this maternal object came the baby, a baby who in Jason's narrative was alone in a "cold" room with his birth mother watching him. In beginning to reimagine what he experienced, he made contact with his longing for her, for her to hold him, to reach through the glass and feel the warmth of her body. Here, desire and longing were closer to their pure forms, with his "first mom" watching him through the glass, someone whom he wants but cannot have because she goes away never to be seen again. With this imagining, he began making a story about his adoption and, in the process, I felt less confined by his communications and with more room to imagine with him.

There was the presence of shame associated with his birth mother giving him up, the feeling of being watched but not claimed as her own, a "broken baby" who felt damaged inside. The closed system that had been more pronounced in relation to me as an object was momentarily breached as he struggled to contain the experience of loss and shame within an interpersonal situation in relation to me as the "perceived other" who bears witness to these bad feelings in him. I experienced myself more as a subject than an object as he told me this dream-thought. I felt a greater capacity for reverie as the projected pieces of his experience congealed around the image of him in the intensive care unit. The chaotic action and streaming movement that had been the scene for his confusion and aggressive play morphed into thought and reflection with his mother and me watching him. The pathways between our minds around this image had opened up, with there being a greater receptivity in me as we became a thinking couple looking in on this baby in the "cold" room, processing previously unrepresented experience and, in doing so, beginning to create a narrative together.

And as Jason watched his birth mother watch him, the splitting that had existed before began to loosen some, making room for longing and separation. In the process, he allowed me to watch him so we could witness together this baby reaching out to be held.

Creating a new medium for communication

As the treatment moved forward, Jason became very interested in YouTube, spending hours watching videos and showing me his latest discoveries. During one particular session, he asked if he could borrow my smartphone to watch his latest interest, a series of animated videos about a duck. With much enthusiasm and anticipation, he told me how much he liked these videos and proceeded to play one of them for me called The Duck Story.

Set within bright, colorful spring scenery, The Duck Story was about a duck that waddles over to a lemonade stand and asks the man, "Got any grapes?" The man tells him that he only sells lemonade and so the duck "waddled away, waddle waddle, 'til the very next day..." (The words are strung together in a catchy, playful tune.) The duck is persistent, returning several times thereafter "and said to the man running the stand, 'Got any grapes?'" Each time the man grows increasingly irritated by the duck's repeated requests and by having to reassert that he only sells lemonade. At one point, the man threatens to glue him to a tree, telling the duck, "So don't get too close," to which the duck replies, "Adios." But the duck is not deterred; returning once again to ask the man for grapes, the man finally relents, taking him to the store "so he won't have to ask anymore." After buying him grapes – the very thing he has been nagging the man for all this time – the duck changes his tune and asks for lemonade. The man is at his wit's end by this point.

This was a creative act on Jason's part, finding a medium through this video where he and I could look at his requests in relation to me (perhaps with Jason as the duck and me as the man running the lemonade stand). Just as we had looked in on him as a baby in the intensive care unit, he had created another tableau for us to look at together, to aid in visually representing something he was trying to understand and give meaning to. The duck, like Jason, was stuck asking for what the man (me) was unable to give, and then when he finally finds a way to give the duck what he's been asking for (grapes), the duck asks for the lemonade. And judging by the man's irritation with the duck, Jason was maybe alerting me to my own irritation with him from our own version of this scenario in the past, with more irritation present in me than I may have been aware of. I could immediately see not only why Jason loved this story, but also why he wanted to play it for me over and over. I was amused and taken with his delight in the video. It was rare to see him so unabashedly joyful.

Asking him about the duck in the context of the story, Jason explained that the duck is never satisfied and that he "annoys" the man because he only wants what the man can't give him.

"Why is that?" I asked.

"Well, I think the duck is really sad, because he can't have everything … he'll never be able to have everything." As he said this, Jason's voice became quieter. I was moved by Jason's quiet reflections.

"But what is it he really wants that he can't find or get?" I asked him.

"I wish I could find my first mom and ask her why she didn't want to keep me," he said as his eyes welled up. I felt that Jason was letting me in, allowing himself to experience this loss and his sadness in my presence and to be curious about his "first mom's" state of mind. Unsure how far we might venture into this territory, I asked him what he thought as to why his first mom gave him up, to which he responded, "I don't know, but maybe I can find out someday."

As the session wound down, Jason gathered his things and, before departing, looked at me and said, "Got any grapes?" We both chuckled, but the sadness in Jason's tone remained and I could see him struggling with what this all meant to him.

Through the development of The Duck Story and the extended reach of Jason's mind to make room for reflection and the use of my mind, he was exploring the psychic relationship with his birth mother by imagining his way into her mind. In recognizing my own otherness that included my flaws as well (voice intonation, etc.), he was now starting to create a reflective space within his own mind and between us for the emotional complications associated with his "first mom." Whereas love and hate had been split prior to this string of sessions, with the maternal object one dimensional and idealized (the image he had been holding on to while disposing of any contact that was felt to be a poor substitute), his growing capacity to think about the subjective state of the other – asking his "first mom" why she "didn't want to keep me" – softened his defenses, as there became less of a sense of urgency to ward off loss. Jason's question about his "first mom" became the seed of a developing narrative, a dream that the analytic space could host as it grew over time. With the evolving story about his birth mother, not only did I become more of a subject to him, but the shift began to open him up as well, making more possible as he developed a growing receptivity to the fullness of others.

Gratitude and the salamander's return

The school year was winding down and the coming summer break meant Jason and I would be apart for several months. In one of our last sessions before the end of the school year, Jason appeared at my office door with the salamander in hand. He quietly told me that he had found it in his desk. Needless to say, I was taken aback, as I had all but given up on the salamander by this point, imagining that it had made its way to the trash or was buried underneath candy wrappers in his school desk. I said to him that I thought he had forgotten all about it, to which he replied, "I did for a while. I didn't care at all about it. It wasn't what I thought it was going to be. But then I realized that there was something about him that I liked."

"What?" I asked.

He said the salamander felt "softer" than it did before and that he was glad to have found him. Considering the salamander as a parting gift of sorts, an expression of gratitude that he had not been able to previously muster, I had the thought that perhaps in some way not only had he rediscovered the salamander, but also together we had retrieved a lost part of Jason.

Notes

1 This chapter was first published as Bonovitz, C. (2015). A child therapist at work: Playing, talking, and the therapist's inner dialogue. *Psychoanalytic Dialogues*, 25:18–28. Reprinted by kind permission of the journal and Taylor & Francis, LLC.
2 While I worked closely with Jason's parents throughout the treatment, my primary focus for the purposes of this chapter is my individual work with Jason.

References

Bion, W.R. (1959). Attacks on linking. *International Journal of Psychoanalysis*, 40:308–315.

Brown, L.J. (2009). Bion's ego psychology: Implications for an intersubjective view of psychic structure. *Psychoanalytic Quarterly*, 78:27–55.

Brown, L.J. (2010). Klein, Bion, and intersubjectivity: Becoming, transforming, and dreaming. *Psychoanalytic Dialogues*, 20:669–682.

Chapter 10

The origins of relationality

The role of pre- and perinatal experience in the structure, psychopathology, and treatment of the relational self[1]

Brent Willock, Ph.D.

Life before birth

"The ego [the I] is first and foremost a bodily ego," Freud (1923) asserted. In a footnote, he clarified: "...i.e. the ego is ultimately derived from bodily sensations, chiefly from those springing from the surface of the body" (p. 26). Six decades later, Thomas Ogden (1989), synthesizing findings from two decades of research in the British Object Relations tradition, postulated similarly that the earliest sense of self derives from contact sensations that gradually give rise to a fundamental sense of a *bounded* sensory surface on which one's experience occurs – the beginnings of a feeling of "the place where we live" (Winnicott, 1971, p. 104). From a sophisticated neo-Kleinian perspective, he proposed the utility of thinking of an *autistic-contiguous position*, a psychic state having primacy prior to the paranoid-schizoid (PS) and depressive (D) positions, though always operating in dialectic tension with them.

The examples that Ogden provided to illustrate his elegant construct suggest that he saw this sensory surface self arising in the context of postnatal interactions (e.g. the baby's cheek on the mother's breast; continuity and predictability derived from the rhythmicity and regularity of sucking; rhythmic cooing dialogue with the mother; feelings of edgedness generated by the infant's gums pressing tightly on the mother's nipple or finger). Extending that perspective back in time, in earlier publications (Willock, 2007, 2015), I highlighted the *prenatal* origins of this autistic-contiguous self.

In this chapter, I will explore the relevance of the autistic-contiguous position for working with children (and adults) whose development has been interfered with by very early developmental trauma. To this end, I will draw on Christopher Bonovitz's (2015) thoughtful clinical work with eight-year-old Jason, supplemented by vignettes from patients with whom I have worked and others reported in the literature.

Dr. Bonovitz's understanding of his young patient's difficulties focused on the loss of his biological mother through adoption at birth. Complementing that formulation, I propose that Jason's core trauma may concern an even more fundamental relational experience. Rather than the loss of his mother per se, could he have been traumatized by the disruption to autistic-contiguity occasioned by the premature loss of his first home, the womb?

In keeping with a contemporary relational and comparative–integrative perspective, I will argue that Jason's premature birth not only interfered with the development of the sensory-based ego ("I") that Freud emphasized, but that it also simultaneously obstructed primal relationality (autistic-contiguity). In accord with this idea, Frances Tustin (1981) spoke of *sensation objects* as the relational complement to the *autosensuous self.* She noted that Winnicott (1958a) demonstrated awareness of this aspect of primitive relationality with his term *subjective object.* Extending Kohut's (1977) ideas concerning the role of selfobjects way back in time, one could say that the foundational separation involved in problematic premature birth is the most fundamental selfobject failure.

Expanding on Spitz's (1965) concept of the *pre-object* and de Jonghe, Rijnierse, and Janssen's (1991) idea of *pre-object relatedness,* Ivri Kumin (1995) described the *primary relatedness* (Kinston & Cohen, 1986) that is present at birth and persists throughout life as the background core, the sense of "being there" and "being with" that accompanies all experience. *Proto-object* relatedness might be an even better term, he suggested, since *proto* means the first or earliest form of something whereas *pre* means in advance of or prior to something. His distinction fits with Ogden's view that this early aspect of relatedness continues throughout the life cycle.

In Ogden's comprehensive framework, the three basic psychological organizations (autistic-contiguous, PS, and D) are always dialectically present, in varying proportions. Each generates a characteristic form of relationship and anxiety. In the autistic-contiguous position, the experience of impending or actual disintegration of one's sensory surface or "rhythm of safety" (Tustin, 1986) results in feelings of leaking, dissolving, disappearing, or falling into endless unbounded space. In Jason's case, I argue that premature rupture of psychobiological containment and sensory contiguity with the womb triggered this terror that his nascent self could depart its autistic-container eternally. In efforts to bridge this breach during his first eight years, he desperately deployed whatever primitive resources he could muster. Finally, in treatment, the right relational conditions were provided for containing and revisiting these anxieties, revising problematic defensive adaptations, and fostering psychological growth.

Perinatal life

Early in Bonovitz's case report, we learn that following an unwanted pregnancy, Jason's mother and her boyfriend gave him up for adoption. Six weeks premature, he spent the first two months of his life in an incubator while in a neonatal intensive care unit (NICU). His adoptive parents visited daily. In long hours at the hospital, they were unable to hold him. Jason believes he "caught" a tic in that NICU. In this motoric habit that he still had when Bonovitz met him, Jason lifts his mouth up into the air as if reaching for something to put in it.

Entering the world with preconceptions, we are psychobiologically preprogrammed to anticipate and respond appropriately to the mother's nurturing breast (Bion, 1962a). When preconception meets realization, a concept (the breast) is born. Out of initial formlessness, a world gradually forms.

What happens when preconception fails to meet realization, when one does not land in Hartmann's (1939) "average expectable environment," when there is excessive difference between original and subsequent milieus? Jason's story reveals what can occur. Spending his first eight weeks in what Sylvia Plath might describe as a bell jar, he experienced something other than an optimally warm, fleshy, nurturing, blessedly scented, human holding environment. This disjunctive start was, I believe, captured in his tic. Repeatedly, Jason lifts his mouth into the air, hoping to encounter something good, only to find nothing. For eight years, this idiosyncratic movement memorialized that anticipated moment of meeting, the time when preconception met absence. This motoric symptom keeps his original hope alive as a dissociated yearning, a perpetual possibility.

Embodying our inborn capacity for repetition compulsion (Freud, 1920) in the service of mastering trauma, Jason's tic embodies the peremptory human need to perpetually return to the "valley of the shadow of death" in hopes of finding something essential to rectify and restore the self. He had to try repetitively to locate some object (nipple) to plug the hole in his self – an oral means of remedying peri-natal trauma.

Not many subscribe to Freud's speculations concerning a death instinct related to repetition compulsion. Nonetheless, in his phylo-genetic fantasy concerning the first living organism's plight in the face of the overwhelming stimulation it encountered, there are parallels to Jason's situation. He, too, entered the world with less than the requisite capacities for coping with stimulation (and the lack thereof) needed to ensure good enough transition from aqueous to terrestrial milieus. He encountered something other than an average expectable environment, with less than average expectable capacities. Finding some successor to the womb's containment, comfort, contiguity, and nurturance was a matter of life or death.

Emigrating from the uterus to the incubator, I believe Jason could not find the anticipated loving, breast-filled arms of a human mother. This breach with expectation challenged his beginning, bounded self based on sensory contact with uterine walls, amniotic fluid, and so forth. Womb loss, combined with violation of breast expectation, constituted a crisis. Urgent repair was required. To fill the hole in the fundamental fabric of his being, he summoned an autosensuous solution, creating a symptomatic safety net – his tic. Failing to find his life-sustaining human object, he resorted to self-generated stimu-lation – something he could control. This emergency operation drew on prenatal experience – a time when it was unclear whether stimu-lation derived from contact with self or other (from touching one's body, the uterine wall, or the umbilical cord). The feeling of contact and the sense of self it gave rise to were what mattered. In that unlit universe, we see as "through a glass darkly," not yet "face to face" (1 Corinthians). In that realm of "primary harmonious interpenetrating mix-up" (Balint, 1968), the autistic-contiguous position rules.

From this point of view, Jason's defensive maneuver (tic) is partially a back-to-the-womb phenomenon (Guntrip, 1969), a symptomatic "regression for the sake of [survival and] progression" (Balint, 1968).

It frantically attempts to repair the autistic-contiguous foundation needed to "go on being" (Winnicott, 1958b, p. 303), to stay sufficiently the same while changing (Bromberg, 1998).

In Freudian terms, Jason's tic "hallucinates the breast". His head rises repeatedly to meet Mama's mammary in what ethnologists call *in vacuo* activity. These biologists report on how birds confined in a giant dome devoid of flying bugs eventually enact their customary flight patterns, searching for, seizing, and swallowing *imaginary* insects. In this "non-average expectable environment", frustrated birds "hallucinate" needed objects. In Jason's vacuous milieu, he similarly "senses" and reaches out for the object biological programming led him to expect.

Since hallucinations (like Jason's tic) do not satisfy fully or for long, we are prompted to turn to reality to seek more sustaining nutriment, Freud stated. When we meet Jason, he has turned to the real world with a vengeance. Unable to find what he needs (heirs to sensory contiguity with the womb, such as the longed-for breast), he is easily and frequently frustrated at home and at school. Yelling and hurling and breaking objects, he also slams his head against walls. "Never satisfied," he becomes "bored" with everything; nothing has lasting value, his parents report.

Caught in traumatic time, Jason's life is suspended between a tic and the void. He is condemned to repetitively revisit the primal crime scene, the moment when the sacred covenant of preprogrammed expectations for sufficient sensory contiguity and for the breast was broken. Months of therapy will be necessary before he can articulate this tragedy as the moment when he became a "broken baby."

From the age of four, Jason was told of his adoption, including why he had been given up. During outbursts, he often screamed that he hated his new parents, wishing he could live with his "real" mother who, he claimed, was nicer. She would give him what he wanted (contiguity, secure holding, the breast, and all derivatives thereof). Particularly denigrating his adoptive mother, he would not allow her to comfort him when he was upset.

"Nature abhors a vacuum," early scientists proclaimed. Into Jason's vacuous world, Klein's bad breast rushes. Any plug, even the bad breast, is better than a hole in the autistic-contiguous membrane. From this perspective, in his tantrums, his adoptive mother might represent the unsatisfying, mechanical, non-womb, non-good-breast, hated NICU experience. Assigned that role, how could she soothe? In contrast, the vanished biological mother might represent the split-off, idealized, reparative, good Mama promising "restoration of the [broken] self" (Kohut, 1977). While Jason never knew his birth mother postnatally, his fantasy of her helps fill the void first encountered in premature transfer from womb to incubator.

Winnicott (1963) usefully differentiated the "environment mother" from the developmentally later "object mother." Jason speaks of his biological mother as if she were his object mother. He laments separation from a pretty, long-haired woman. I believe this beautiful lady is a stand-in for something more fundamental. For defensive purposes, he confuses a more oedipal, object mother (attractive, long-haired woman) with a developmentally earlier, far less differentiated, autistic-contiguous environment mother. He can call upon this fantasy mother when he needs something solid to stuff the hole in his self-membrane. In his tantrums, the intense physical sensations he generates are likely even more important than the visual aspects of his pretty biological mother. These outbursts appear to be noisy versions of his quiet tic.

Patients often cling to higher ground, such as a seemingly oedipal-level object, as a defense against succumbing to earlier terrors (Fairbairn, 1952; Guntrip, 1969). Rather than being oedipally organized, Jason was usually more like a fish out of water, struggling to get supplies needed, like oxygen, to survive. In his turmoil, he was sometimes mistaken as to what would truly fill the void. Nothing he found satisfied for long. Nonetheless, various entities (like his beautiful birth mother image) temporarily helped him avoid more profound horrors – Winnicott's (1974) "primitive agonies" and Bion's (1962b) "nameless dreads."

In the above (and what will follow), some might find it unusual to bring together Freudian, Kleinian, British Object Relational, self psychological, and other schools of thought. From a comparative–integrative perspective (Willock, 2007), multiple viewpoints provide fuller, more multidimensional understanding of complex phenomena.

The opening act

Jason's first sessions featured fenced-in farm animals. Bonovitz's attention was especially caught by the enclosure. It kept animals from walking away and getting lost, whereupon "their owners might never find them again," Jason said. Bonovitz believed his patient was communicating that it would be critical to help maintain this structure, otherwise he and Jason might be separated.

Anticipated breakdown typically represents one that happened long ago (Winnicott, 1974). Snared in trauma, past, present, and future merge in a timeless trap. I would therefore complement Bonovitz's future-oriented understanding of fence failing with the idea that Jason was simultaneously conveying his core trauma – disintegration of his primal (womb) boundary. From this viewpoint, the fallible fence represents the line between his nascent autistic-contiguous self and the void. He must strive to maintain this damaged boundary that has already leaked essential self components and may fail to contain what remains.

"*Après moi, le déluge*," Louis XIV proclaimed, perhaps fusing birth and death imagery. Jason's narrative similarly suggests a time when natal and thanatotic anxieties intermingled. The therapeutic challenge, as I see it, will be to recapture aspects of his autistic-contiguous self (*le moi*) that was severely tried, significantly contorted, partially lost, and primitively patched in the deluge of premature birth.

Jason's agrarian scenarios typically terminated when he randomly threw all the animals into the air. Games were similarly abandoned, regardless of whether he was winning or losing. These actions interrupted any momentum, connection, or rhythm that had been established. Relational rhythm (Tustin's [1986] "rhythm of safety") is a core component of secure autistic-contiguity. Abandoning activities, Jason typically asked what else there was to do, seeming to hope activity might fill these "self-precipitated" gaps in the continuity of *being*.

In these premature play disruptions (Erikson, 1950), Jason functions in the traumatic zone beyond the pleasure principle (Freud, 1920). He endeavors to master anticipated discontinuity by causing it, rather than waiting to become the passive, overwhelmed victim. "Choosing" the defense of turning passive into active (Freud, 1948), explosive endings beat being blindsided.

Countertransference clues

For the first several months, Bonovitz felt pressure to keep something good going. In my mind, this experience parallels the biological mother's (ambivalent) wish to sustain her pregnancy. From this perspective,

Bonovitz was struggling to hold on to his fetus and avoid fence breach (miscarriage). He was nervous. What might happen if he could not hold Jason's attention? In this antediluvian anxiety, doomsday will surely arrive. "My time was running out, and the tension was building," he shared ominously.

Bonovitz wondered about how dyads negotiate the anxieties and unarticulated affect states that move back and forth, the undercurrents of the exchange that are difficult to translate into words. Central to these challenges are terrors unleashed when there is a felt breach in the rhythms ("undercurrents of the exchange") and sensory contact ("difficult to translate into words") that characterize autistic-contiguous, fragmentable bedrock (toys scattered every which way).

Like the folkloric Dutch boy who shoved his finger into a dyke hole to prevent catastrophic flooding (the deluge), with primordial fence failures we use whatever we can. Bodily features and functions are usually closest at hand. With Jason's tic and other omnipotent defenses, he endeavored similarly to pack the hole in his self-boundary to prevent his nascent self being swept away in a traumatic tsunami.

Bonovitz began thinking he was not good enough. He felt like an incapable parent, unable to establish a meaningful connection. This unsettling shift, or intensification in the countertransferential therapeutic ambience, was precipitated by Jason's family's first vacation. Tentative though the analytic matrix (from Greek *metra*, meaning womb) was, it had managed to some degree to contain "the anxieties and unarticulated affect states that move back and forth, the undercurrents of the exchange that are difficult to translate into words." The holiday disrupted the therapeutic frame's autistic-contiguous rhythms, exposing weakness in the analytic membrane. Fraying threads in the psychanalytic fabric raised the specter that the animals (Jason and Bonovitz, hitherto contained and sustained in their regular, reliable space) could depart from their fence forever.

Jason's vacation and Bonovitz's "inability to keep up with his desperate hunger for novelty and failed search to find something that was lastingly satisfying to him, gave rise to an intense futility and an agonizing frustration." Bonovitz's words suggest his powerful identification with Jason's failed, postnatal search for the new environment mother – the novel "good breast", heir to the good womb – needed to bridge/heal the autistic-contiguous breach.

Carrion culture

Post-vacation, Jason's body language conveyed that Bonovitz was the last person in the world he wanted to see. With their regular contact rhythm disrupted, his analyst seemed to become as undesirable as the NICU. While Bonovitz may have incubated positive feelings and hopes during their separation, something very different brewed in his young patient's soul.

With his fingertips, Jason held a toy dinosaur as if it were a piece of "rotten carrion." Hollering that he hated being in Bonovitz's office (incubator), he complained that his therapist made him miss his favorite television show. With these words and actions, Jason conveyed his reawakened sense of unbearable separation. Deprived of his environment mother (transferentially via vacation), he was struggling to defend against shock. In his "new" milieu, he found nothing promising to hang on to. Grasping at straws, he clutched a metaphorically disintegrating entity – rotten carrion – that embodied his dissolving, autistic-contiguous, primal sense of self.

Always attuned to the intersubjective field, Bonovitz encapsulated its subtleties in strikingly evocative language (dinosaur as putrefying flesh). In the earliest stages of development, self and object are organized as relatively undifferentiated events (Fast, 1985). This nascent structure permits fluid, primary process, self-protective, identificatory shifts when needed. In the prehistoric raptor image, hinting at the basic struggle for survival, Jason could be everything, the whole event (primary narcissism). Rather than being carrion, he could selectively narrow his focus to become the omnipotent metabeing holding the dinosaur's fate in his hands. He could drop, devour, or otherwise devastate his totally controlled captive. "He's got the whole world in His hands ... He's got the itty bitty baby in His hands ... He's got the whole world in His hands" (American spiritual).

The mummy

What happens when Jason puts himself in charge of the "itty bitty baby's" fate? He proceeded to wrap a boy figure from head to toe in pipe cleaners. Bonovitz's association – a "mummified boy" – evokes more death imagery: a child prepared for journeying to the afterlife.

On a more hopeful note, this swaddling fabric afforded warmth, comfort, love, and security – the autistic-contiguity needed to ensure safe transition from womb to postnatal "afterlife". Music for this momentous voyage could be furnished by altering just one word in a popular song's title (*Don't Fence Me In*), making it: *Do Fence Me In.*

As Bonovitz contemplates this encircled boy, for a fleeting moment he imagines the incubator. This image evaporates when Jason, a steely gleam in his eyes, stares at his analyst, fiercely declaring the boy is his brother. Could it have been his (unconscious) intention to erase any such NICU image from both their minds?

According to Jason's organizing principles (Stolorow, 2005) as I see them, wished-for swaddling is no more likely to be found than the illusory breast he seeks with his repetitive tic. Instead of a relatively seamless transition to comforting love wraps, his love maps warn him he is destined for discontiguity. For self-preservation, he would need to aggressively render that imminent trauma not-me (Sullivan, 1940). Therefore, steeling his soul, he projected that awful fate onto his "brother".

Bonovitz's description of the *steely* gleam in Jason's eyes suggests to me the possibility of Jason's defensive identification with the cold, inanimate, indifferent incubator materials and milieu. Such *imitative* identification with the "aggressor" (Steele, 1970) occurs before clearer boundaries between self and object are established (those involved in later, familiar versions of this defense).

In the drama following the fraternal proclamation act, Jason is scarcely his "brother's keeper". He is destined instead to become his abuser, perhaps his killer. In such projective identifications, a tie to the object is characteristically maintained. Accordingly, Jason fastens a string around his toy sibling. Swinging him about, bashing him into walls, stomping on him, he omnipotently rewrites his own tumultuous, near-death, postnatal scenario (Aron, 2014; Willock, 2014). This time around, he can manically be "the Lord thy god ... an angry god" instead of the impotent victim of the deity's (parents') neglectful absence. In this maelstrom, potential postnatal primary intersubjectivity (Trevarthen, 1979) collapses into sadomasochistic, doer/done-to complementarity (Benjamin, 2004). Buberian I–thou intimacy is eclipsed by I–it brutality.

Bonovitz highlights the chaotic nature of this play. I would add that Jason, fancying himself as the drama's god-like director/creator, is endeavoring to organize chaos and catastrophe. To sidestep autistic-contiguous disaster, he grasps at a more advanced, PS level of psychic organization. Visiting cruelty on brother animal is far preferable to permitting creatures (self fragments) to eternally exit a damaged perinatal fence. Choosing more advanced organizing principles (kill or be killed), sadistic part-object relations replace dissolving, autosensuous, pre-object relations. The breached autistic-contiguous barrier is plugged by the intense barrage of sensorimotor physicality. Doing dodges the grave threat to "going on being". He becomes the traumatizer rather than traumatized.

Confronted by Jason's violent play, Bonovitz observed his own mental space closing up. Unable to generate thoughts and meaning, there was just "physicality to respond to." In this intense countertransference, the depressive position in which there is a subject who can contemplate situations (Ogden, 1986) has dissolved, just as it did for Jason as he struggled to patch the rent in the flimsy fabric housing his threatened soul.

Jason was consumed with envy for his sibling who did not have the learning problems and other difficulties with which Jason was saddled, Bonovitz believes, as he struggles to comprehend Jason's vicious attack on his "brother". I would add that some of these learning disabilities and other challenges may be partly attributable to prematurity. Beyond these possibilities, at this moment, I think his brother has a different meaning. Here, Jason desperately needs this "brother" to be a "toilet-breast" (Meltzer, 1967) into which he can dump his greatest terrors. Meltzer's term "nicely" captures the expulsive aim of this part-object relationship. "The basic problem is one of psychic pain and the need for an object in the outside world that can contain the projection of it" (p. 20).

Stuff it

Suddenly, the "climate in the room" shifted. Jason wanted to leave. He accused Bonovitz of making him think about sad memories, like his pet frog dying. *Post coitum omne animal triste est* (After intercourse every animal is sad). Having discharged orgastic violence onto his "sib", sadness set in. Omnipotent defenses (explosive physicality) had briefly countered autistic-contiguous terror. Instead of being a self with a hole, he had become a holy terror. Nonetheless, he still ended up feeling like the NICU infant lifting his orifice into the air and finding a dead frog, and other sad images of André Green's (1983) dead mother.

Jason asked if he could take something home. I believe he wanted something to concretely meet his gesture, his request, his body/ mouth/mind's yearning to repair autistic-contiguity. Seizing a stuffed salamander (a relatively "live", present toy as opposed to the dead, departed frog/mother), he declared, "I need it!" His request felt desperate, as though something of great consequence were at stake, Bonovitz remarked. In this significant moment, Jason was "driving a bargain, seeking a compromise between rampant narcissism [battering his "brother"] and full-blown infantile dependence" (Meltzer, 1967, p. 30).

Bonovitz wondered what this urgency to take something home was about. Jason had a plethora of toys. Losing their value after a day or two, these objects were repeatedly replaced by something "new and better" that soon also ceased to hold his interest. I think Jason's urgency pertained to his need to fill the breach in his autistic-contiguous membrane lest he drain into eternal nothingness – the terror forecast in his opening story of the fallible fence. Clutching the stuffed salamander provided autosensuous stimulation, helping block the time–space gap that was emerging as Jason contemplated the session ending and prepared to leave the therapeutic womb to face the rest of life with its unappealing, NICU-reminiscent moments and challenges.

Helping mend the self-enclosing membrane, the salamander served as a stopgap rather than being a tenderly beloved transitional object. Jason might lose interest in this toy when his crisis passed, much as one ceases to be interested in a bandage after the bleeding stops and a scab forms. Nonetheless, grabbing the salamander represented a significant step beyond clutching carrion (putrefying flesh) and defensively battering the "brother". While not a transitional object, it was a move beyond "rampant narcissism" toward "full-blown infantile dependence" ("I need it!").

Experiencing a sinking sensation, Bonovitz felt this could be the last time he would see his salamander. Eight years earlier, when Jason's amphibian self first landed on *terra non firma*, his former watery milieu was never replaced with comparably cozy conditions supporting illusions of continuity. Problematic prematurity taught Jason much about disappearances. Now he undoubtedly preferred being the magician orchestrating the vanishing of objects rather than being the one mystified and devastated by loss.

Bonovitz raised interesting technical questions about whether it was correct to allow Jason to take the toy. All child (and some adult) analysts can resonate with this predicament. Rather than disrupting this discussion's continuity by engaging that technical issue directly, I will stay with Bonovitz's feeling coerced into allowing Jason to "take something of mine without my having fully given it to him." From my transferential, perinatal point of view, Jason would have felt entitled to grab whatever he needed, what he had been psychobiologically preprogrammed to expect from the environment mother in terms of autistic-contiguous stimulation, containment, and nurturance. What's yours is mine – your nipple, your salamander, your "primary maternal preoccupation" (Winnicott, 1958b).

In their next session, Bonovitz asked Jason where the stuffed animal was that he had promised to bring back. Jason shrugged his shoulders, as if that creature were the furthest thing from his mind. He had no idea where it was. It had clearly gone way beyond the fence, though perhaps with projective identificatory strings attached. "What do you care anyway? There's other stuff here," Jason quipped. (You've got a nice incubator. Why are you so hung up on that old uterus you lost? Let it rot in peace, like the afterbirth carrion it has surely become.)

Transferring his sense of loss into his analyst worked temporarily. Negative hallucination (banishing his sense of deprivation or privation) is often as unsustainable as positively hallucinating the breast (or the autistic-contiguous matrix, as many autistic children and others do via autosensuous stimulation). Soon, therefore, Jason reverted to his omnipotent deity defense. Holding a series of toys to his face, he established brief contact (autistic-contiguity) before hurling each across the room. With each toss, he yelled in an angry, aching voice how much he hated these stupid toys.

This aggressive "play" can be seen as Jason's rendition of Freud's (1920) grandson's *fort* (gone) game. Before that Viennese child could add *da* (return) to his famous pastime, throwing objects was the only means he had for coping with his mother's comings and goings. Similarly with the salamander, Jason was more skilled at enacting gone, rather than reunion. One senses it will be some time before he may be able to choreograph the amphibian's reappearance.

Away but not forgotten

After flinging toys – becoming womb exiler rather than exiled – Jason complained about his therapist speaking in a high-pitched voice, as if Jason were a baby. In the next session, he shared that he had not liked his early postnatal experience. The birthing room had been cold. His biological mom had been watching him, he believes, but he never saw her again (brief facial contact before throwing him away, as in his previous toy play). Sitting with unprecedented stillness, heavy sadness settled in. With sunken eyes, Jason looked at his analyst. Turning away, the following tidbit rolled out of his teary mouth-mind: "I was a broken baby." Ever in sync, Bonovitz felt heartbroken.

This moving moment represents a treatment milestone. It highlights Jason's shift from an aggressive, action-oriented, omnipotent defensive style to one allowing for profound verbal/emotional communication. Recall Meltzer's (1967) statement that "The basic problem is one of psychic pain and the need for an object in the outside world that can contain the projection of it." Previously, not feeling he had a human object that could receive his agony, Jason had to transfer his suffering into other objects, such as his mummified brother. Now, brutal projective identification was no longer necessary.

"The 'heir' … to the relinquishment of massive projective identification is the 'toilet-breast' dependence on an external, and eventually, on an internal object" (Meltzer, 1967, p. 24). Jason could now use his analyst for toilet-breast dependence rather than endlessly repeating his primitive modes of defensive object relating. As he trustingly conveyed his "broken baby" bits to Bonovitz, he was sharing his new conviction that between the two of them, containment could be accomplished. Via continuing treatment, this toilet-breast would become an increasingly useful, internalized object.

Paraphrasing Winnicott (1975), we might say that at birth there is no such thing as a broken baby. What is more likely is a broken autistic-contiguous connection. My three-year-old autistic patient, Anika, poignantly portrayed this stark reality. Although she rarely spoke, at the end of one session she pointed to the toys on the rug, uttering one word: "Broken." Her facial expression matched her bleak descriptor. In a subsequent session, she shared her storybook depicting a little girl separating from her mother by boarding an airplane for an exciting trip. Pointing to the illustration, Anika uttered that same word: "Broken." These rare verbalizations suggested that relational breaks shattered Anika's autistic-contiguity, the condition necessary for going on being. Despite this sadness, it was a promising development that she was beginning to want to communicate the nature of her core trauma.

Trevor, a sophisticated, accomplished, troubled adult, was prone to feeling like an empty sack of skin lying on the sidewalk. This awful feeling would especially plague him when he was struggling with separations. His creepy image conveyed a concrete, hopeless reality. When partings ruptured his fragile sense of autistic-contiguity, self components vacated his vulnerable self sack, leaving the depleted membrane abjectly alone, to rot in a world of indifference.

Unlike desolate patients such as Anika and Trevor, Jason typically shifted into raucous emergency action to avoid experiencing autistic-contiguous catastrophes. To dispel feelings of powerlessness, emptiness, and death, he called on primitive, omnipotent defenses, pumping himself full of "lively", energizing aggression. Hurling toys, he became the sack emptier, the spewer of objects, not the emptied entity or the inanimate, scattered, broken, abandoned, lifeless objects.

On Rorschach card IX, a young psychopath perceived a baby's head and body (Meloy, 1988): "They didn't tie the umbilical cord and the guts are shooting out. Can that really happen? Can it bleed to death?" During inquiry, this man noted: "He's red when he comes out, this is the green and orange guts coming out" (pp. 412–413). Meloy does not say whether this criminal's birth had been premature, but the imagery he produced certainly conveys catastrophic transition to a negligent, incompetent, life-threatening, postnatal environment. Any pre-existing autistic-contiguous security and self-boundary that may have been achieved has been obliterated. As self-contents exit violently, annihilation seems imminent.

From this psychopath's ensuing response, one can understand and predict his violent, defensive style (Willock, in preparation). "Some guy's handing another guy something. Looks like a bug here, drilling through one leg, the handle and power unit here." In inquiry, he referenced cockroaches. From the perspective of problematic nativity, to halt his infantile (psychic) hemorrhaging, he defensively transforms passive into active traumatization. Via projective identification, he becomes the grandiose sadist (the "power unit") drilling into his debased victim (cockroach). By inflicting suffering on others, personal pain and potential death are dodged. In similar fashion, I believe Jason projectively identified his life-threatening perinatal situation into his toy brother, then battered the life out of him mercilessly.

Would anyone be surprised to learn that Meloy's 22-year-old psychopath bound and gagged then torture-murdered an older homosexual gentleman? Recall Jason binding his brother doll prior to brutalizing him. In the adult sociopath's crime, there was similar tight containment – no comforting swaddling for his doomed crybaby. His screams would never be heard, let alone responded to lovingly. The Lord thy god is an angry god.

Returning to Jason's impressive transition from violence to sadness, he now longed for his birth mother to reach through the glass and hold him. Her warm body would dispel the room's coldness, repairing the autistic-contiguous rent with warm, sensuous, "primary object love" (Balint, 1968). In this yearning, Jason creatively fused his biological and adoptive mothers, for it was the latter who looked at him every day through the glass. Now able to imagine a very different perinatal experience, Jason was effectively rewriting his traumatic birth phantasy (Willock, 2014).

Regarding the salamander, why should Jason return that creature when he himself had been so ripped off at birth, robbed of his entitlement? Only if the sacred, parent–child covenant were miraculously (re)established would he have to live up to his half of that contract. Revisiting his birth trauma ever more consciously, one senses he was locating/creating ingredients for repairing that primal bond. Making ever more significant contact with Bonovitz, Jason was shoring up basic trust (Erikson, 1950) that, eventually, might include commitment to loving reciprocity (primary intersubjectivity, returning the salamander).

Lining up his ducks

Jason became very interested in YouTube. Recall his earlier complaint that his analyst had interrupted his favorite television (boob tube) show. Now that autistic-contiguity had been revitalized via ongoing empathic attunement that facilitated surviving serial crises and plugged holes in the sensory self membrane, restoring an increasingly fine fence, the show was back on. Psychological development could resume and proceed on a more solid footing.

Jason's new favorite program concerned a duck. Surely it is more than coincidental that he was attracted to creatures who are at home on land and water – salamanders, frogs, ducks. All these animals are eminently suitable perinatal symbols.

Repeatedly, the duck visits a lemonade stand, requesting grapes. The frustrated vendor finally threatens to glue the duck to a tree – a perverse form of otherwise desirable, adhesive identification for a boy who so easily becomes unglued. In face of the duck's relentless persistence, the man eventually finds some grapes, whereupon the duck wants lemonade.

While this story lends itself to being understood as being about a creature who is difficult or impossible to satisfy (as Jason certainly used to be), one could also interpret it as being about a being who, once he feels his idiosyncratic needs have finally been understood and gratified, can accept and even desire what the world originally had to offer. (When life gives you lemonade...)

In treatment, Jason came to feel held and contained by his *sense* that his analyst was trying hard to comprehend and help him, tolerating a fair amount of grief in the process. This analytic attitude strengthened the autistic-contiguous floor beneath Jason that hitherto had been prone to cracking up and caving in. Archaic gaps in perceived primary maternal preoccupation were being filled by psychoanalytic preoccupation.

Jason delighted in watching the duck video over and over with his therapist. This activity helped rebuild, reinforce, and reinflate intersubjective, potential space. In this revitalized container, the duck story was a cherished transitional phenomenon. Rewarding, calm, cultural make-believe was now possible based on Jason's new feeling that a good life is feasible. Pre-symbolic sensory problems had been sufficiently attenuated, making symbols and other transitional phenomena available for use and growth.

"Psychopathology can be thought of as a collapse of the generative dialectical interplay of modes of experience ... Collapse in the direction of an autistic-contiguous mode ... precludes the development of 'potential space' (Winnicott, 1971)" (Ogden, 1989, p. 137). Implosion in the PS direction results in a sense of entrapment in a world of things-in-themselves. There, one does not experience oneself as the author of one's thoughts and feelings. Rather, cognition, affect, and sensation are experienced as objects or forces bombarding, entering into, or propelled from oneself. Desperate defenses against that sort of implosion were evidenced in Jason's throwing toys and battering his "brother" and in the psychopath's guts shooting out from his untied umbilical cord prior to his fantasy of drilling into a cockroach.

On the rocky road to transitional and intersubjective space, the salamander served as an important intermediary between repetitively disrupted, explosive play and narrative cohesion. That "I need it!" stuffed toy facilitated the necessary "dialectical interplay between the sensory and the symbolic" (Ogden, 1989, p. 138), between autistic-contiguous and depressive positions.

Jason explained that the duck had been really sad because he could not have everything. When Bonovitz asked what the animal really wanted, Jason responded: "I wish I could find my first mom and ask her why she didn't want to keep me." A psychoanalyst could hardly hope for a more direct response to an indirect question. Jason was communicating that he did not need the defensive barrier afforded by displacement into play space (what "duck" really wanted). He now felt comfortable talking intersubjectively, heart to heart. Underscoring the soulful flow now possible between patient and analyst, Jason's eyes welled with tears. As autistic-contiguous holes healed, he and Bonovitz were connected in an increasingly warm, solid, sensuous, interpersonal, affective rhythm.

Although Jason knew why his birth mother could not keep him, he yearned to hear it from the horse's mouth. Direct sensory transmission would help restore fractured autistic-contiguity. In analogous fantasy, he/duck must at last hear the right words from the fruit vendor and see/touch/taste the anticipated, elusive grapes (nipples). When Jason finally contacted that magical fruit (formerly grapes of wrath) in his mind's eye, his mind's mouth, and the psychoanalytic matrix, he became able to move forward, accepting what life interrupted now had to offer (lemonade, therapeutic incubator, adoptive parents, Bonovitz, and the world).

Returnables

As the next summer vacation approached, rather than breaking down as he had prior to the previous holiday break, Jason was now in much better shape. With an increasingly solid, autistic-contiguous platform beneath him, he found the salamander and restored it to its "rightful" owner. This act of reparation typifies depressive position object relations, which were now possible for Jason. Prior to sufficient analytic repair of the relational covenant that had been smashed by problematic prematurity, he had felt no need to live up to his end of the agreement about returning the stuffed toy. In fact, he had needed to break his word to let Bonovitz taste how that feels, to see if his toilet-breast analyst could tolerate (and perhaps transform) that unbearable experience.

Bonovitz had all but given up on ever seeing his amphibian friend again. He imagined it had made its way to the trash or was buried beneath copious candy wrappers in Jason's school desk (where, in fact, Jason had found it). Bonovitz intuited that the salamander had been exiled into a toilet-breast.

Infantile dependence may be increasingly held in a split-off position outside the analytic situation "as the oral introjective relation to the breast becomes more clearly differentiated from other zones and modes of infantile transference" (Meltzer, 1967, p. 30). As this splitting-off lessens, reunion of feeding-breast with toilet-breast can manifest. After functioning for a long time in expulsive, toilet-breast mode, Jason worked earnestly on his dependency relationship to the feeding-breast via the duck video, "the projective relation to the mother (toilet-breast) being more easily established than the introjective (feeding breast)" (Meltzer, 1967, p. 32). At school, Jason found a toilet-breast suitable for holding his salamander. This important, behind-the-scenes development seems to have facilitated bringing oral issues into treatment. "The projective 'toilet-breast' relationship forms the dependency background of the analytic work" (Meltzer, 1967, p. 25).

Meltzer (1967) warned of a dangerous tendency in the transference for a "reversal of the splitting, i.e. – to bring the feeding breast into the playroom and to split-off the toilet-breast elsewhere" (p. 30). While Jason used some dissociative processes, he also found ways to creatively overcome that division. Integrating toilet- and feeding-breasts, he established an increasingly cohesive, internalized, transformative object.

When Bonovitz said he thought Jason had completely forgotten about the salamander, Jason replied, "I did for a while. I didn't care about it at all. It wasn't what I thought it was going to be. But then I realized that there was something about him that I liked." These articulate sentiments indicate that as internalization and integration progressed, he became able not only to hold the salamander in his toilet-breast desk, but also to nurture (care for, like) it. Having obtained his grape nipples, he was able to bestow some love on his baby. Blessed by this benevolent cathexis, the "dead" (fecalized) salamander was resurrected. The dialectic between sensory and symbolic, between autistic-contiguous and depressive positions, was restored. In this process, Jason's relationship to reality was revitalized.

The salamander signified Jason's unloved, abandoned self (Willock, 1986, 1987). Exiling that self to the toilet-breast was also returning it to the womb, which I regard as precursor to both toilet- and feeding-breasts. In his school womb, Jason's forgotten, unloved, uncared-for self could be safely contained, quietly nurtured. Waste disposal was not an issue. In that toilet-womb, Jason's salamander self matured until ready for rebirth (Willock, 2014). There was no prematurity this time. In fact, from Bonovitz's perspective, the stuffed animal arrived well past the expected delivery date.

The born-again salamander felt "softer," Jason remarked. His tactile adjective speaks to a desirable, sensuous quality, providing self/womb/breast/world autistic-contiguity, something so lacking in his initial postnatal incubator experience. Jason was glad to have found the stuffed toy. Instead of holding rotten carrion, now he had the good breast. "He's got the whole world in his hands."

Perhaps already, or soon, Jason would no longer need to bash his head against hard walls at home and school. Such painfully symptomatic stimulation would not be so necessary. Nor would he have to inflict analogous brutality on his mummified "brother" or any other object. In a world of increasingly internalized soft salamanders (breasts/wombs/bodies/minds), violence would no longer be so needed.

With the salamander's return, the analytic couple retrieved a lost part of Jason, Bonovitz remarked. I would add that an important aspect of that previously lost component was the sense of self derived from autistic-contiguity with the original, presymbolic, maternal matrix (womb). When Jason was no longer so preoccupied with sustaining his threatened self-boundary (fence), he could advance beyond the autosensuous aspects of objects and emergency plugs (rotten carrion, the salamander, tantrums, and omnipotent defenses) to transitional phenomena (the duck). With potential space restored, intersubjective relatedness became possible. Treatment had promoted a far healthier balance in the autistic-contiguous/PS/D trialectic.

Summary

Christopher Bonovitz provided a fruitful therapeutic relationship. In that good relational womb/breast, grapes for sacred communion wine could be created and nurtured to maturity. The analyst, his salamander, and YouTube's grapes and lemonade all proved sufficiently succulent and sweet, affording much-needed hope regarding goodness in the world. These communion essentials elevated Jason from his earthly or hellish trials and tribulations to a more heavenly plane. Re-establishing sensory contiguity and promoting symbolization, this nurturant holding environment gave him something substantial to latch onto. The promising new world contrasted sharply with the nothingness that hitherto had met his expectant mouth.

New grapes made from "old whine" and other ingredients made "sense" of the previously frightening, chaotic void, transforming it into potential space. The life-sucking vacuum was filled with expanding, narrative meaning ("memories" of traumatic parturition; the duck's delightful odyssey from frustration to fulfillment; the salamander's resurrection and return). The collapsed, disintegrating self envelope no longer had to be pumped up with hot air, explosive violence, and other grandiose defensive maneuvers. Relational remediation had succeeded. Jason had not only located his good breast (the soft salamander, succulent grapes), but, more fundamentally, the autistic-contiguity he had lost long ago when transitioning from womb to incubator and beyond. Restoration of this "broken baby" exemplifies the miraculous repair psychoanalysis can achieve.

Bonovitz's case presentation, including his reflections on the child analyst's mind at work, facilitates exploring the roots of relationality. The symptoms that I believe emanate from his patient's problematic prematurity permit us to contemplate the importance of the prenatal, sensory beginnings of self, object, and relationship. Fetal transition to a not expectable environment (neonatal intensive care) affords opportunities for considering serious challenges to sustaining the embryonic self and its capacity for relatedness. Intensive psychotherapy with children struggling with sequelae of these difficult perinatal experiences enables us to better understand the foundations of relationality, their ordeals and self-protective endeavors, and the processes involved in remedying such basic vulnerabilities in self-structure and relational capacity.

Note

1 An earlier version of this chapter, first published with a somewhat different focus, appears in Willock (2015). Psychoanalysis of prematurity. *Psychoanalytic Dialogues*, 25:34–49. Reprinted by kind permission of the journal and Taylor & Francis, LLC.

References

Aron, L. (2014). With you I'm born again: Themes and fantasies of birth and the family circumstances surrounding birth as these are mutually evoked in patient and analyst. *Psychoanalytic Dialogues*, 24:341–357.

Balint, M. (1968). *The basic fault: Therapeutic aspects of regression*. London, UK: Tavistock.

Benjamin, J. (2004). Beyond doer and done to: An intersubjective view of thirdness. *The Psychoanalytic Quarterly*, 73:5–46.

Bion, W. (1962a). A theory of thinking. *International Journal of Psycho-Analysis*, 43:306–310.

Bion, W. (1962b). *Learning from experience*. London, UK: Heinemann.

Bonovitz, C. (2015). A child therapist at work: Playing, talking, and the therapist's inner dialogue. *Psychoanalytic Dialogues*, 25:18–28.

Bromberg, P. (1998). *Standing in the spaces: Essays on clinical process, trauma, and dissociation*. Hillsdale, NJ: Analytic Press.

de Jonghe, F., Rijnierse, P., & Janssen, R. (1991). Aspects of the analytic relationship. *International Journal of Psycho-Analysis*, 72:693–708.

Erikson, E.H. (1950). *Childhood and society*. New York, NY: W. W. Norton & Company.

Erikson, E.H. (1959). *Identity and the life cycle*. New York, NY: International Universities Press.

Fairbairn, W.R.D. (1952). *Psychoanalytic studies of the personality*. London, UK: Tavistock Publications.

Fast, I. (1985). with Erard, R.E., Fitzpatrick, C.J., Thompson, A.E., Young, L. *Event theory: A Piaget–Freud integration*. Hillsdale, NJ: Lawrence Erlbaum Associates.

Freud, A. (1948). *The ego and the mechanisms of defense*. New York, NY: International Universities Press.

Freud, S. (1920). Beyond the pleasure principle. *S.E.*, 18.

Freud, S. (1923). The ego and the id. *S.E.*, 19.

Green, A. (1983). The dead mother. In: A. Green (Ed.), *On private madness* (pp. 142–173). London, UK: Hogarth Press.

Guntrip, H. (1969). *Schizoid phenomena, object relations and the self*. New York, NY: International Universities Press.

Hartmann, H. (1939). *Ego psychology and the problem of adaptation*. (trans.: D. Rapaport). New York, NY: International Universities Press.

Kinston, W. & Cohen, J. (1986). Primal repression: clinical and theoretical aspects. *International Journal of Psycho-Analysis*, 67:337–355.

Kohut, H. (1977). *The restoration of the self*. New York, NY: International Universities Press.

Kumin, I. (1995). *Pre-object relatedness: Early attachment and the psychoanalytic situation*. New York, NY: Guilford Press.

Meloy, R. (1988). *The psychopathic mind: Origins, dynamics, and treatment*. Northvale, NJ: Jason Aronson.

Meltzer, D. (1967). *The psycho-analytical process*. London, UK: Karnac.

Ogden, T.H. (1986). *The matrix of the mind: Object relations and the psychoanalytic dialogue*. Northvale, NJ: Jason Aronson.

Ogden, T.H. (1989). On the concept of an autistic-contiguous position. *International Journal of Psycho-Analysis*, 70:127–140.

Spitz, R. (1965). *The first year of life: A psychoanalytic study of normal and deviant development of object relations*. New York, NY: International Universities Press.

Steele, B.F. (1970). Parental abuse of infants and small children. In: E.J. Anthony & T. Benedek (Eds.), *Parenthood: Its psychology and psychopathology* (pp. 449–477). Boston, MA: Little, Brown.

Stolorow, R.D. (2005). Prereflective organizing principles and the systematicity of experience in Kant's critical philosophy. *Psychoanalytic Psychology*, 22:96–100.

Sullivan, H.S. (1940). *Conceptions of modern psychiatry*. New York, NY: W. W. Norton and Company.

Trevarthen, C.B. (1979). Communication and cooperation in early infancy: A description of primary intersubjectivity. In: M. Bullowa (Ed.), *Before speech* (pp. 321–348). Cambridge, MA: Cambridge University Press.

Tustin, F. (1981). *Autistic states in children.* Boston, MA: Routledge & Kegan Paul.

Tustin, F. (1986). *Autistic barriers in neurotic patients.* New Haven, CT/ London, UK: Yale University Press.

Willock, B. (1986). Narcissistic vulnerability in the hyperaggressive child: The disregarded (unloved, uncared-for) self. *Psychoanalytic Psychology*, 3:59–80.

Willock, B. (1987). The devalued (unloveable, repugnant) self: A second facet of narcissistic vulnerability in the aggressive, conduct-disordered child. *Psychoanalytic Psychology*, 4:219–240.

Willock, B. (2007). *Comparative–integrative psychoanalysis.* New York, NY: The Analytic Press.

Willock, B. (2014). The mutually facilitating maturational matrix. *Psychoanalytic Dialogues*, 24:364–373.

Willock, B. (2015). Psychoanalysis of prematurity. *Psychoanalytic Dialogues*, 25:34–49.

Willock, B. (in preparation). *The colonel and the cannibal.*

Winnicott, D.W. (1958a). Birth memories, birth trauma, and anxiety. In: *Collected papers: Through paediatrics to psycho-analysis* (pp.174–193). London, UK: Tavistock.

Winnicott, D.W. (1958b). Primary maternal preoccupation. In: *Collected papers: Through paediatrics to psycho-analysis* (pp. 300–305). London, UK: Tavistock.

Winnicott, D.W. (1963). The development of the capacity for concern. In: *The maturational processes and the facilitating environment: Studies in the theory of emotional development* (pp.73–82). New York, NY: International Universities Press.

Winnicott, D.W. (1971). *Playing and reality.* New York, NY: Basic Books.

Winnicott, D.W. (1974). Fear of breakdown. *International Review of Psycho-Analysis*, 1:103–107.

Winnicott, D.W. (1975). *Through paediatrics to psycho-analysis.* London, UK: The Hogarth Press and the Institute of Psycho-Analysis.

Chapter 11

"Is this chair alive?"

Interpersonal relating and the beginnings of the self

Seth Aronson, Psy.D.

Noah tentatively peered into my office. It was his first session and he was testing the waters.

In his flat, monotone voice, he remarked, "Oh, you have a dollhouse – how terrifying." With virtually no affect, the comment seemed ridiculous, even comical, but I suspected it betrayed his seeking the familiar in the toys in the consulting room while concurrently acknowledging his terror at the unknown.

Noah was a slight, light-haired, and fair-skinned boy of four. His parents had consulted me after he had been asked to leave a third preschool program because of his extreme aloofness and tantrumming whenever he was asked to participate in any social group activity. Left to his own devices, Noah would stand alone, talking to himself, and treating the other children, in his parents' description, "as if they were furniture." He was close with his mother and father, demonstrating affection toward them, but was extremely fearful when confronted with anyone or anything that was new. Noah appeared to be quite withdrawn from the world, his experience severely restricted, with little, if any, room for exchange and interaction. His constriction and fearfulness, together with his tantrumming, led me to wonder about his aggression and his object world's reaction (phantasied and real) to it.

In this chapter, I describe a model of therapeutic action that incorporates elements of a contemporary Kleinian approach, emphasizing projective identification, while highlighting the interpersonal aspect of the interaction. Change occurs via several key components: the therapist, through reverie, provides containment for the various projections; through the mutual exchange of projections (and projective identifications), which is inherently an interpersonal exchange, child and therapist create meaning together, becoming "partners in thought" (Stern, 2010); the various and mutual projective identifications (notably positive ones) that allow the child to begin to integrate previously dissociated aspects of self and other, "standing in the spaces" (Bromberg, 1998); and through this acknowledgment of repudiated self-states, the child learns to bridge the gap between him or her and the therapist, while maintaining a sense of integrity of self and other.

And so we began our first session together. Noah delicately stepped around my office, not daring to touch any toy or object, instead simply labelling them.

"Oh, a puppet." "That's a cat." "A chair." "That's a desk." His verbalizations were quiet, short, and not elaborated. An ambulance siren sounded outside. He became extremely fearful and ran to the door, covering his ears. I explained that it was simply a siren and far away from us. After a few seconds, he resumed his tentative exploration of the toys.

While beginning treatment with me, Noah had been enrolled in a therapeutic nursery program, the first acknowledgment by his parents that he needed more intensive intervention. His speech was unclear and there were moments when he spoke in garbled, nonsensical words. He had floppy muscle tone, as if his limbs were made of rubber and had no resistance. His fears of the outside world were extensive, ranging from loud noises (his mother could not vacuum while he was in the house) to elevators, animals, any physical activity, and, of course, people. Despite evident strengths such as intelligence, it seemed clear that he was on the autistic spectrum.

His first few weeks were spent examining the office and toys. He didn't seem to quite know what to do with them. I attempted to engage him in some rudimentary symbolic play, feeding puppets, arranging a dollhouse with a family, but he appeared uninterested.

And then he engaged in his first attempt at some sort of play.

He found a soft Nerf ball and began to lightly throw it against objects in the office.

"Is this chair alive?" he would ask while tossing the ball against it.

"No!" he and I would say together in an exaggerated comical way that indicated "of course not."

"Is a desk alive?"

"No!"

"Is a door alive?"

"No!"

And so began our first foray into the realm of separating inner from outer, animate from inanimate, a sense of fantasy from an inchoate sense of reality, self from other, and the beginnings of our relationship.

This type of call and response seemed reminiscent of how young children often talk to themselves in bed before falling asleep. Stern (2010) asks:

> To whom are they talking? ... [I]t is plausible to imagine that they are talking to their parents and attempting to imaginatively listen to themselves through their parents' ears and thereby lend their experience a credence, coherence and depth of feeling it otherwise could not have.
>
> (p. 113)

In his early efforts to name and contain experience, Noah was beginning to parse Noah from chair, Noah from desk, Noah from a vague and undifferentiated world. In a rudimentary way, Noah was attempting to give rise to a self, demarcating it from other, separating live from not-alive and calling out to the other (me), hoping and wishing for a response of recognition.

The creation of mind

Recent authors have described "the close connection that exists between what happens *within* an individual's mind and what happens *between* one person and another" (Hobson, 2002, p. 22, original emphasis; see also Fonagy, 1993; Alvarez, 2012). The discovery of mirror neurons (Gallese, Fadiga, Fogassi, & Rizzolatti, 1996; Ammaniti & Gallese, 2014) suggests that our capacity to learn to share emotions and sensations with each other is inherently rooted in the interpersonal dyad. Once we learn via mirroring patterns of interpersonal relating, we gradually internalize these patterns, putting our own individual stamp on them, and then can engage in joint attention exchanges, which necessitate the monitoring of the other person's focus of attention in relation to the self and the object (Ammaniti & Gallese, 2014). Or, as Hobson (2002) puts it, the infant, in engaging with the world, requires an Other who in turn can engage with the world and, in this way, learns how to relate via both his/her own engagement as well as the Other's relation to the world.

What are the conditions necessary for this to occur?

In the Kleinian model, the infant requires a caregiver who can tolerate and accept the baby's projections. These projections initially consist of sensations the baby experiences that come from within and without. Such early physical experiences (such as hunger or needing to have one's diaper changed) are overwhelming to the young infant and the baby's inability to tolerate them leads the infant – in phantasy – to expel them.

Where do these aspects and elements of experience go?

The answer is, they go into the caregiver, who accepts the baby's projections, modifies them, and transforms them via containment into experiences the baby is then able to take back, accept, and introject. Bion (1962) postulated that this process represented the beginning of thought, as the baby not only introjects the caregiver's transformed material, but also, through the exchange with the caregiver, learns how to begin to metabolize these overwhelming experiences; in essence, how to think about things.

The caregiver who is able to contain these early difficult experiences does so through reverie. Reverie is "an emotional experience in which the mother does something for the baby akin to mental digestion which the baby cannot do for him/herself ... it is an unconscious activity of the mother" (Riesenberg-Malcolm, 2001, p. 169). The caregiver must experience what the baby is feeling in order to correctly respond to the baby's distress and, in this way, identifies with the baby's projected material. Simultaneously, the baby identifies with what he/she has projected, which now resides, so to speak, in the caregiver. It is only when the material is transformed – made palatable – that it can be safely taken back by the infant.

Bion (and Herbert Rosenfeld) went on to develop the notion of the communicative aspect of projective identification. In order for reverie and containment to occur, the caregiver must somehow understand/identify with whatever the infant is trying to get across. The baby's projections must be understood as a form of communication, not simply material to be evacuated without meaning.

This entire cyclical process is, of course, inherently interpersonal. It takes place within the dyad. Furthermore, it strongly suggests that in order for the baby to begin to build up his/her mind, the infant requires a "partner in thought" (Stern, 2010). As Hobson (2002) writes, "When an infant is engaged with someone else's mind, she is in a position to find out about other minds" (p. 143) – and, I would add, her own.

As the child interacts with the world, he or she relies on the other to respond, optimally in a consistent and predictable fashion. For example, when a balloon accidentally pops, the parent might register the child's fear and startled response (accepting what is projected). In turn, the caregiver might remark, "Oh, that was just the balloon. It was an accident," which returns the projected material (fear) in a transformed way that allows the child to feel safe and understood. The popping of the balloon, together with the startled reaction, becomes symbolically represented as the anxiety is shifted away from the direct and actual event and put into words by the attuned caregiver. There is a mind out there thinking about the child's experience. This acknowledgment of the child's mental state by the parent is what Meins et al. (2003) called "mind-mindedness". Such attunement by the caregiver helps to create meaning for the child – experience can be registered, understood, and affect-regulated.

The role of projective identification

Klein recognized that not only painful affects (such as the infant's distress) are involved in projective identification, but good elements as well. As Klein (1975/1997) wrote, "It is not only what are felt to be destructive and 'bad' parts of the self which are split off and projected into another, but also parts which are felt to be good and valuable" (p. 142).

In Klein's 1955 paper in which she deconstructs the French novel *If I were you* by Julian Green, she made clear that projecting good parts of the self is not accompanied by depletion (which characterizes pro-jective identification in the paranoid–schizoid position), but rather can serve to enrich the ego by securing a relation between it and a world endowed with goodness (Bell, 2001). Positive projective identification emphasizes the communicative aspect of the process, providing the object with a portion of the self experience, that which is character-ized by pleasure, in hopes of sharing the experience. Love is commu-nicated as " 'good' psychic entities" (Likierman, 1988, p. 33) that are put into the other. Further, this allows one to retain an empathic tie to the other, a tie that can be characterized by warmth, tenderness, and love (as Meira Likierman [1988] describes in her paper on maternal love and positive projective identification). It can also help with the development of empathy and perspective. One of the aims of therapy is to help the child with this important developmental task of connect-ing to a world full of goodness; in Klein's (1955) thinking, "the breast in its good aspect [which] is the prototype of maternal goodness, inex-haustible patience and generosity as well as of creativeness" (p. 180). The therapist, in engaging in reciprocal projective identification with the child, serves as a guide to a different world, one filled not only with hate, but also with love. The reciprocity of the projective identifica-tion is undoubtedly aided by the nature of child therapy; we do not sit on high, making pronouncements from our chair. Rather, we sit on the floor, in close physical proximity and contact with the child, which I believe allows the child to know us in a deeper, more intimate way.

Thus, the child can learn to recognize the other within a context of relatedness rather than within a context of destructiveness and oblit-eration of all meaning. A connection is formed for the sake of bridg-ing, relating, while learning to begin to respect difference. There is no attempt to colonize or control but to find, in Milner's (1955) phrasing, "the familiar in the unfamiliar," enhancing development and enriching relationship. There is, ultimately, in Sodre's (2004) words, "a peaceful welcoming of the object into the inner world" (p. 57) rather than the fear of warlike invasion by a persecutory object.

Noah's characteristic approach to people was to expect the worst – warlike invasion, colonization, or being overrun by the other (as well as his own aggression and destructiveness). His extreme constriction precluded meaningful contact with others and didn't afford him the opportunity to learn to regulate affective experience. In this sense, he was much like Klein's (1930) patient, Dick, whose fear of his own destructiveness inhibited him from exploring the world.

My first direct encounter with Noah's aggression and his terror of it came many months into our work together once Noah discovered a small toy cat with a long fluffy tail. Noah enjoyed waving the long tail and gradually over time brought it closer and closer to me. (He was still averse to any physical contact.) He indicated that he would swish the tail near my nose and I was to pretend to sneeze. And so began our game – a game that we played over and over (and over) again, in a repetitive and obsessive way, much like previous games (such as tossing the Nerf ball at objects).

One day, I pretended to sneeze so strongly that my yarmulke accidentally flew off my head. (I am an observant Jew and wear a yarmulke; see Aronson, 2007). Noah froze in his tracks, turning ghostly white, terror stricken.

I immediately said something like, "That's OK." But he was already in an extreme dissociated state, panicked, not listening. Noah's self-state of aggression and sadism toward the object had been activated, leading to dissociation, flight from the self, as it were, as well as the other, and extreme panic. He turned and fled, hiding beneath my desk. It was clear that his perceived act of aggression toward me had terrified him.

I spoke to him softly, telling him I was OK, we were simply playing a game, I was not injured. But he remained under my desk until the session's end when I had to enlist his mother's help to get him to come out.

Anxiously, I awaited the next session. Would he refuse to come into my office? Would he hide under the desk? Noah entered the room, somewhat apprehensively, but then, to my surprise, chose the cat and indicated that we were to play the "sneezing game." Once again, he swished the tail under my nose. Once again, I pretended to sneeze. He checked to see that my yarmulke remained in place. Again, the swishing of the cat's tail. Again, I "sneezed" and my yarmulke became dislodged. Noah turned pale. He froze.

I said, "But you see – the cat made my cap (his word for my yarmulke) come off, but I'm still here, still OK." Noah didn't run or hide.

And thus, with some gentle coaxing from me, we initiated a new version of the "sneezing game," one in which the "naughty cat" knocks off my cap. I began to offer some thoughts about our game. Perhaps the cat was curious as to what was underneath my cap (in what I hoped might address his extreme fear of exploring the world). Perhaps the cat didn't like that I wore a cap and he didn't (denoting envy, greed, and a wish to possess what the object had). Perhaps the cat enjoyed being naughty toward me (his taking some comfort and even sadistic pleasure in his aggression). In this way, Noah and I began taking tentative steps as companions in making meaning of experience. It also allowed me to call his attention to affective experience associated with the game, increasing the possibility of interactive contingency (Beebe & Lachmann, 2014).

I believe Noah was beginning to formulate his experience of himself as aggressive, assertive, curious ("desire for knowledge" is a trait Klein [1930] connected with sadism). He was beginning to know himself through my reflected appraisal (Sullivan, 1940) as a boy who could be curious and aggressive and that the world (and I) could withstand his forays. As Donnel Stern (2010) writes:

> We need to feel we exist in the other's mind, and that our existence has a kind of continuity in that mind and we need to feel that the other in whose mind we exist is emotionally responsive to us, that he or she cares about what we experience and how we feel about it.
>
> (p. 111)

I was serving as a new object, one in whose mind Noah began to emerge as forceful, envious, competitive, and capable of aggression. I also attempted to remain steadfast and unswerving in my recognition, acknowledgment, and acceptance of his aggression, as in the Greek myth of Aeneas' helmsman who holds on to the ship's tiller throughout the night, even after he is thrown by the gods into the sea, an image of remaining true to one's belief (Caper, 1999, p. 53).

Our game also allowed Noah to begin to develop less anxiety toward the unknown. The unfamiliar was fraught with anxiety, projected into the world, making it a terrifying and unpredictable place. The beginnings of our play together helped him incorporate in piecemeal fashion less fear and a greater capacity for experience of previously uncharted territory.

Over time, Noah began to learn that I, as the other, would not overrun him, but that he could gradually begin to take me (and his experience of being with me) in, a rudimentary form of positive projective identification. The new version of the sneezing game ushered in another surprising behavior. One day, Noah asked if he could wear the cap and if I could then swish the cat's tail, making *him* sneeze, knocking the cap off *his* head. I wondered somewhat anxiously to myself what would his (non-Jewish) parents think? What might this say about his identification with/relationship to me? Ultimately, I thought that this was about returning the projected material to him and how perhaps this new perception of himself as one who can be aggressive and me as one who tolerates/withstands/contains his aggression was crystallizing. Once the projected/dissociated material could be safely returned to Noah, he could then begin to experience new relational patterns of himself and other. As for his wearing my cap – mirror neurons indeed!

And so, with some trepidation on my part, I took off my yarmulke, allowing Noah to wear it during the session. We enacted, then, my being the cat, causing Noah to sneeze, knocking the cap from his head, and Noah's learning to tolerate my aggression toward him. Noah with cap and me without cap, Noah with cat, me with cat, represented precursors of playing at being me, himself, aggressor, victim, boy, animal – shifting states and roles within the kaleidoscope of play. As the child learns how to hold disparate states of mind (Alvarez, 2012) and "pretends" to be multiple "players" simultaneously via the interpersonal dimension of play, there can begin to be a rudimentary integration of states into an illusory (Bromberg, 1998) self and other. Previously dissociated states associated with terror can be played with, lived in, embodied, and the spaces between such states may begin to be bridged (Bromberg, 1998; Frankel, 1998).

Furthermore, our new way of being with each other allowed Noah to project and locate his experience in me while he played at being me. I could understand what it was like for him to be aggressor and he, in turn, could experience being the recipient of the aggression (and the sneezer!). New perspectives of the other could, via our changing of roles, begin to develop.

The sneezing game led to other explorations of aggression. Among the toys, Noah discovered a policeman's whistle. At first, he tentatively blew into it, barely making a sound. I commented on his curiosity and wondered how it would be if he blew the whistle more forcefully. Would the noise be so loud that it would frighten him? Me? He quickly put it away, only to return to it in our next meeting. Again, he tentatively blew into it, this time (inadvertently?) registering a much louder sound. He froze, dropped the whistle, and once again fled beneath my desk. I went over to him, describing how he hadn't expected to have such a loud sound come from within, but that he and I had both survived the ordeal. This time, I was able to get him to come out from the desk, but he safely chose puppets to play with for the remainder of the session. In the next session, he returned to the whistle, tweeting a louder sound. He turned pale, then looked at me to register my response. I assured him we were both fine and he continued blowing the whistle. In a move that demonstrated his developing capacity for symbolization, he then decided he would be a policeman and he wanted me to be a child crossing the road (something he had witnessed in his hometown at a school crossing). His controlling of the loud noises emanating from the whistle seemed to allow him mastery of his fear, expression of aggression, and a new way to be with me. At the session's end, his mother inquired as to what was going on in the room since she heard the tweeting sounds coming from my office!

My work with Noah's parents was focused on helping them to accept Noah's nascent exploration of the world, which meant accepting his (and their) aggression. Noah was an only child. His parents were trying to have another child, but thus far had been unsuccessful, and there was tension and sadness around this. His father worked as an architect, his mother a graphic artist. Both his parents were gentle, soft spoken, and, I suspected, not comfortable themselves with aggression. I wondered how their quiet, reserved demeanors might be contributing to Noah's fear of the world and his inability to assert himself in a healthy way. Early on, the infant's wish to learn about the world is via phantasied sadistic attacks to penetrate and possess the mother's body. These attacks give rise to fears of retaliation from the object as well as fear of the child's own aggression residing within. Defenses get set in motion to protect the infant from both of these sources of danger – within and without – including projection and projective identification. Over time, with the building of a good internal object, the child's anxiety and dread lessens and he is able to project his aggression farther into the world, away from the object, displacing it, creating a symbol that stands for the perceived sadistic, retaliatory object, while keeping it at a safe and tolerable remove. This, of course, requires a caregiver who is comfortable withstanding the child's phantasied (and real) attacks, without retaliating or shutting down the child's developmentally healthy need for aggression. Without such containment and an interpersonal response demonstrating acceptance of assertion, the child is left with an excessive sense of sadism and an ego unable to cope with the strain of such strong affects. As in Klein's (1930) case of Dick, on an interpersonal level, the child withdraws from interaction with the world, while psychically, their withdrawal and refusal to acknowledge others effectively obliterates and destroys the object world. Anxiety and affects are violently expelled, no interactions occur, and no symbolic meaning is made (recall Noah's initial inability to play symbolically, much like Klein's description).

In parent meetings, then, we discussed how to best help Noah become more comfortable with his aggression. His parents agreed that this was a worthy goal, but with hesitation. They expressed their fear that he would turn into a wild, unmanageable child, which I believe spoke volumes about their discomfort containing Noah's aggression (as well as their own). I tried to explain how I was trying to help him learn to better express his aggression and see that it could be tolerated. I linked for them the connection between Noah's extreme withdrawal and fear with his discomfort with others as well as himself. At Christmas, once we were well into the sneezing game, I gave Noah a punching balloon on a rubber tether. He was delighted – it not only allowed him sanctioned aggression, but also was a mode of helping with his physical coordination, which was quite poor. His mother looked at me quizzically when Noah left the office and triumphantly displayed his gift. Needless to say, our next parent meeting was about my choice of gift!

Over time, Noah's mother and father did come to see the value of his forays into physicality, but it remained a significant focus of the parent work.

Development of self and other

Making sense of his mind with its aggression, terror, desire – as well as mine – would begin to allow Noah to tolerate the separation of self and other. As Klein suggests (as does Hobson, 2002), the child must develop the capacity to symbolize, which Noah had difficulty doing when we first met. He could not engage in even primitive symbolic play.

The development of symbolism comes via the separation of self and other with the achievement of the depressive position. By creating symbols, the child projects his or her anxiety farther and farther away from the original object, with the various symbols ultimately representing the object (or connection to the object). The symbols allow the child to tolerate loss as they connote distance from the object, while maintaining a tie to that object through their representation of it. Noah's senses of curiosity, healthy assertion, and symbolic capacities, as well as other qualities, were so dissociated and out of reach that his experience was severely restricted. He could not allow himself to get near another person, much less try to make sense of or represent his or the other's experience. For optimal development, the child must be able to adopt others' perspectives, seeing the world from different points of view, acknowledging their separateness. Initially, Noah could only envision a world from his rather constricted perspective, and this in turn forced those around him to bend to his worldview. There was no other, only a confusion of Noah and the world. In order for all this to occur, Noah had to begin to develop a self, with a capacity to think, to symbolize, and to tolerate and regulate affect – and this self can only develop in relationship. He had to learn to communicate in the sense of effecting change in an other *and*, in turn, being affected by the other person. Such change can only occur in a dyadic–interpersonal exchange, with projection and projective identification as driving forces.

Through our play, Noah began to discover aspects of his self experience previously disavowed. He could locate these heretofore repudiated elements in my office, in our sessions, and in me. Through containment, I tried to be someone interested in all facets of his experience – his curiosity, his aggression, his naughtiness. Eventually, he began, on occasion, to ask me questions about myself – did I live in my office? How old was I? Who else played with the toys? We began to develop elementary conversations and exchanges. He told me some information about his week, home life, what he ate for lunch that day. There were the beginnings of the "to and fro" described by Winnicott (1971) across the interpersonal space, as together we were helping Noah to build a way to think, regulate affect, and be more present in his relationship to me.

Conclusion

Michelangelo's famous statue of Moses depicts him with horns – based, in fact, on a mistranslation of the Biblical verse that describes Moses' descent from Mount Sinai. The Hebrew word *keren* can mean horn, but in this context, it refers to the rays of light emanating from Moses' face.

Rabbi Naftali Zvi Yehudah Berlin, a 19th-century Talmudist, in his Biblical commentary, *Delve into the word* (1975), discusses the phenomenon of Moses' luminousness. He wrote that the light originated in Moses' encounter with the divine and that Moses did not attempt to cover his face when he spoke with the people because he wanted them to see and feel his experience of being lit up with such great joy after speaking with God:

> In this way, the treasure of the experience of Moses' teaching would be seen in his face, lit up with joy, which in turn, would light up the faces of his students, (literally) reflecting the joy and pride of their teacher.
>
> (p. 164)

What I believe Berlin is describing is positive projective identification and the power of interpersonal exchange. The teacher's face emanates light, which is then reflected in the face of the student so that they both can mutually revel in the shared delight of the experience.

In a strikingly parallel passage, Winnicott (1971) wrote:

> What does the baby look like when he or she sees the mother's face? I am suggesting that ordinarily, what the baby sees is him or herself. In other words, the mother is looking at the baby and what she looks like is related to what she sees there.
>
> (p. 112)

These authors are describing an interpersonal exchange across psychological space and how such exchange impacts the formation of self. The students described by Berlin see themselves in Moses, and Moses in turn finds his reflection in their glowing faces. Moses, witnessing the delight in the reflected appraisal, cannot help but respond favorably to his students, who in turn benefit from the positive affirmation.[1] Winnicott's baby looks into the eyes of his mother, finds himself, and the mother is in turn created by what she finds in the face of her infant. The baby sees himself in his mother's eyes and responds with delight, eliciting his mother's love. Each of the partners needs each other, utilizing the mutually projected experience – there is reciprocal engagement; they are partners in the work of the creation of the self.

Noah, through witnessing his self (Siegel, 2007) in relationship with me, could begin to locate those parts of his experience too fraught to accept and call his own. By playing with at first being him and then me, he could begin to gain some perspective of the other.

Later that spring, Noah's parents reported that they had been to a park over the weekend. Some children were playing with a soccer ball. Noah, still hesitant, watched the game from the sidelines, the other children still presenting a formidable challenge to his slowly expanding awareness of people. When the game finished, Noah's father noticed his son continuing to eye the ball. He asked the other children if Noah might take a turn with the ball. They agreed, and no sooner had Noah's father brought the ball over, to everyone's surprise, Noah, without missing a beat, ran up to the ball and kicked it hard – a sign of newfound strength, release from inhibition, and assertion of self.

And so, much in the way that we cannot be sure where the ball we aggressively kick will land, we learn to live with the ambiguity, the not-knowing, the hopes, wishes, and fears we all harbor, Noah's ball sailed off into the sky – hopefully landing softly, contained, somewhere out in the distance.

Note

1 I am indebted to Avivah Zornberg, Ph.D., for this insight.

References

Alvarez, A. (2012). *The thinking heart.* London, UK: Routledge.

Ammaniti, M. & Gallese, V. (2014). *The birth of intersubjectivity: psychodynamics, neurobiology and the self.* New York, NY: W.W. Norton & Co.

Aronson, S. (2007). Balancing the fiddlers on my roof: On wearing a yarmulke and working as a psychoanalyst. *Contemporary Psychoanalysis*, 43:451–459.

Beebe, B. & Lachmann, F. (2014). *The origins of attachment.* New York, NY: Routledge.

Bell, D. (2001). Projective identification. In: C. Bronstein (Ed.), *Kleinian theory: A contemporary perspective* (pp. 125–147). London, UK: Whurr Publishers/Wiley.

Berlin, N.Z. (1975). *Delve into the word*, Vol. 2. Jerusalem, Israel: El Hamekorot.

Bion, W. (1962). *Learning from experience.* London, UK: Maresfield.

Bromberg, P. (1998). *Standing in the spaces: Clinical essays.* New York, NY: Analytic Press.

Caper, R. (1999). *A mind of one's own.* London, UK: Routledge.

Fonagy, P., Steele, M., Moran, G., Steele, H., & Higgitt, A. (1993). Measuring the ghost in the nursery: An empirical study. *Journal of the American Psychoanalytic Association*, 41:957–989.

Frankel, J. (1998). The play's the thing. *Psychoanalytic Dialogues*, 8:149–182.

Gallese, V., Fadiga, L., Fogassi, L., & Rizzolatti, G. (1996). Action recognition in the premotor cortex. *Brain*, 119:593–609.

Hobson, P. (2002). *The cradle of thought.* London, UK: Macmillan.

Klein, M. (1930/1975). *Love, guilt, and reparation.* London, UK: Vintage.

Klein. M. (1955/1975). *Envy and gratitude.* London, UK: Vintage.

Likierman, M. (1988). Maternal love and positive projective identification. *Journal of Child Psychotherapy*, 14:29–46.

Meins, E., Fernyhough, C., Wainwright, R., Das Gupta, M., Fradley, E., & Tuckey, M. (2002). Maternal mind-mindedness and attachment security as predictors of theory of mind understanding. *Child Development*, 73:1715–1726.

Milner, M. (1955). The role of illusion in symbol formation. In: M. Klein, P. Heiman, & R. Money-Kyrle (Eds.), *Directions in psychoanalysis* (pp. 82–108). New York, NY: Basic Books.

Riesenberg-Malcolm, R. (2001). Bion's theory of containment. In: C. Bronstein (Ed.), *Kleinian theory: A contemporary perspective* (pp. 165–180). London, UK: Whurr Publishers/Wiley.

Siegel, D. (2007). *The mindful brain: Reflection and attunement in the cultivation of well-being.* New York, NY: W. W. Norton & Co.

Sodre, I. (2004). Who's who? Notes on pathological identifications. In: E. Hargreaves & A. Varchevker (Eds.), *In pursuit of psychic change* (pp. 53–65). London, UK: Routledge.

Stern, D. (2010). *Partners in thought.* New York, NY: Routledge.

Sullivan, H. (1940/1953). *The interpersonal theory of psychiatry.* New York, NY: W. W. Norton & Co.

Winnicott, D. (1971). *Playing and reality.* London, UK: Tavistock.

Section IV

Reimagining gender

Chapter 12

What's your gender?

Diane Ehrensaft, Ph.D.

Introduction

Recently, I was walking my dog on an early, gray California morning. I passed a parked city bus, doors open, the driver lounging in his seat. He looked out the open doors, smiled, and called out, "What a cute dog." I smiled back and thanked him, and then he asked, "Boy or girl?" Without a second's thought, still walking, I yelled back, "Boy," and continued on my way. Then I began to wonder, "I'm probably never going to see this person again, so why did he have to know whether my little 11-pound dog is a boy or girl? Does the assigned sex change the driver's perception of my dog? Did the information help the driver psychologically locate my dog in his own categorizations of girl dogs versus boy dogs?" My thoughts then wandered from bus drivers, dogs, and dog owners to therapists, children, and children's parents. Binary gender has been so deeply instilled in our psyches that we reflexively organize our relational dyads into "boy or girl", whether it is a child, a dog, or a pet rat. It is exactly this internal, reflexive binary gender organization that child clinicians need to bring to consciousness and shift if we are to establish empathic and effective therapeutic approaches to children who are neither, both, or not what you think they are – boy or girl.

Historically in psychoanalytic discourse, children who did not accept the sex assigned to them at birth or who demonstrated extreme variations from culturally dictated appropriate gender behaviors for their sex were diagnosed as having a disorder that needed to be treated. In 1973, the removal of homosexuality as a diagnosis in the Diagnostic and Statistical Manual of Mental Disorders (DSM) marked a paradigm shift from homosexuality as pathology to homosexuality as normal variation; the year 2013 followed suit in the removal of the diagnosis Gender Identity Disorder from the DSM, de-pathologizing gender nonconformity and making it a problem only if the person is in distress.

Yet the conceptual framework of gender as disease still remains fixed in many practitioners' lexicons, particularly in work with children. To correct this bias and establish best practices for children who go against the cultural gender grain, a new developmental framework, along with a matching set of clinical guidelines, has emerged to replace the model of gender as disease. Known as the gender affirmative model, its underlying principle is that gender in all its variation is a sign of health, not illness. The clinical goals are not to fix gender, but to provide the space for children to explore and establish their authentic gender self and for those children who are gender-nonconforming to build or strengthen gender resilience in the face of a social world that is not always ready to accept them, while simultaneously challenging that world to be more gender inclusive. Although the gender affirmative model is adaptive to many schools of clinical practice, it is particularly suited to psychoanalytic child therapy, where through listening, playing, mirroring, observing, relating, and interpreting we strive to get to the heart of the gender matter – what's on the child's mind, what are the developmental obstructions preventing the child from moving forward, and what are the intrapsychic and interpersonal knots that require untangling so that a child can discover their authentic gender self and go on being and growing with vitality and harmony. This chapter offers an excursion into this gender affirmative psychoanalytic model of child therapy.

Relearning gender

The first step in this model is to re-educate ourselves about gender. The developmental theory of gender upon which many of us cut our training teeth began with Freud (1938) and funneled into Stoller's (1985) model. A child is born and assigned a sex, male or female. If ambiguous, genital surgical procedures to establish a stable singular gender assignment should be done as soon as possible, as after 18 to 24 months a child is firmly in a core gender identity – I am male, I am female – and thereafter it becomes very difficult to change that identity. Once knowing one's gender label, which is both facilitated and mediated by parents' conscious and unconscious messages and reflections, a child's next developmental task is to learn how to "do" gender – gender role socialization. This activity is done in close relationship with one's mother and father (with the assumption that all children will have both). During this same period, a tumultuous drama unfolds – children have intense erotic fantasies about their parents: boys will want to marry their mothers, girls their fathers. Through successful negotiation of these fantasies, facilitated by parents' empathy and boundary setting, children will emerge from the Oedipal phase relinquishing those infantile incestuous desires, firming their own heterosexual identities as they forestall gratification and await an opposite sex partner of their own when they reach adulthood. Within that process they will establish a firm gender identity with a new understanding that one is and always will remain the sex listed on one's birth certificate or assigned early in life (for intersex children). If this developmental trajectory takes a course other than that described above, it was thought, there would be cause for concern, and parents would usually be to blame for the child's anomalies. To quote Stoller (1985) speaking of "primary transsexual" boys (those non-intersex boys who have been feminine from the first year of life):

> As an infant, such a boy usually has an excessively intimate, blissful, skin-to-skin closeness with his mother. This, unfortunately, is not interrupted by his father, a passive distant man who plays no significant part in bringing up his son.
>
> (p. 16)

In family situations like the one Stoller described above, professional help should be sought to cure the child's gender anomalies and to treat the parents so they cease veering their child's gender development in wrong directions because of their own neurotic conflicts.

For a theory of development to be robust, it should be evident in empirical observation. The above theory fails that test: many individuals continue renegotiating their gender throughout childhood or adulthood, with no observable detriment to their mental health. Children may establish a gender identity in concordance with their assigned sex, be firm in that identity, yet not embrace a heterosexual identity, with no aspersion on their emotional well-being. Whereas core gender identity is typically concordant with assigned sex based on observable external genitalia, for a minority of people this is not the case, with increasing evidence that gender identity lies not between our legs but between our ears, in our brains and minds (Diamond, 2000). Therefore, one's assigned sex at birth may differ from one's core gender identity, not because of poor parental handling or infantile confusions, but because of brain and mind gender messages overriding signals from genitalia, chromosomes, or parental expectations.

In a revised theory of gender development, gender identity is differentiated from gender expressions. Core gender identity is defined as the gender one knows oneself to be; it may or may not match the sex assigned at birth; it may not be binary. Whereas core gender identity is the "being" of gender, gender expressions are the "doing" of gender – how one puts together a gender presentation. We could otherwise understand gender identity as the existential core of the self, while gender expressions are a synonym for what we have come to know as the performance of gender, which leads me to a critique of Judith Butler's assessment of all gender as performance. Specifically, Butler has challenged essentialist binary gender categorizations and proposed instead that all gender is a performance, rather than an innate given (Butler, 2004). While an accurate assessment of gender expressions, Butler's stated position on gender as performance is less pertinent to one's core gender identity, which appears to have much more of a constitutional foundation than being solely a product of cultural sculpting and social transactions. Indeed, gender identity is communicated to those around us not just through our words and actions, but also in the sense of ourselves as experienced by others through nuance, feelings, and unconscious transmissions, factors far more amorphous than performance.

The role of the parent in this model is not to legislate, shape, or educate the child in the proper "doing" of gender, but to mirror back to the child an authentic rather than distorted image of that child's gender. In a transactional feedback loop, the infant or child, while influenced by the parents in the parents' conscious and unconscious communications about gender expectations, is also the driving force in communicating to the parents the child's specific gender desires and sensibilities.

Whereas, as mentioned above, gender identity is less amenable to environmental manipulation, gender expressions are much more malleable and influenced by environmental pre- and proscriptions. Borrowing from Winnicott's model of the true and false self (1960, 1965), the infant begins with a kernel of a true gender self, which is the baby's own constitutional possession. It may or may not match the sex identified on the birth certificate. The responsibility of the parents, as the holding environment, is to leave room for the child's gender individuality to unfold. If the parents impose their own gender wishes too strongly at the expense of the child's authentic gender desires, the child may be forced to establish a false gender self, either to accommodate environmental expectations or to protect the more fragile true gender self from harm. In this psychological mediating process, the child calls on gender creativity to put together an individualized gender self that is drawn from both the inside and the outside (Ehrensaft, 2011a, 2011b, 2012, 2016).

Put in different terms, the child uses the psyche to weave together a unique three-dimensional "gender web" from three major threads: nature, nurture, and culture (Ehrensaft, 2011a, 2012, 2016). If the environment around the child should impinge on the child's spinning of the web by grabbing the threads from the child, a child's true gender self is at risk of being suppressed or even annihilated. If the parents are able to keep their hands at their sides and instead appropriately mirror back to the child the child's unique gender self, the true gender self will more easily unfold, albeit still under the influence of the larger surrounding environment. In this model of development: (1) there are infinite possibilities, rather than just two (male/female) for the true gender self; (2) neither constitution nor environment prevails – they both live in dialectical tension with each other; and (3) the true gender self encompasses both core gender identity and chosen gender expressions. Neuroscience interfaces with genetics; genetics interfaces with intrauterine environment; physiology and the organism interface with environmental provisions; the social–cultural–political landscape both wraps around and is pushed in new directions by all the aforementioned forces.

This model of development is informed by the recent psychoanalytic theoretical constructs that posit multiple rather than binary categories of gender (Dimen, 2003; Goldner, 2003; Harris, 2005; Corbett,

2009). Rather than "either-or" we can now think about "all-or-any", "both-and", and "neither-nor" (Goldner, 2011). The gender affirmative model, developed in concordance with the theory of gender multiplicity, has recently been validated in both clinical observation (Corbett, 2009; Ehrensaft, 2011b, 2012, 2016) and empirical research, most poignantly in an Israeli study (Joel et al., 2014) that investigated the gender narratives of a sample of 2155 Israeli subjects who reported fluid feelings about their own gender. The researchers concluded:

> Taken together, our findings suggest that dichotomous gender categorisation does not reflect the complexity and multiplicity of gender experience. Rather, our study provides supportive evidence to non-binary theories of gender that perceive gender as fluid rather than dichotomous, and consider all human beings, not just gender nonconforming individuals, to have complex assemblages of gendered selves.

> (p. 22)

So now we come to the key question: how does this gender multiplicity model of development translate into work with children in the therapy room?

Who's that knocking at my door?

A child's gender can bring that child to our clinical door for many reasons. In one family, the parents cannot make sense of their child. They have four daughters, but only this one has been consistently resistant to conforming to being the girl that child is supposed to be. Their child is upset, they are worried, and the grandparents are putting pressure on them to fix this problem – it just is not right. In another family, the parents are in full support of their child being gender-nonconforming or transgender, but they worry *they* may not have it right. In yet another family, a child is in distress about gender and asks to go see someone for help. The list could go on, but suffice it to say that children will show up on our clinical doorsteps for a variety of gender-related reasons and always the relational task for the psychotherapist will remain the same: to listen to the child and facilitate that child in getting their gender footing.

Circling back to the nonbinary developmental gender theory, an extrapolation of Irene Fast's theory of gender inclusivity (1984, 1999) provides an enlightening portal into the psyches of children who are defying the gender norms of their culture or the sex assignment given to them at birth. In Fast's theory, there is a pre-Oedipal stage of gender inclusivity, in which the toddler believes that all genders are in the range of that child's possibilities. (More accurately, Fast only posits two genders, with the child's belief that it is possible to be both a boy and a girl or to switch between the two.) With the advent of the Oedipal stage comes the sobering realization that one cannot be all genders, only one, and with sorrow but acceptance, the child accomplishes the developmental task of gender constancy, coming to understand that there are no backsies when it comes to gender. The gender-nonconforming children knocking at our doors may not have moved on, but rather continue to operate from the earlier sensibility that gender in flux, in transition, or in transformation is within the realm of possibility as long as we are not so restricted in our thinking as to assume that gender is dictated by the body. In a traditional psychoanalytic framework, we would interpret this as a developmental arrest, with serious concern for the child's reality testing and body–psyche integration. Within the constructs of the gender affirmative model, however, this sensibility is understood instead as a manifestation of gender creativity, evidence of a rebel with a cause – to claim the true gender self and to challenge an essentialist notion of gender: if gender lies more between my ears than between my legs, then I can envision, imagine, and compose within my mind, both consciously and unconsciously, my own unique mosaic of gender possibilities that come together from the inside, the outside, and somewhere in-between.

Sometimes these children come to our offices only whispering this gender revelation; sometimes they belt it out loud and clear; sometimes they bury it from consciousness but it leaks out in their play, in their actions, in their gender stress or distress, and in the conscious and unconscious transmissions within the relationship they establish with us as their therapists. It is not uncommon for a little boy whose parents have come to me to have had the following dialogue with his parents:

Parent: We know you love to play with Barbies and dress up in princess gowns and boys can do that, too, you know.

Child: I know, I know, but that's not what I said. I said I'm a *girl* who likes to play with Barbies.

Another common dialogue:

Child: My new name is Gregory. Don't call me Gigi anymore.

Parent: But, honey, you're a girl, not a boy. That's why you have a girl's name.

Child: Well, maybe for now, but then when do I get to be a boy?

If a frog can turn into a prince, then surely a girl can turn into a boy or a boy into a girl or a half-and-half and, truth be told, it is a lot more realistic for a girl to become a boy than for a frog to become a prince. With the influence of changing cultural norms and the introduction of medical interventions (puberty blockers, cross-sex hormones, and surgeries) to better align one's affirmed gender self with one's sexed body (Ehrensaft, 2011a, 2016; Hidalgo et al., 2013), the gender-inclusive, gender-creative child can maintain the vision of gender fluidity and transformation long after that child knows that frogs will be frogs and princes may turn into kings (or queens), but never frogs. In that light, the children's gender inclusivity counts as developmental expansiveness rather than developmental arrest, an eventuality that needs to be kept in mind as the children who are neither, both, or not what we think they are – boy or girl – come to us for mental health support. Long before reaching adulthood, these children who are knocking at our door with their persistent, unrelinquished gender inclusivity offer us, in their jouissance and naiveté, a window into the construct of gender fluidity, articulated by Goldner (2011) that "[as] genders morph and multiply, it becomes clearer that gender is a circulating, transferable property, an 'improvisational possibility'" (p. 166).

As we open the door to children who are questioning, exploring, or declaring their gender, the greatest clinical concern is for the children who are in distress or in states of stress about their gender. Most likely, these children will fall under one of two umbrellas, or perhaps move from under one to under the other, or stand beneath both:

1. Under the first umbrella are the children who do not conform in their gender expressions to what is expected from them in the culture in which they are growing and are discomforted about that,

because of either internal angst or external pressures or a combination of both.

2. Under the second umbrella are the children who become aware that the sex assigned to them at birth does not match the gender they know themselves to be, often with significant angst about the mismatch between their sexed body and their gendered psyche.

Many of these children come from families who support them, yet they are still in distress. Some will come from environments that do not support them and are at higher risk not only for stress, but also for some significant psychological difficulties, including anxiety, depression, self-harm, and suicidality (Grossman & D'Auguelli, 2007; Roberts et al., 2012). Many, with all their gender inclusivity, may nonetheless mourn the life they can never wholly have. As expressed most poignantly by a 17-year-old transfeminine patient of mine, "In my heart, I know that I will never have everything I want to become the woman that I am." Even at a very young age, gender-dysphoric children experience this sense of loss and frustration, as illustrated by a six-year-old patient: "Why couldn't my mommy put me back inside her so I could come out the right gender? Why did God get it wrong? I thought God knew everything. Well, He sure didn't know about me." Our role as clinicians is to help the child deal with these losses and establish a relational space where we can get down to the work of "knowing about me" and, where indicated, fortifying gender resilience, which involves holding true to one's gender even in a world not supportive of that gender.

The therapist: An ear, a mirror, and a translator

The basic principle of the gender affirmative clinical model is simple: if you want to know what a child's gender is, listen and the child will tell you. It is not for us to say but for the child to affirm. If taken at face value, this rubric generates waves of anxiety and reflexive criticism, leading to a misinterpretation of the practice modality as a thoughtless, speedy process in which the clinician pulls out a tablet, asks the child what their gender is, and then promptly rubber stamps what the child says – because, after all, it is not for the clinician to say. Nothing could be further from the truth. The simplicity of the basic principle can only be understood when converted into the complicated clinical processes that ensue and the role of the clinician in those processes.

Just as there is no infant without a parent (Winnicott, 1975), there is no gender journey without the child in relationship with a holding environment, be it parents, therapist, or the social world surrounding the child. In the traditional psychoanalytic model in which gender variations are seen as neuroses or anomalies to be cured, the analyst, as an agent of change, is assigned the task of identifying distortions in masculinity and femininity and working to repair them by getting boys to be more masculine and girls to be more feminine, typically with the intent of warding off a transgender or homosexual outcome and, ironically, often with a slippage into behavior modification techniques to reinforce "appropriate" gender performance. In the gender affirmative model that acknowledges an infinite range of gender possibilities that transcend assigned sex at birth and its accompanying social proscriptions and prescriptions, no such agent of change is needed. Instead, the intent is to establish a therapeutic relationship that facilitates children living as their most authentic gender, be it male, female, or other, and be it matching or different from their assigned sex. The job of the clinician is not to ward off a homosexual, transgender, or gender-nonconforming outcome, but to facilitate the child's discovery of the authentic gender self, making relational use of the child's and the clinician's gender creativity to open up the intermediary space where this discovery can take place.

As a child therapist in training, I was taught to wait until a child brings material to you; you do not force it on the child. This should fit in very nicely with the gender affirmative model of "listen and the child will tell you", except for one problem. In a social world replete with angst about gender variations, the child who comes to us with gender conundrums may have read cues, either consciously or unconsciously, and internalized at a very young age that their gender transgressions in thought or action are things of which we do not speak, not even to the nice lady who knows about gender and is supposed to help with those things. Therefore, one can wait until hell freezes over and a child will still remain sealed off, either to the clinician or to themselves if the gender material is buried under layers of the unconscious. So the first seeming contradiction in the listening approach is the sometimes necessary "breaking of the rules" by initiating the conversation about gender, rather than waiting for it to unfold. We can consider it an invitation and initial facilitation, offering a potentially "safe" space, one which the child can eagerly or tentatively accept or alternatively throw in our face as trespassing on the child's private internal space, at which point, like in any other treatment, we back off, watch, and wait.

At the same time that we offer a hand to the child, we work to build an alliance with the parents. In this model, there will be no child in therapy without active participation of the parents, who are typically the first to tip the clinician off with their own perceptions of their child's gender behaviors and feelings, along with whatever weight they carry about their own responsibility for or reactions to their child's gender presentations. As we meet with the parents, we may also experience an intense push from without or a pull from within to quickly arrive at a conclusion. The parents are often anxious if not desperate to get some answers so they can locate their child in gender space. In Western culture, for both clinician and parent, gender has typically been embedded in our psyches as bedrock – we have to know: boy or girl, man or woman. The child may be in no such hurry or under no such binary gender orders, so the second relational complication about the gender affirmative listening model involves training oneself to overcome the need-to-know angst and live in an intermediate space of gender ambiguity, of gender-not-knowing, and to help parents do the same. This is exactly why, far from the misperceived instantaneous rubber stamping of gender authenticity based on a child's initial report, the child's discovery of the authentic gender self and the clinician's acknowledgment of that self may move as slow as molasses and only come months – if not years – after a therapeutic dyad has been firmly in place. So to listen is also to wait.

Over time, the function of the therapist while waiting and listening parallels the task of the parent in a child's early development: to mirror back to the child what the child is presenting to the parent. From the oft-quoted passage in *Playing and reality*, Winnicott (1970) states:

> Psychotherapy is not making apt and clever interpretations; by and large it is a long-term giving the patient back what the patient brings. It is a complex derivative of the face that reflects back what is there to be seen.
>
> (p. 117)

This quote applies almost to an exaggerated degree to the relational work with a child who is coming to us to discover their true gender self, finding the gender that is there to be seen, whether it be in expressions, identity, or both. Let us return to the example of my little patient who bemoaned: "Why did God get it wrong and make me the gender I'm not?" If I were to interpret to this child that he was externalizing his frustration on others rather than accepting and mourning the loss of what he wished he was but was not, at a minimum he would feel let down, experiencing me as not hearing what he was telling me. At a deep level, he might experience himself as having entered a funhouse where the mirrors are all distorted and reflect back to him some grotesque image of himself, rather than the person he was trying to tell me he was – not based on his birth certificate, but on what his psyche told him. This child was communicating not that he *wished* he were a girl, but that he *was* a girl, a state of being that even the deities got wrong by giving this child the wrong external genitalia in light of his own internal reflection of self as a girl, one who liked to wear dresses and have long, flowing hair, rather than the shaved buzz cut he was forced to have under his father's critical and watchful eye. To mirror back to this child what was there to be seen was to articulate, "You so much want me to see you as the girl you are, not the boy everyone thinks you are, because of the mistake God made with your body."

Finding the face that is there to be seen is another one of those deceptively simple formulas for relationship when it comes to gender, because of the required stretching, imagining, and pushing oneself out of one's comfort zone, as the therapist has to rewire their own brain synapses to hold in mind that penis does not equal boy and vagina does not equal girl and that boy and girl clothes are really all just people clothes, and so forth. In searching for the face there to be seen, therapists may be encumbered by their own gender histories; the reflection back to the child may have shades of the therapist's own gender sensibilities, which may in turn color the child's understanding of the child's own gender within the relational matrix of gender discovery. So cleaning the mirror to rid it of the therapist's own projected gender distortions and thumb prints is a necessary component of facilitating the child's discovery of the authentic gender self. In that reciprocal process, the therapist may simultaneously discover something new about their own gender self.

If getting the mirror in place was not enough of a challenge, the therapist also has to strain to translate what the child is showing or alternatively hiding through feelings, speech, fantasies, dreams, ruminations, and actions about both the true gender self and the false gender self that may be cloaking the inner gender identity and/or expressions. Children do not necessarily have cohesive narratives about their gender any more than any of us do. They cannot communicate the *why* of gender, only the *what* and *how* of gender, so it is absurd to pose the following question to a child: "Why do you want to be a girl?" With a blank face, a child might respond, "Because I am one." The same blank stare might ensue if a boy is queried, "Why do you want to wear a dress?" The often-heard response: "Because I like dresses."

To make matters even more complicated, the reflection of the child's "gender face" that we search to give back is often opaque or shrouded, particularly in the context of a social world not necessarily welcoming of a child who goes against the gender grain, creating either conscious suppression or unconscious repression. Concurrent with suppression or repression may be manifest anxiety or depression because of contemporary or historically distorted or inaccurate gender mirroring by the child's social environment, beginning with the parents, contributing to the gender face that may be hard, if not impossible, to find because the child is not willing to expose it and/or it is unsafe to show that face to the light of day. The therapeutic hope is that through the relationship between therapist and child, if it is not compromised by the therapist's gender angst or inflexibility, the conditions will be set for the child to come out from under the shell of self-protection, fear, or denial and find the safety to both explore and communicate about the gender web they are constructing from the threads of nature, nurture, and culture.

There are indeed some children who are not so hard to read: they demonstrate clearly from a very young age that they are not the gender that is indicated on their birth certificate; they are either the opposite one or some other one altogether. Their declarations are often made clear in a single verb – "am" rather than "wish to be". They are persistent, insistent, and consistent from an early age in their communication through word, action, ideation, and affect about their affirmed gender identity. Over time, we discover that these children are relatively impervious to the relational matrix: they will revert back to their insistence on knowing their gender identity, no matter what distortions the environment or their social or therapeutic relational matrices may reflect back to them. In these cases, their gender is not a wish; it simply "is" – an existential knowledge of the self embedded deep in the psyche, certainly arrived at only after entry into a relational world that informs the child of the concept of gender as a category of life, but stubbornly of the child's own making. Far more than performance, for these children, we experience the "being" of gender, a psychologically bounded sense of self that is out of synch with the sex-coded embodiment of gender as the culture has defined it. Relationally, these children are often our easiest patients: we listen and they tell us very directly. This is in contrast to the children who truly do not know but are anxious to untangle the biopsychosocial knots and discover the pathways to their authentic gender identity and/or expressions. I will highlight the relational challenges of this latter group of children by presenting snippets of my work with a gender-nonconforming child over time as I attempted to translate and mirror back what the child was telling me about her/his gender.

Maddie/Matt

Maddie was nine years old when she first came to see me. In an initial parent consultation, I learned from Maddie's mother and father that when she was three, she asked her mother, in all earnestness, "Am I going to turn into a boy when I'm five?" Maddie was clearly immersed in Irene Fast's stage of gender inclusiveness, in which the essentialism of the body is overridden by the imaginings of the psyche. By the age of four, she refused to wear dresses, but in her activities, up until the age of seven, she gravitated toward activities more typically "girl" in our culture, especially art. She eschewed any type of sport. Her friends were primarily girls. At around her seventh birthday, she began to become obsessed with playing sports – basketball, football, and taekwondo. She started dressing more and more like a boy, choosing all of her clothes from the boys' section of stores. If sitting at a table in a restaurant, a waiter would most likely ask, "And what would *he* like to drink?" Maddie would never correct these perceptions of her and was genuinely pleased when taken for a boy. Over the next year, Maddie began using the boys' bathroom in public places.

At about that same time, Maddie's mother was diagnosed with a serious illness that could prove to be fatal. Coincident with her mother's diagnosis, Maddie began to ask people to call her Matt, but indicated that she still wanted to be referred to using female pronouns. Just before my first visit with Maddie, she had attended a cousin's bar mitzvah in a shirt, tie, and sports coat.

Maddie's parents also reported that since infancy, Maddie had been sensitive to loud noises, finding them intolerable. She was also hyper-alert to her physical surroundings. Always very adept with words, she became a very early reader, voraciously reading whenever given the chance. She was also very scientifically minded, and had a pronounced curiosity to know how things worked. Related to her early hypersensitivities, Maddie in recent years was laden with fears, which she felt intensely – of the dark, of bad stories on the news, of tongue depressors and injections at the doctor's office. Maddie's parents observed that she played with both boys and girls, but had no real friends and was never invited to classmates' birthday parties.

Maddie's parents had long been aware of their daughter's gender nonconformity and were simultaneously supportive and puzzled – was this about gender or something else? Was Maddie transgender, fluid in her gender, or unstable in her gender identity? By their observation, Maddie had long ago ceased asking when she was going to turn into a boy, but appeared to have simply seized fate in her own hands as she evolved toward a more masculine presence in dress, activities, and name. Like many parents of their generation, Maddie's mother and father had read up on transgender children and were aware of medical interventions for transgender or gender dysphoric children, particularly gonadotropin-releasing hormone agonists, commonly known as puberty blockers, to halt the advent of a potentially unwanted puberty and buy a child more time to explore gender. They both shared, in their own gender histories, a rather expansive and accepting sensibility about gender. In fact, the father demonstrated many traits that in our culture would be on the "feminine" side of a binary gender scale, while the mother also exhibited cross-gender expressions, some of them survival tactics related to her participation in a male-dominated, highly competitive professional field. While perplexed by Maddie's gender presentation, neither of them appeared to be threatened by her gender nonconformity. Their own mirroring back to Maddie about her gender could best be described as "whatever floats your boat." As a reflection of their sensitivity to Maddie's gender explorations and concerns, although Maddie was now only nine and showing no signs of the early stages of puberty (when puberty blockers are first considered), her parents thought it would be helpful to set up an informational consultation with a pediatric endocrinologist to learn more about these procedures for putting a pause on puberty. After meeting with the family, the endocrinologist referred Maddie to me for the purpose of gaining insight into Maddie's gender status.

So our work began, not as a weekly psychotherapy, because of geographic distance, but within the model of ongoing therapeutic consultations over time, sessions that have continued into the present. During that time, we have built a strong relationship in which Maddie holds me in mind as the person who writes books about gender and helps kids figure out theirs.

The nine-year-old child who first walked into my office was stiff, formal, and reasonably shy, dressed in a white button down shirt over a t-shirt, shorts, and sneakers, with long, cascading curls. Her parents had informed me that she was now starting to ask people to call her Matt, so my first query was to ask what name she would like me to call her. Without a moment's hesitation, she replied, "You can call me Maddie and you can think of me as a girl, although actually, I'm in the middle." I should note that Maddie's parents were quite surprised to learn this later, as she had been insistent with every other new person she met that they refer to her as Matt. As I heard Maddie describe herself, the thought ran through me, "How exactly do you mirror back 'in the middle'?" a clear indicator of my own emotional experience of being knocked off balance by Maddie's self-report of gender fluidity, despite all my clinical experiences and my writing, teaching, and lecturing about the multiplicity of gender.

Maddie went on to tell me that she had three best friends, all boys; one second best friend, a girl; and a whole list of boys who were definitively in the category of "not friends." She echoed her parents' report by explaining, "I like flag football and baseball, but—" she paused "—I still like to do girl things, too." Noting the formality of Maddie's speech and her observable social discomfort in the room, I tagged another thought: "Has anyone done an evaluation for or suggested

Asperger's?" More questions came to me: "What about the mother's illness, how does that factor in? If it's Asperger's, is gender really the issue? Could it be inability to read social cues about gender or obsessive preoccupations, presently focused on gender?"

Historically, a child's disavowal of their assigned sex or confusion about their gender has been posited to be a result of early trauma, attachment disruptions, or parenting neuroses (Stoller, 1985; Coates et al., 1991; Zucker & Bradley, 1995). Maddie had none of the three, as far as I could tell, and recent investigations have debunked any of these factors as primary determinants of gender nonconformity (Ehrensaft, 2007, 2011a, 2016). However, even though Maddie's expressions of gender nonconformity and queries about gender transitions preceded her mother's major illness, I could not discount the possibility that anxiety about her mother's recent diagnosis had catapulted Maddie into a more extreme position on her gender, with a move from Maddie to Matt (except with me). In our early visits, Maddie was able to talk about her mother's illness, but somewhat dispassionately – just reporting the facts. Although her parents indicated Maddie's verbal precocity, she was fairly taciturn with me. I found that I was able to learn much more about her from her play than her words. Among the vast possibilities of toys and figures from which to choose, Maddie pulled out all the hospital and dentist toys, and then proceeded to line up every form of military figure, ancient to modern, set up to surround and protect a figure of indeterminate gender lying on a stretcher outside a meticulously organized doctor's office. I wondered with her whether she was trying to tell me something about her mother's recent illness. Maddie just looked at me and shrugged. Much of the work I was doing was in my head, rather than in dialogue with Maddie, as intuitively I thought it most important to just offer a holding space. I was impressed that gender might not have been the first thing on Maddie's mind right now, with her mother being so ill. I was concerned that perhaps her parents felt more of an urgency to fast forward on Maddie's gender status as her mother might not be around that much longer and would want to know before dying.

As so much of children's play is overdetermined, the hospital scenes Maddie repeatedly constructed were not just about her mother's illness; they turned out also to be about her. Her parents had previously explained to her what puberty blockers were and why some children took them, either by injection or subcutaneous implant. Maddie brought up the subject herself with me in one of our early visits. She told me in minimal words that she did not like the puberty blocker idea because "I HATE SHOTS." Therefore, she would be just fine staying in the middle. Did the blockers, morphed into feared and hated shots, symbolize an intrusion into Maddie's gender inclusivity where she could be any and all rather than have to choose between either/or? Had the blockers gotten conflated with the drugs her mother had to take for her illness and therefore repudiated as something not to be thought about? After we had met a number of times and had woven together some threads of connection, I tried floating a balloon by sharing my ruminations with Maddie. Although I was still experiencing Maddie's relational woodenness, I felt fortified to go forth based on her mother's earlier report that while Maddie was extremely anxious about coming to see me, she left the first appointment reporting to her mother, "That was really OK. She's nice." But perhaps I had gone too far, for as I finished sharing my thoughts that blockers might be an intrusion and too much like her mother's medicines, Maddie grew stiff and anxiously hopped from foot to foot; she could only respond by staring ahead.

So what could I translate about Maddie's true gender self at that time? Maddie appeared to be living in some middle ground between boy and girl, but it was far too early to tell if she was transgender. Typically, the transgender child communicates, "I am a [gender other than the gender matching the sex assigned at birth]," whereas the gender fluid child states, "I wish I were a [gender other than the gender matching the sex assigned at birth]" (Ehrensaft, 2012; Steensma et al., 2013). Maddie had not definitively communicated either. There were some soft signs of Asperger's, which could compromise Maddie's thinking and lead to idiosyncratic solutions to life problems or an inability to read social gender cues, clouding rather than lighting the way toward Maddie's true gender self. However, findings from the gender clinic in Amsterdam indicate a statistically significantly higher percentage of the children definitively diagnosed with primary gender dysphoria at their clinic having a diagnosis of an autism spectrum disorder than is found in the general public (de Vries et al., 2010), suggesting a coexisting phenomenon rather than gender nonconformity as a solution to or sequela of underlying social communication struggles. The repudiation of puberty blockers was confounded by Maddie's morbid fear of injections, so giving me little clarity about Maddie's gendered self. What puzzled me most was this child's insistence that I recognize her as a girl named Maddie, while demanding that others begin addressing her as a boy named Matt.

I will leave the reader with that puzzle and fast forward two years. Maddie is now Matt full time – with male pronouns. Referred by me for a full neuropsychological workup early in our consultations, Matt qualified for a diagnosis of Asperger's and gender dysphoria in the context of an intellectually gifted child. Matt has seen a therapist on a weekly basis to treat his social anxieties, while seeing me periodically for "gender check-ups." He got over the fear of injections enough to be able to express a desire to go on puberty blockers to put physiological puberty on hold and buy some time while he explored his gender further. He actually got a "get out of jail free" card by opting for a blocker administered as a yearly subcutaneous implant through an outpatient surgical procedure rather than enduring monthly shots. His speech is still formalistic, but Matt is far more outgoing and articulate than in our first meetings. His main preoccupation right now is making it onto the boys' basketball team. I could not say that Matt now feels totally comfortable in his skin as a boy, but rather that, for the present, he has found a male identity to be the best fit for him, even though there is still quite a bit of girl and girl/boy within him. His transition from Maddie to Matt has been an evolutionary unfolding and my own reading of Matt's gender face is that he is one of those youths who will benefit from putting a halt on puberty with blockers, allowing him more time to explore his gender identity before consolidating his true gender self, which could conceivably be other than binary. His mother is still very ill and he is now able to speak openly and with deep feeling about his worries for her, bringing into focus that his angst about his mother runs parallel to his cross-gender identification, rather than causing it.

In a recent visit, he explained that in his last bimonthly meeting with the pediatric endocrinologist at the local gender clinic, the doctor neglected to ask him (which he always had done before), "On a scale of 1 to 10, if 1 is girl and 10 is boy, what number would you give yourself?" (Of note is that the interdisciplinary staff team at the clinic had just decided to eliminate that question from their clinical protocols because it was too binary in conception, leaving little room for gender multiplicity.) Matt was indignant about the clinic dropping the protocol, because he had some important news: "Last time I was a 5. But now I'm a 6." Because we went back a long way with each other, I shared with Matt the gender concept I had learned from another child who presented as a boy in the front but then spun around to display a long, blonde braid with a bow in the back: "You see, I'm a Prius. Half boy/half girl. I'm a hybrid." Matt sat thoughtfully for a moment, and then lit up: "Hmmm. Then I think I might be moving toward a Tesla." Translation: hybrid = living in the middle; electric = all boy. Over the years, I have worked to translate and to mirror back to Maddie/Matt what she/he has presented to me. In return, with a glint in his eye, Matt told me excitedly in our last visit, "You know, you should write a book about me."

Conclusion

According to Gabbard (2003), "A theory of therapeutic action must describe both what changes (the aims of treatment) and what strategies are likely to be useful in facilitating those changes (technique)." The gender affirmative model, using listening, mirroring, and translation as its tools, appears to qualify as a therapeutic action theory, with its aim of helping the child discover the true gender self. To evaluate the effectiveness of the technique, I would like to propose, letting Matt be our guide, that we hold off on a final assessment until Matt is old enough to write his own book about himself.

References

Butler, J. (2004). *Undoing gender*. New York, NY: Routledge.

Coates, S., Friedman, R.C., & Wolfe, S. (1991). The etiology of boyhood gender identity disorder: A model for integrating temperament, development, and psychodynamics. *Psychoanalytic Dialogues*, 1:481–523.

Corbett, K. (2009). *Boyhoods: Rethinking masculinities*. New Haven, CT: Yale University Press.

de Vries, L.C., Noens, I.L.J., Cohen-Kettenis, P.T., van Berckelaer-Onnes, I., & Doreleijers, T.A. (2010). Autism spectrum disorders in gender dysphoric children and adolescents. *Journal of Autism and Developmental Disorders*, 40:930–936.

Diamond, M. (2000). Sex and gender: Same or different? *Feminism & Psychology*, 10:46–54.

Dimen, M. (2003). *Sexuality, intimacy, power*. Hillsdale, NJ: The Analytic Press.

Ehrensaft, D. (2007). Raising girlyboys: A parent's perspective. *Studies in Gender and Sexuality*, 8:269–302.

Ehrensaft, D. (2011a). *Gender born, gender made: Raising healthy gender-nonconforming children*. New York, NY: The Experiment.

Ehrensaft, D. (2011b). Boys will be girls, girls will be boys: Children affect parents as parents affect children in gender nonconformity. *Psychoanalytic Psychology*, 28:528–548.

Ehrensaft, D. (2012). From gender identity disorder to gender identity creativity: True gender self therapy. *Journal of Homosexuality*, 59:337–356.

Ehrensaft, D. (2016). *The gender creative child: Pathways to nurturing and supporting children who live outside gender boxes*. New York, NY: The Experiment.

Fast, I. (1984). *Gender identity: A differentiation model*. Hillsdale, NJ: The Analytic Press.

Fast, I. (1999). Aspects of core gender identity. *Psychoanalytical Dialogues*, 9:633–661.

Freud, S. (1938). Three contributions to the theory of sex. In: *The basic writings of Sigmund Freud* (pp. 562–563). New York, NY: Random House.

Gabbard, G. (2003). Rethinking therapeutic action. *The International Journal of Psychoanalysis*, 84:823–841.

Goldner, V. (2003). Ironic gender/authentic sex. *Studies in Gender and Sexuality*, 4:113–139.

Goldner, V. (2011). Trans: Gender in free fall. *Psychoanalytic Dialogues*, 21:159–171.

Grossman, A.H. & D'Augelli, A.R. (2007). Transgender youth and life-threatening behaviors. *Suicide and Life Threatening Behavior*, 37:527–537.

Harris, A. (2005). *Gender as soft assembly*. Hillsdale, NJ: The Analytic Press.

Hidalgo, M.A., Ehrensaft, D., Tishelman, A.C., Clark, L.F., Gorofalo, R., Rosenthal, S.M., Spack, N.P., & Olson, J. (2013). The gender affirmative model: What we know and what we aim to learn. *Human Development*, 56:285–290.

Joel, D., Tarrasch R., Berman Z., Mukamel M., & Ziv E. (2014). Queering gender: Studying gender identity in the normative population. *Psychology and Sexuality*, 5:291–321.

Roberts, A.L., Rosario, M., Corliss, H.L., Koenen, K.C., & Austin, S.B. (2012). Childhood gender nonconformity: A risk indicator for childhood abuse and post-traumatic stress in youth. *Pediatrics*, 129:410–417.

Schwartzapfel, B. (2013). Little boxes. *The American Prospect*, 24:36–47.

Steensma, T.D., McGuire, J. K., Kreuls, B., Beekman, A., & Cohen-Kettenis, P. (2013). Factors associated with desistence and persistence of childhood gender dysphoria: A quantitative follow-up study. *Journal of the American Academy of Child and Adolescent Psychiatry*, 52:582–590.

Stoller, R. (1985). *Presentations of gender.* New Haven, CT: Yale University Press.

Wallace, R. & Russell, H. (2013). Attachment and shame in gender-nonconforming children and their families: Toward a theoretical framework for evaluating clinical interventions. *International Journal of Transgenderism*, 14:113–126.

Winnicott, D.W. (1960). Ego distortion in terms of true and false self. In: D.W. Winnicott, *Maturational processes and the facilitating environment* (pp. 140–152). Madison, CT: International Universities Press.

Winnicott, D.W. (1965). *Maturational processes and the facilitating environment.* Madison, CT: International Universities Press.

Winnicott, D.W. (1970). *Playing and reality.* London, UK: Tavistock Publications.

Winnicott, D.W. (1975). *Through paediatrics to psycho-analysis.* New York, NY: Basic Books.

Zucker, K. & Bradley, S. (1995). *Gender identity disorder and psychosexual problems in children and adolescents.* New York, NY: Guilford Press.

Chapter 13

Holding futurity in mind

Therapeutic action in the relational treatment of a transgender girl[1]

Avgi Saketopoulou, Psy.D.

My six-year-old patient, Jenny, and I worked together in analytic play therapy for a year and a half before she was able to share with me something I had only known from her parents: Jenny had been born male. Careful and patient work, which I'll describe in detail, made it possible for Jenny to move from being deeply invested in my not knowing about her natal body to wanting to share with me this fact that was painful to her. When she did, rather than saying to me, as one might expect, that she had been born male, Jenny framed the disclosure as follows: "I don't want you to think I've been lying to you, but there is something I haven't told you: Dad thinks I am a boy." Jenny paused, scanning my face for a reaction, then added sadly, "Sometimes I wear boy clothes so his heart doesn't keep breaking."

Jenny's statement captures something crucial about the experience of trans children like her: for her, it is of course the father who makes a mistaken gender attribution. This brings into sharp focus a key controversy: is the child confused about their gender or is the environment failing to understand that which does not meet expectable forms of gender?

These kinds of questions juxtapose external reality with internal experience, pitting psychic and social forces against each other instead of attending to their interpenetration. This makes them unnecessarily facile. Jenny, for instance, was unquestionably a liar, if only a Winnicottian one. Much like other trans children her age (Ehrensaft, 2011; 2013), she was hard at work developing a false, male-presenting self (Winnicott, 1954) to protect her father from his distress about her femaleness.[2] Aware that body morphology determines how one's gender is perceived, Jenny's negation ("I don't want you to think I am a liar") concealed her concern that if I knew, I, too, would think of her as a boy. Still, Jenny's problem did not exclusively derive from without; that is, from living in a world that treats gender as fixed by biology. Jenny's was also a problem of inner life. Since her gender experience painfully and perplexingly clashed with her bodily morphology, Jenny was *herself* confused about how it was possible to be a girl when her body spelled "boy".

Tackling therapeutically any single one of these issues would be in itself a difficult task. To deal with all of these, as well as with the unconscious fantasies and defensive strategies that undergird them, is an extraordinarily challenging clinical endeavor (DiCeglie, 2009). Psychoanalysis is well equipped to address such nuanced therapeutic needs precisely because it can help illuminate how inner and outer synergistically complicate and amplify each other. Relational psychoanalysis is particularly helpful in that task because it comes with an armamentarium of conceptual and clinical tools that, as I'll show, can be incredibly useful in the treatment of transgender children.

In this chapter, I will eschew the much-debated quest for etiological factors. I will do so because I believe that we can work well with transgender children only if we treat their gender not as a symptom but as a *viable subjective reality*. My particular focus thus will be to try to comprehend how unconscious fantasy may be mobilized to manage the painful experience of gender/body mismatch *once it has already been formed*. One possible such dynamic deployed to deal with the distress that arises from the discontinuities between body and gender experience is, I will propose, the unconscious fantasy that one has been born into the wrong body. The work of mourning, of coming to terms with the body one has, is critical in order for a child to have a healthy social transition.

Massive gender trauma

I use the term *massive gender trauma* to describe a developmental trajectory that captures the struggles of some transgender children (and of some transgender adults, though I'll be focusing on child work in this chapter). Massive gender trauma arises at the frequent, yet oner-ous intersection of two critical, often paired, psychic events:

a. The experience of being misgendered; that is of being mis-recognized by one's primary objects as belonging to one's natal sex despite the child's insistent claims to a different gender identity. When gender is tenaciously conflated with bodily morphology, such children often feel unseen and unknown (Ehrensaft, 2013a).
b. Gender-inflected body dysphoria: the painful feeling that one's physical body and one's gender are misaligned (e.g. a female child who understands themselves as a boy). Such dysphoria can present as early as two or three years of age (Coates, 2006; Edwards-Leeper & Spack, 2013) and is often accompanied by a powerful wish for coherence between one's experienced gender and bodily anatomy.[3]

Massive gender trauma issues from the melange of these two distinct but inter-implicated psychic events. It is a particularly toxic, psychi-cally combustible blend that shares some of the formal features of traumatic experience like dissociation, anxiety, and depression. In my discussion of process material from Jenny's treatment, I will illustrate that the fact that children have to negotiate these difficulties together with, and sometimes through, the synchronous burdens of normative psychic growth leaves the developing psyche porous to psychiatric ill-ness. The dynamic solutions some such children may adopt to manage these challenges and the way in which unconscious fantasy can become recruited in dealing with the discontinuities between the sexed body and gender experience can then become folded into the very structure of the personality, leading to serious characterological problems, dif-ficulties with emotional regulation, and even impaired reality testing. Notably, research has shown a propensity to mood-disordered presen-tations in children who struggle with their gender (Edwards-Leeper & Spack, 2013).[4] As these problems get woven into the very fabric of how a child negotiates their intrapsychic and intersubjective worlds, strate-gies that originated in the attempt to manage massive gender trauma may become a part of their character (Krystal, 1978, 1985) and overall psychological functioning. The ensuing emotional difficulties and psy-chiatric problems, I am thus proposing, often *result from* the traumatic

and unmentalized impact of being trans, rather than being their originary cause, as is often assumed.

Parents frequently react to children's body dysphoria with anxiety,
alarm, and bewilderment. Overwhelmed by their own affect, they often
seek help. The anguish felt in response to the body's primary and secondary sexual characteristics is a critical feature of these children's experience and, yet, it is a rarely addressed issue in their treatments. The
focus rather tends to be on social transitioning, on their frequent mis-
gendering, and on educative efforts to be made with the familial environment, school setting, and so on. However, such interventions that are
organized solely around supporting the child's gender identification are
inadequate. Oriented toward disaggregating the body from gender, these
approaches usually derive from a misreading of gender theory's emphasis
on gender performativity (Butler, 1993) as positing that gender is something that people choose to enact rather than something that people are
(Serano, 2013; Meadow, 2014). As such, these interventions fail to capture the clinical importance of helping body-dysphoric children mentalize their overwhelming and unbearable somatic feelings. This anguish
issues from the child's inability to resolve the conflict between the reality
of their gender experience and the child's own, heavily defended against
attachment to the notion that the body spells gender's reality.

To resolve this conundrum, some of these child patients resort to the
unconscious fantasy that one's natal sex is not and, in fact, has never
been real. This defensive maneuver permits them to hold onto their
own sense of their gender without having to confront the discrepancy
with the material reality of their sexed body. On a conscious level, this
can manifest as the belief that one was born in the wrong body. It
is thus that, for example, a child born male who has been unable to
process the incongruity between their corporeality and their gender
may come to believe that they were mistakenly born in a male body
when, in fact, they *should* have been born female. How are we to understand such beliefs if not as issuing from the exorbitant pain that mas-
querades as a sense of a cosmically perpetrated injustice? "Ungrieved
grief," Cheng tells us, "becomes grievance" (2001, p. 46). This grievance and its behavioral correlates, I am suggesting, are underwritten
by the unmetabolized turbulence of body dysphoria. For such patients,
mourning the body about which they've fantasized but do not have

is a crucial part of the therapeutic process. I use mourning here to describe the experience of loss that Steiner (1992) has described often accompanies the relinquishment of omnipotent control. In the case of the transgender child, this control has been installed in the first place as a way of keeping pain at bay and its gradual resolution involves a confrontation with the deep suffering that is aroused in giving up the conflation of wish and reality. The therapeutic task is to help the child de-link gender and body in their own psyche, to help them disturb the fixed relationship between the materiality of the flesh and gendered experience so that language and symbolism can become possible.

Bearing the knowledge of their natal bodies is critical in work with body-dysphoric transgender children. By "knowledge" here I am drawing on Bion's notion of K that treats knowing not as a cognitive act of intellectual perception but rather as an emotional event that involves contact with inner life and with the pain that saturates it, as well as the capacity to stay still and observe one's suffering before one moves to act (1962). This kind of knowing requires that cognitive acknowledgment and psychic torment can be reconciled rather than evaded and denied.

Naming and processing the anguish brought to the child by their body, exploring its psychic meanings, and eventually accepting the body one was born into is crucial to psychological health. Yet, contrary to the position argued by many analytic writers (Chasseguet-Smirgel, 1985; Stein, 1995a; Chiland, 2000), I do not see this kind of acceptance as necessarily resolving the question of whether these children will later require hormonal and surgical interventions. Rather, coming to terms with the body one has is a gateway to a psychologically healthy social, emotional, and, should this become necessary over time, medical transition process. This distinction matters greatly because it should guide our clinical technique: the body one has needs to be known to the patient *so that, when necessary, it may eventually be given up.*

Jenny

A Caucasian, five-year-old child from an upper-middle-class family, Jenny was referred to me by Dr. A, an experienced and gifted psychoanalyst who had consulted with her family. Uninformed of the extent of her gender conflicts, Dr. A had approached Jenny in the waiting room and crouched down to her height to say, "Hi. I am Dr. A. And you must be Johnny." What followed was an agonizing outburst, part fury and part despair. Jenny cried inconsolably and, amidst her tears, named her parents' betrayal: "You told, you told!" Jenny's parents tried to reassure her it was OK, that Dr. A had met other kids like her, but she was impossible to soothe. Jenny was unable to tolerate the full 45 minutes and the session had to be terminated early. It had become apparent that a blend of the unintended misnaming and Jenny's pronounced fragility had destroyed the likelihood that a therapeutic relationship could be established with Dr. A.

Dr. A called me to make the referral and as we talked, we both appreciated how devastating that particular address must have been. We assumed that Jenny had perhaps heard it as "You *must*, you *have* to be Johnny". And yet, Dr. A and I were also struck by Jenny's inability to modulate the intensity of her feelings: once the experience of distress had been elicited, Jenny could not be comforted. I wondered what else, other than the evident pain of misrecognition, might have landed Jenny into this throbbing tantrum.

When I met with her parents, they reported to me that Jenny had been saying she was a girl since she was two years old, that she had always expressed anguish about her body, and that she felt resentful about being perceived as a boy. Over the years, she had moved from distress to depression to violent acting out. And most recently she had become persistently suicidal. Her parents were incredibly concerned. Despite being able to provide an otherwise detailed developmental history, their memory regarding her subsequent gender development was rather vague. This suggested to me that although they appeared to be on board with Jenny's gender identification, they were, perhaps, struggling with it more than they could acknowledge to me or to themselves. The mother was less able to voice her ambivalence than the father, yet contrary to common parental reactions of distress (Brill & Pepper, 2008; Hill & Menvielle, 2009), both appeared to find it crucially important to present as unconflicted about Jenny's femaleness.[5] I wondered: had not having informed Dr. A of the degree to which Jenny was female-identified been an enactment of the parents' ambivalence? Had Dr. A been unconsciously recruited to enact that which they could not bear to think or to mourn?[6]

A year prior, the parents reported to me, in a meeting with Jenny's coach they were informed that their child had been identifying as a girl. The coach asked the parents how to handle that when Jenny stepped in, announcing it was she who should be asked and her name from now on was to be Jenny. Her parents were deeply shaken. Neither had heard the name before and they had not realized that Jenny's femaleness had a life that spread outside their home. On the other hand, Jenny's gender was not news to them. And since, as I soon learned, they had both experienced their own parents as having mishandled their autonomy as children, they felt strongly about not wanting to repeat the same with their own child. Both took considerable pride in their daughter's advocating for herself. From thereon they followed her lead, and soon Jenny was fully socially transitioned to living as a girl: she was in dresses, wore hair barrettes, and routinely introduced herself as a girl. The parents also fully complied with Jenny's instruction that since she had been born "in the wrong body," all evidence of her male past should be instantly erased. Acting as if Jenny had been born female, the parents dutifully obliterated all references to her bodily anatomy (e.g. at bath time) and avoided all discussion of her natal maleness.

With these changes at home and in school, Jenny's suicidality quickly receded. Yet, another set of behavioral problems started surfacing. Jenny began getting into vicious arguments with her younger brother when he struggled with pronouns or the name change. Any accidental mention of her maleness by relatives or schoolmates sent Jenny into unending fits of tears that would cascade into prolonged tantrums that were traumatic for the entire family. What had originally looked like open-minded acceptance was beginning to spiral out of control. The parents started to worry about how Jenny's refusal to acknowledge her past would evolve and what it would mean for her future. What were they going to tell those who had known Jenny as Johnny and who naturally had questions? How should they manage her tearful and occasionally rage-filled demands that she be introduced to her new school as a natal girl? Where was the line between respecting her need for privacy but not colluding with a near-magical transformation that could be neither acknowledged nor remembered?

Soon Jenny's problems with emotional regulation started spreading to areas well beyond gender. Jenny's ability to self-soothe began to erode and she became increasingly unable to utilize caregivers' efforts to comfort her. This eventually culminated to her insisting that she did not and, in fact, never had had a penis. A large-scale process of denial seemed to be taking root. Jenny started responding to casual references about her body either by altogether ignoring them or by appearing genuinely surprised that her natal body might exist in the minds of others; that is, that it might survive despite the deployment of her omnipotent defenses against it. These defensive maneuvers were beginning to exceed the contours of a wish generated in response to gender pain; Jenny, it seemed to me, was moving into the territory of psychotic operations.

Correctly interpreting these as signs of psychological difficulty, her parents took seriously my opinion that Jenny might suffer from mood dysregulation, something with which the child psychiatrist with whom the family had initially consulted also agreed. Was her gender a symptom of an early-stage bipolar disorder, the psychiatrist wondered? To me, the problem seemed to be the inverse: while Jenny had received a lot of support and mirroring by her environment in regard to her identified gender, the horror aroused in her by her male body had gone fully unaddressed. I believed that her nascent psychotic solution and the accompanying mood dysregulation were indexical of Jenny's inability to process and digest the complicated discrepancies between her body and her gender experience. There must be something profoundly disturbing and deeply disorienting in feeling that one is a girl only to look down at one's body to encounter a penis. This discrepancy makes significant demands on one's capacity to think coherently: against the powerful and unremitting feelings of being a girl, Jenny's body answered back a vociferous "no". How is a body-dysphoric child to process this mind-numbing dissonance?

Jenny felt tremendous discomfort with her penis, but she dealt with that discomfort by rapidly moving into shaky psychological ground. In substituting her feelings of distress about her penis and her wish that she had been born female with the construction of a reality in which her penis did not *and never had* existed lay the prodromal stages of an unfolding psychotic process. For Jenny, perceptive reality was becoming increasingly subordinated to the unconscious fantasy that her body had in fact never been male: a realistic perception of her bodily materiality was losing to the edict of gender coherence. I felt that Jenny urgently needed help to become able to tolerate knowing the material reality of her body's contours, to tolerate the fact that these were agonizingly incongruent with her sense of self. For Jenny, sanity would have to involve an undoing of the notion that her body delivered gender's verdict.

In the play therapy, I let Jenny take the lead. I never asked her about her name or inquired about her gender. I offered opportunities for her to introduce these herself by indicating my openness to narratives around identity changes in how I entered her play scenarios (e.g. she played often with a stuffed cocoon which, turned inside out, would become a butterfly). For the most part, though, Jenny ignored me. I understood this to signal her need to bring her body into our work on her own terms.

Outside the sessions, when forced to deal with her penis, Jenny was still unraveling. Looking for a bathing suit to take swimming lessons, for example, had been disastrous. Jenny insisted on a girls' suit, but when she tried it on her penis and scrotum impenitently announced themselves as they bulged through the fabric. The experience left her disorganized for days.

Within our sessions, Jenny was enjoying in the presence of another the fantasy that she had always been a girl. Giving her the space within our relationship to experience her gender as a reality that was not delimited by history felt critical to me for several reasons. First, her clearly articulated and very profound distress around her body indicated to me that Jenny might be a transgender girl rather than a proto-gay boy. In that, I was trying to imagine and protect a *possible* future evolution of her gender into an adult trans woman as well as a gay man. Furthermore, the incident with Dr. A had cautioned me that to relate to her gender in any way other than how she presented herself to me would seriously jeopardize, if not preclude, the establishment of a therapeutic relationship. I also found it essential to resist any pressure to become recruited into policing what she did and did not tell me about herself and her body. To do so, I thought, would be tantamount to allowing her anxieties about her body – and those of her parental environment – to be extruded into me.

The room this afforded Jenny permitted her to come into contact with her own anxiety about her magical resolution. Jenny's struggle began to materialize in our sessions through enactment: in the third month of our work, a pattern emerged such that a few minutes into every session Jenny would have a pressing need to use the bathroom. I would walk with her to the ladies' room and from inside the stall[7] she would issue her instructions: "Don't come in. I don't want you to see my private parts." Sometimes while urinating she would anxiously yell out, "You can't see anything, right?" These scenes were painful and comical at once. Our "bathroom play" came complete with a ritualized series of interactions around locking the door, testing the strength of the lock, checking the range of visibility in the crack between the bathroom wall and the door hinged on it, and even a whistling code to warn her of further risks to privacy when others entered the shared space.

The frequency of these bathroom trips and her active enlisting of me in the securing of her privacy served a double purpose: they both controlled my access to her body and unconsciously invited me to hold it in mind. Back in the consulting room, though, Jenny ignored any reference I made to our bathroom visits. I soon came to realize that what was happening in the bathroom was to remain unspoken in my office not in some dissociative pact, but as something that needed to be protectively sequestered to a separate space.

In my work with Jenny, the restroom became the paradigmatic encapsulation of where the bodily and the social meet. A meaning-saturated space, it required of Jenny to interact privately with her male anatomy while publicly claiming her gender as female in choosing the ladies' room. It is because of this complexity that the restroom became the site where Jenny routinely encountered her body/gender split and why it became a liminal space that served the transitional function of trying to work out her omnipotent grip over reality (Winnicott, 1953). In its confines, her body could be both known and not known; it could belong to our intersubjective experience and to her intrapsychic life alone; it could be contemplated and then unceremoniously abandoned.

While I refrained from referencing the content of our bathroom excursions, I did nevertheless focus on her affect. I might, for instance, comment on how anxious she seemed that her privacy was protected or ask if the whistling code we employed felt reassuring. We could then imagine together who would walk in, what they would do, and how we would deal with the intrusion. Once these feeling states were imported into the consulting room, the rigidity of Jenny's bathroom play began to soften. She started to occasionally "forget" to close the door to the stall. She would then emerge, frantically asking me whether I had seen anything. We were getting closer, I felt, to her "revealing" to me – and to "discovering" herself – the fact of her body.

For these reasons, I felt that it would be crucial for Jenny's penis to become thinkable (Bion, 1962) to her before she could shed her reliance on fantasy-based, omnipotent solutions. She would then, perhaps, become able to interact better with others around the fact of her natal sex. With her school friends who remembered that Jenny used to be Johnny starting to whisper in the school corridors, the need for her to acknowledge her past became even more pressing.

As I continued interpreting Jenny's affect around our bathroom trips, our play shifted, revolving now around animals and animal transformations. Could one animal really turn into another? Jenny began drawing in our sessions. As she drew one such transfiguration after another, she started becoming doubtful. Could a cow actually become a bird? If an ostrich put its head in the sand, did the world around it *really* disappear? In beginning to question whether such untraceable transformations were possible, Jenny was, I sensed, trying to push back against the intrapsychic erasure she had enacted. We played through these themes for a while. In one such session, Jenny drew several renditions of a donkey: as the animal raced across the page, its form changed to a horse, and by the finish line it had convincingly transformed into an ostrich. We talked about the animal's successive bodily changes and as we reached the final one Jenny turned to me questioningly. I told her I thought she felt confused as to whether this kind of change could actually happen and that I could tell how much that horse wanted everyone to know it was really an ostrich.

Jenny nodded, giggled loudly, and then, unexpectedly, lifted her skirt over her head in a grand gesture of exhibitionism. The contours of her genitals protruded through her underwear. And that was it: Jenny was coming out to me. She peeked down from over her lifted skirt, stared at her genitals, then lowered her skirt and looked at me expectantly. How was I to treat this communication? Was it an invitation to name that which she could not bear to put into words? Was the naming going to disorganize her? Would it shame her? Injure our relationship? Time presses on us at such unexpected clinical moments: it both dilates and contracts. It seemed to take me a very long time to decide how to respond. Soon the silence would be too long and perhaps Jenny would think that her penis was unthinkable to me, too. I told her, "What I just said about what the horse wanted, it made you feel a lot of things. I think you want to tell me about them but can't find the words." It sounded awkward. She asked if it was time to go. It was.

Jenny started out our next session in an unusual way: rather than making her usual beeline for the toy closet, she sat on my couch and announced she had something she needed to tell me: "Dad thinks I am a boy. Sometimes, I wear boy clothes so his heart doesn't keep breaking." Jenny's statement opened up the floodgates for us. She and I spent much time over the following months trying to understand together what it meant to her to be a girl and what it meant that her dad thought she was a boy. Those discussions paved the way for us to talk about her body and, eventually, to her admission that it was not just her dad but that she, too, was confused about how she could be a girl when she had a penis. Jenny was able to enact in her play her panicked sense of being a "fake," her fear that she had "deceived" everyone, and the unremitting anxiety that she would be "discovered" by classmates, her parents' friends, even by strangers.

As her male anatomy was becoming knowable to us in the room, we were also able to start talking concretely about her penis and about how much she disliked it. She explained to me with considerable delight that she had discovered how to tuck[8] and wondered if her penis did in fact disappear when she could not see it. Would I take a look and tell her if she took her clothes off? As we continued with these discussions, our excursions to the bathroom began to subside and eventually stopped. Some of her play began to revolve around gender per se, while some migrated into scenarios exploring whether she was black or white, Chinese or Mexican, of the earth or an alien, an animal or human. All revolved around questions of categorical identification and of legitimacy: did she possess the right attributes that would firmly and indisputably locate her within one class? As these issues made it into words, her anger began to subside, and while she still disliked talking about her penis, her reliance on magical solutions began to wane. The tension around her gender and her conflicts with her parents did not disappear, but they did significantly mellow. Jenny began recovering her capacity for affective regulation when she found herself being misgendered by her brother or her classmates.

It was such that Jenny started dreaming, a sign of her emerging ability to form representations of her affect states. In one of her dreams, an ostrich put its head in the sand: there had been others like it where the ostrich would re-emerge headless, a hoped-for – albeit gruesome – castration. In this particular dream, though, Jenny felt anxious that the sand would get in the ostrich's eyes: "This won't work!" she thought in the dream in a panic. When the bird lifted its head, however, Jenny found that its neck had shrunk. It now looked more like a chicken, "but not like a regular chicken, because you can kind of tell it used to be an ostrich." Jenny paused to search for language, and in a eureka moment, she exclaimed with excitement: "It was not an ostrich or a chicken: it was an ostricken!" This dream, which was laced with relief, condensed the ostrich's omnipotent control over reality (the head in the sand) and her emerging insight as to how problematic the unconscious fantasy had become (the sand that will get in the animal's eyes) with the coveted absent penis (the shrunken neck). Having been able to move away from her omnipotently concocted fantasies, Jenny dreamt up an *ostricken*, a reassuring and generative neologism that inscribed memory, temporality, and history.

Therapeutic action

How can we understand what was ultimately helpful in my work with Jenny? It seems to me that what was of use to my patient was orienting the work around registering, appreciating, and eventually helping her mentalize the fact that the incoherence she experienced between her gender and her body was the very site of a near psychic catastrophe. Focusing the treatment on helping her bear the pain this brought her, but without pressuring her to do so prematurely, was what may have ultimately made it possible for her to come into contact with this anguish in graduated, manageable doses. As the clinical narrative shows, this happened first through the enactment of the bathroom trips and bathroom play, which forced her to interact with her male anatomy even as she was able to claim herself as a girl. This was followed by her increasing efforts to form representations, which were captured in her drawings becoming less disorganized. The process culminated in her dreaming and the alpha function at work that produced her brilliant condensation of the ostricken.

The question of therapeutic action is, of course, not only a question of technique. From a relational viewpoint, it must also include an accounting of the analyst's internal process and psychic/conceptual work, for it is this process that informs clinical technique in the first place. "Technique" is a not a term used frequently in contemporary relational work because of its association with a level of conscious and precise intentionality that I clearly did not have during the treatment. I use it, however, to help me draw a distinction between what we do in the consulting room, and the psychic states we attend to and cultivate in ourselves so that we may be able to tune into the patient and follow her in ways that respect her pace and rhythm, rather than acting out our own internal pressures as a way of quelling our own countertransferential anxieties; or, in those instances when we work with children, to prevent acting out that aims to relieve our identifications with the parents' anxieties.

The question of therapeutic action, then, can also be reframed to ask: what was the orienting framework that helped me, as Jenny's therapist, prioritize her gender experience even when, in the immediate, one might have read the clinical progression as further compromising her capacity for self-regulation? What was it that afforded her and me the intersubjective space to believe in her gender and to live it out together for a year and a half, which, in turn, helped her confront her body's forceful disagreement and yet still maintain her gender identity? And what about that internal work is uniquely relational?

I worked with Jenny with two sets of relational tools in mind that enabled the treatment to develop as it did. The first issued from relational psychoanalysts' revamping of traditional gender theory to propose and convincingly articulate the socially constructed nature of gender (Benjamin, 1991; Dimen, 1991, 2007; Goldner, 1991, 2003; Harris, 1991; 2005a; Corbett, 1996, 1997). This work, wonderfully summarized in Dimen and Goldner (2005) and in Corbett (2011), draws on feminist and postmodern theory (Butler, 1993, 1990; Halberstam, 2005; Stockton, 2009; Salamon, 2010) to show that the question of whether gender and sexed body do or don't align bears no relation to mental health. Without the help of these tremendously important theoretical innovations, we would not, as a field, be able to conceptualize patients like Jenny with the confidence of belief.

The second important element in Jenny's treatment was the temporal framework orienting the work. While most schools of psychoanalysis rely primarily on the past (conscious memory and the archival unconscious) to drive the work, relational work also privileges the role of futurity (Seligman, 2016). With transgender children, and Jenny in particular, this was especially important because so much of what made clinical sense in the here and now also hinged on what would be possible for her in the future. In some ways, the analyst working with transgender patients not only is required to work with the historical past, with defenses and relational facts and fantasies, but is also in the position of having to imagine a world that, as far as transgender experience is concerned, does not yet exist.

To explain what I mean in more detail, I turn to Loewald's classical paper on therapeutic action. I rely on Loewald, whom I, along with many others, think of as the first relational thinker, and specifically on a somewhat undertheorized part of his paper on therapeutic action (1960). In this essay, Loewald speaks powerfully to the transformational potential held by new objects whose novelty resides in *the envisioning of the patient's future*. This has especially potent implications when it comes to trans children because their otherness can often make their futures seem especially tenuous. I'll follow the trail of Loewald's thinking on futurity to reflect on trans kids and to flesh out how thinking about futurity has been critical to my treatment of Jenny.

Loewald's essay has been celebrated for its progressiveness in marrying the topographical model with an understanding of the early dynamics between caretaker and infant, and for recognizing the centrality of the patient–analyst relationship (Chodorow, 2008, 2009). The place of futurity in his work, however, remains mostly unexplored. With a few notable exceptions (Cooper, 1997; Jacobs, 2008), his belief in the clinical power inherent in analytic imaginings of a patient's future has not been given its clinical due. Loewald (1960) tells us that, ideally, the parent relates empathically to the:

> ...child's particular stage in development, yet ahead in his vision of the child's future and mediating this vision to the child in his dealing with him. This vision, informed by the parent's own experience

and knowledge of growth and future, is, ideally, a more articulate and more integrated version of the core of being that the child presents to the parent. This "more" that the parent sees and knows, he mediates to the child so that the child in identification with it can grow. The child, by internalizing aspects of the parent, also internalizes the parent's image of the child – an image that is mediated to the child in the thousand different ways of being handled, bodily and emotionally ... The bodily handling of and concern with the child, the manner in which the child is fed, touched, cleaned, the way it is looked at, talked to, called by name, recognized and re-recognized – all these and many other ways of communicating with the child, and communicating to him his identity, sameness, unity, and individuality, shape and mould him so that he can begin to identify himself, to feel and recognize himself as one and as separate from others yet with others. *The child begins to experience himself as a centered unit by being centered upon* ... In analysis, if it is to be a process leading to structural changes, interactions of a comparable nature have to take place.

(pp. 229–230, emphasis added)

Loewald writes evocatively of the process of being able to imagine a future for an other. That process, he tells us, is mediated not only through language, but is also transmitted through multiple avenues, including embodiment. Drawing on Laplanche (1999), I would add that such communications oftentimes exceed conscious registration and/or intent. As the ability to empathically envision a future becomes internalized, an experience of the self "as a centered unit" arises, constituting subjectivity.

It's easy to see how this passage can generate clinical controversy due to: worry about infantilizing patients by imagining for and, therefore, in lieu of them; over-investment in particular outcomes; and narcissistic overvaluing of the analytic role (Friedman, 2008). These critiques notwithstanding, Loewald's recommendation is especially productive when what is imagined does not reside in anticipated outcomes as sites of stable meanings, but rather lies in the potential for envisioning growth and emergent possibility. Having a future made imaginable through an other can be doubly powerful for children, because the future lies ahead as something adults promise but is not yet known to be possible.

The need for a different orienting temporal framework is especially pronounced in working with transgender children like Jenny because temporality is mapped differently onto their lives than in those of normative others (Stockton, 2009; Bruhm & Hurley, 2004; Harris, 2005b). Oftentimes deemed too young to be seen as able to claim their gender,[9] trans children's otherness is considered retrospectively. Only when they look back as adults to announce that early kernels of their queerness had been there all along can others take their childhood seriously. Paradoxically, then, queer children's deferred identities are often only recognized as having existed after their expiration date has passed. This nonlinear relationship to time literalizes *nachträglichkeit*, "putting past and present ... side-by-side almost cubistically" (Stockton, 2009, p. 14).

The therapeutic action in work with trans children inheres, then, among other things, in allowing one's imagination to "go queer" when it, most canonically, goes straight (Corbett, 1997). Part of what made it possible for me to be patient and wait for Jenny's disclosure as long as I did – part of what made it feasible for me to "trust" in her gender – was my sensing that despite the complicated nexus of wish and defense, Jenny had to be treated *as a girl in real time*, with no qualifications as to her gender and with no need to make any anxious proclamations about her body. This permitted a kind of imagining *for* Jenny of how her life might be lived should she be able to settle into her knowledge of her body despite its discrepancies from her sense of self. It is through this extended period of my accepting her gender of experience rather than her gender of assignation – that is, of working from within a framework of futurity – that Jenny was able to take me in enough to tolerate confronting her body. She did so by introducing me to it and, I think on some level, by encountering it anew as the body of a trans girl – rather than as a body that was burdened with the "untenability" of her gender.

Conclusion

I have shared a clinical story of having watched my child patient waver on the precipice of psychotic dysregulation because I want to underscore that when we fail to see that pathology follows from the mismanagement of body dysphoria and when we are unable to imagine a future for our transgender child patients, we can, without intending to, iatrogenically fence trans patients *into* the psychotic mechanisms that some of them may resort to in order to manage unbearable affect. Having worked for many years with severely mentally ill young children, I have had many occasions to observe how a mechanism that originates in the attempt to cope with one particular area of trauma can acquire a life of its own and how it can become autonomous from its origins to install itself as the dominant strategy of dealing with all emotional difficulty (Krystal, 1978, 1985). By the time this solution coalesces into a pattern of interacting with the world, character runs the risk of becoming colonized by the pathological strategy as if surrounded by poison ivy.

We are in a strange place in history. We know more about trans issues than we did a mere ten years ago. Our analytic discourse on gender is becoming more nuanced and textured. Side by side with the multiple questions that remain unanswered regarding clinical work with transgender children, there are, quite likely, also numerous others we have not yet even imagined asking.

Notes

1 This chapter first published as Saketopolou, A. (2014). Mourning the body as bedrock: Developmental considerations in treating transsexual patients analytically. *Journal of the American Psychoanalytic Association*, 62:773–806. Copyright © 2014 by American Psychoanalytic Association. Reprinted by permission of SAGE Publications, Inc.
2 Defenses deployed against experiencing oneself as a disappointment to one's primary objects can often become confusing to their environment, which can misinterpret them as evidence of the child's "confusion" regarding gender identification (Lev, 2004).
3 My focus here is on children who experience body dysphoria from very early in life. Obviously, not all transgender children share this characteristic.
4 This symptomatology tends to recede with social and medical transition.
5 During the course of the family work this shifted, with the father becoming able to get in touch with and to express more openly his discomfort with his child's gender. This, as we came to discover, was something that Jenny had already been sensing long before her father became aware of it himself.
6 Parents' mourning of their fantasy of their child's gender is an important facet of the family work necessary in these treatments. Discussing it

is beyond the scope of this chapter, but the interested reader can consult DiCeglie (2012) and Riley, Sitharthan, Clemson, and Diamond (2011).

7 In the building where I practice, a shared bathroom space serves the entire office floor. Several stalls are separated by divides that ensure privacy, while the washing basins are located in the common space.

8 This is the practice of concealing the penis to achieve a flat appearance in the crotch area.

9 Normative inflections of gender are, of course, exceptions. Natal girls who play with Barbie dolls and natal boys who play at being Superman are considered perfectly capable of enacting and claiming their gender.

References

Benjamin, J. (1991). Father and daughter: Identification with difference. *Psychoanalytic Dialogues*, 1:277–299.

Bion, W.R. (1962). *Second thoughts*. London, UK: Karnac Books.

Brill, S. & Pepper, S. (2008). *The transgender child: A handbook for families and professionals*. San Francisco, CA: Cleis Press.

Bruhm, S. & Hurley, N. (2004). *Curiouser: On the queerness of children*. Minneapolis, MN: University of Minnesota Press.

Butler, J. (1990). *Gender trouble: Feminism and the subversion of identity*. New York, NY: Routledge.

Butler, J. (1993). *Bodies that matter: On the discursive limits of "sex"*. New York, NY: Routledge.

Chasseguet-Smirgel, J. (1985). *Creativity and perversion*. New York, NY: Norton.

Cheng, A.A. (2001). *The melancholy of race: Psychoanalysis, assimilation, and hidden grief*. London, UK: Oxford University Press.

Chiland, C. (2000). The psychoanalyst and the transsexual patient. *International Journal of Psychoanalysis*, 81:21–37.

Chodorow, N.J. (2008). Introduction: The Loewaldian legacy. *Journal of the American Psychoanalytic Association*, 56:1089–1096.

Chodorow, N.J. (2009). A different universe: Reading Loewald through "On the therapeutic action of psychoanalysis". *Psychoanalytic Quarterly*, 78:983–1011.

Coates, S. (1990). Ontogenesis of boyhood gender identity disorder. *The Journal of the American Academy of Psychoanalysis and Dynamic Psychiatry*, 18:414–438.

Coates, S. (2006). Developmental research on childhood gender identity disorder. In: P. Fonagy, R. Krause, & M. Leuzinger-Bohleber (Eds.),

Identity, gender and sexuality: 150 years after Freud (pp. 103–131). London, UK: Karnac.

Cooper, S.H. (1997). Interpretation and the psychic future. *International Journal of Psychoanalysis*, 78:667–681.

Corbett, K. (1996). Homosexual boyhood; notes on girlyboys. *Gender and Psychoanalysis*, 1:429–461.

Corbett, K. (1997). Speaking queer; a reply to Richard C. Friedman. *Psychoanalytic Dialogues*, 2:494–514.

Corbett, K. (2011a). *Boyhoods: Rethinking masculinities.* New Haven, CT: Yale University Press.

Corbett, K. (2011b). Gender regulation. *Psychoanalytic Quarterly*, 80:441–459.

Davenport, C.W. (1986). A follow-up study of 10 feminine boys. *Archives of Sexual Behavior*, 15:511–517.

DiCeglie, D. (2009). Between Scylla and Charybdis: Exploring atypical gender identity development in children and adolescents. In: G. Ambrosio (Ed.), *Transvestism, transsexualism in the psychoanalytic dimension* (pp. 55–73). London, UK: Karnac.

DiCeglie, D. (2012). Response to Alessandra Lemma – APP lecture research off the couch: Revisiting the transsexual conundrum. *Psychoanalytic Psychotherapy*, 26:290–293.

Dimen, M. (1991). Deconstructing difference: Gender, splitting and transitional space. *Psychoanalytic Dialogues*, 1:335–352.

Dimen, M. (2007). Ma vie en rose: A meditation. In: M. Suchet, A. Harris, & L. Aron (Eds.), *Relational psychoanalysis, Vol. III: New voices* (pp. 53–60). New York, NY: The Analytic Press.

Dimen, M. & Goldner, V. (2005). Gender and sexuality. In: A. Cooper, G. Gabbard, & E. Person. *The American Psychiatric Publishing textbook of psychoanalysis* (pp. 93–114). Washington, DC: American Psychiatric Publishing.

Drescher, J. & Byne, W. (2013). Introduction: The treatment of gender dysphoric/gender variant children and adolescents. In: J. Drecher & W. Byne (Eds.), *Treating transgender children and adolescents: An interdisciplinary discussion* (pp. 1–6). New York, NY: Routledge.

Drummond, K.D., Bradley, S.J., Peterson-Badali, M., & Zucker, K.J. (2008). A follow-up study with gender identity disorder. *Developmental Psychology*, 44:34–55.

Edwards-Leeper, L. & Spack, N. (2013). Psychological evaluation and medical treatment of transgender youth in an interdisciplinary "Gender Management Service" (GeMS) in a major pediatric center. In: J. Drecher & W. Byne (Eds.), *Treating transgender children and adolescents: An interdisciplinary discussion* (pp. 27–42). New York, NY: Routledge.

Ehrensaft, D. (2011). *Gender born, gender made.* New York, NY: The Experiment.

Ehrensaft, D. (2013). From gender identity disorder to gender identity creativity: True gender self child therapy. In: J. Drecher & W. Byne (Eds.), *Treating transgender children and adolescents: An interdisciplinary discussion* (pp. 43–62). New York, NY: Routledge.

Friedman, L. (2008). Loewald. *Journal of the American Psychoanalytic Association,* 56:1105–1115.

Goldner, V. (1991). Toward a critical relational theory of gender. *Psychoanalytic Dialogues,* 1:249–272.

Goldner, V. (2003). Ironic gender/authentic sex. *Studies in Gender and Sexuality,* 4:113–139.

Goldner, V. (2011). Gender in free fall. *Psychoanalytic Dialogues,* 21:153–158.

Halberstam, J. (2005). *In a queer time and place: Transgender bodies, subcultural lives.* New York, NY: New York University Press.

Harris, A. (1991). Gender as contradiction. *Psychoanalytic Dialogues,* 1:197–244.

Harris, A. (2005a). *Gender as soft assembly.* New York, NY: Relational Perspectives Book Series.

Harris, A. (2005b). Gender in linear and nonlinear history. *Journal of the American Psychoanalytic Association,* 53:1079–1095.

Hill, D.B. & Menvielle, E. (2009). "You have to give them a place where they feel protected and safe and loved": The views of parents who have gender variant children and adolescents. *Journal of LGBT Youth,* 6:243–271.

Jacobs, T.J. (2008). Hans Loewald: An appreciation. *Journal of the American Psychoanalytic Association,* 56:1097–1104.

Krystal, H. (1978). Trauma and affect. *Psychoanalytic Study of the Child,* 33:81–116.

Krystal, H. (1985). Trauma and the stimulus barrier. *Psychoanalytic Inquiry,* 5:131–161.

Laplanche, J. (1999). *Essays on otherness.* London, UK: Routledge.

Lemma, A. (2012). Research off the couch: Revisiting the transsexual conundrum. *Psychoanalytic Psychotherapy,* 26:263–281.

Lemma, A. (2013). The body one has and the body one is: Understanding the transsexual's need to be seen. *International Journal of Psychoanalysis,* 94:277–292.

Lev, A.I. (2004). *Transgender emergence: Therapeutic guidelines for working with gender variant people and their families.* New York, NY: Haworth Clinical Practice Press.

Loewald, H.W. (1960). On therapeutic action. In: *Papers on Psychoanalysis* (pp. 221–255). New Haven, CT: Yale University Press.

Meadow, T. (2014). Being a gender: A new conceptual framework. Lecture given at Princeton University, April 2, 2014.

Riley, E.A., Sitharthan, L. Clemson, L., & Diamond, M. (2011). The needs of gender variant children and their parents according to mental health professionals. *International Journal of Transgenderism*, 13:54–63.

Salamon, G. (2010). *Assuming a body: Transgender and rhetorics of materiality*. New York, NY: Columbia University Press.

Seligman, S. (2016). Disorders of temporality and the subjective experience of time: Unresponsive objects and the vacuity of the future. *Psychoanalytic Dialogues*, 26:110–128.

Serano, J. (2013). *Excluded: making feminist and queer movements inclusive*. Berkeley, CA: Seal Press.

Steensma, T.D., Biemond, R. de Boer, F., & Cohen-Kettenis, P.T. (2010). Desisting and persisting gender dysphoria after childhood; a qualitative follow-up study. *Clinical Child Psychology and Psychiatry*, 16:499–516.

Stein, R. (1995). Analysis of a case of transsexualism. *Psychoanalytic Dialogues*, 5:257–289.

Steiner, J. (1992). The equilibrium between the paranoid–schizoid and the depressive positions. In: R. Anderson (Ed.), *Clinical lectures on Klein and Bion* (pp. 46–58). London, UK: Routledge.

Stockton, K.B. (2009). *The queer child, or growing sideways in the twentieth century*. Durham, NC: Duke University Press.

Winnicott, D.W. (1953). Transitional objects and transitional phenomena: A study of the first not-me possession. *International Journal of Psychoanalysis*, 34:89–97.

Winnicott, D.W. (1954). Metapsychological and clinical aspects of regression within the psycho-analytical setup. *International Journal of Psychoanalysis*, 31:16–26.

Index